# EVANGELIZING ADULTS

First printing, March 1985

Library of Congress Catalog Card Number 84-62350
ISBN 0-8423-0793-1
Copyright 1985 by the Paulist National Catholic
Evangelization Association
Printed in the United States of America

# EVANGELIZING ADULTS

### GLENN · C · SMITH · EDITOR

PAULIST
NATIONAL CATHOLIC
EVANGELIZATION ASSOCIATION
WASHINGTON, D.C.

TYNDALE HOUSE
PUBLISHERS, INC.
WHEATON, ILLINOIS

First printing, March 1985

Library of Congress Catalog Card Number 84-62350
ISBN 0-8423-0793-1
Copyright 1985 by the Paulist National Catholic
Evangelization Association
All rights reserved
Printed in the United States of America

# CONTENTS

Throughout American history, indeed from the very moment the discoverers of this great land set foot on this soil, Christianity has been an integral part of the American way of life. However, there have been special seasons of great revival, growth, and vitality within the churches of our land.

Historians point to what they call the Two Great Awakenings. The first was in the early colonial times when men such as John Wesley, Jonathan Edwards, John Carroll, and George Whitefield brought the early settlers into church participation and membership.

A second great awakening occurred when the settlers moved West. Just prior to the Civil War, such a stirring throughout the land for spiritual revival occurred, that historians estimate almost 75 percent of the population became churched. As the settlers moved West, so did the church, until the entire land was covered with churches of every denomination.

We are now on the threshold of what church growth experts call the Third Great Awakening. Never before in American history have so many of our citizens been so involved in their church as they are today. For the first time since Jesus Christ's time, the rate of church growth exceeds the rate of population growth. There are more people attending church in America per capita than ever in history. There are more Christian schools of all levels in America than ever before. There are more and better trained clergy today, the churches are larger and better attended, and as we are all aware, churches are using radio, television, and the printed page more than ever.

When we consider how men such as Billy Graham have personally spoken to almost every citizen within the United States, and how television and radio offer the gospel message on a daily basis to every man, woman, and child, the potential effect upon our spiritual lives is astounding. Never before in our history do we find millions of children attending Sunday schools, teenagers involved in Young Life, or college-aged students involved in Campus Crusade and Youth For Christ, International.

Thousands of well-trained lay leaders leave hundreds of Bible colleges and seminaries each year to seek to evangelize. It is their intent that every citizen in America personally be invited to consider Jesus Christ and his church by the end of this century. We are living in what has been named the Age of Evangelization.

This book on the art of evangelization is, in itself, somewhat of a miracle. That Southern Baptist, Assembly of God, Roman Catholic, Methodist, Presbyterian, and many other leaders would combine their experience and scholarship to make such a volume possible is amazing and encouraging. This is the shared wisdom and experience of some of the most talented people in America's growing churches. In this effort, the spirit of competition for members has been abandoned for the greater task of presenting the glorious message of Jesus Christ.

We trust that clergy and lay leaders alike will read through each exciting story of how these great men and women have led others to Jesus and his church, whatever the denominational label. May it be, for you, a presentation of contemporary methods for reaching out to the inactives, the alienated, and the unchurched throughout our nation.

May this indeed be the Third Great Awakening within our nation, and may we have an active part in reaching every soul for Jesus Christ by the end of this century.

—*Dr. Glenn C. Smith*

## STORMING THE GATES OF HELL

Caesarea Philippi was a city famous for its ancient worship of nature gods, and also the site of a massive white marble temple built by Herod the Great, dedicated to the veneration of Caesar Tiberius. It was here one day that Jesus asked his disciples what people were saying about him. What a place to pose such a question! It was as though the carpenter from Nazareth was placing himself against the power of the prevailing world's system and demanding a comparison.

Forced to make some response, the disciples replied that some regarded Jesus as one of the prophets that was to precede the coming Messiah. "But whom do you say I am?" he asked. Let everyone speak for himself. To this challenge, Peter answered, "Thou art the Christ, the Son of the living God." More than a forerunner of the anointed one, Jesus was incarnate deity, the King of glory, who would reign forever.

With this divine revelation clearly in focus, Jesus told the perceptive speaker of the congregation: "Upon this rock I will build my church; and the gates of hell shall not prevail against it" (Matthew 16:13-18; cf., Mark 8:27-30; Luke 9:18-20). The big fisherman depicted in his faith and testimony how the new community would be formed out of the world.

Jesus recognized that the building would not be completed without conflict. The work would be assailed by treacherous forces of evil from the "very gates of hell," a picturesque metaphor for the place where designs and plans are born, as well as the point from which hosts will attack. All the powers of the underworld were seen unleashed against Jesus' people. Yet he saw, too, the church emerging victorious—not merely surviving the assaults, but taking the offensive, gaining mastery over the enemy, until every foe was defeated. Nothing could ultimately prevail against them. However fierce the battle in this world, the church will be triumphant.

## ETERNAL VERITIES

We live with this thrilling sense of destiny. What may be viewed as failures and hardships are only temporary sequences in the will of him who has determined the end from the beginning. The past and the future are always present in God. Indeed, if we contemplate eternal reality, the redeemed from every tongue and tribe and nation can be seen now in heaven, clothed with white robes, and palms in their hands, crying with a loud voice, saying, "Salvation to our God which sitteth upon the throne, and unto the Lamb" (Revelation 7:9, 10; cf. 5:9).

Here, from the vantage point of heaven, we get a better perspective on what really matters. At the feet of Jesus, permanence dispels the passing contingencies of time. Though now we see only vaguely the outlines of the coming Kingdom, we know that it is certain and that someday every knee shall bow before Christ, in the realms above and on earth below, and every tongue shall confess that he is Lord (Philippians 2:10, 11).

## PURPOSE OF CREATION

This adoration of the Son was in view when God created mankind in his image. As the psalmist said, "All nations whom thou hast made shall come and worship before thee, O Lord; and shall glorify thy name" (Psalm 86:9; cf. Isaiah 43:21; Revelation 4:11).

Sin is the repudiation of this divine order, worshiping the creature rather than the Creator (Romans 1:20-25). Judgment is certain, of course. An infinitely holy God cannot ignore the perversion of his will. Still he loves that which he has made, and is ever seeking restoration of the fallen race.

God's purpose unfolds awesomely in the call of Abraham, through whom he will raise up a special people to show his glory to the nations (Genesis 12:1-3; 18:18; 22:18; 26:4; Acts 3:25). The patriarch obeyed, utterly committing himself to follow the will of God, prefiguring that quality of devotion which characterizes children of the Kingdom. Though the promise was never realized in the faltering experience of Israel, it would be fulfilled when Shiloh came, their Messiah, in whom the Spirit would rest without measure. He would be a light to the Gentiles, and call out a people to serve him from the ends of the earth (Genesis 49:10; Isaiah 49:6). "Of the increase of his government and peace there shall be no end" (Isaiah 9:6, 7).

The promise eventuates in the coming of the King. One as the Son of Man will appear with the clouds of heaven, coming "to the Ancient of Days" for a formal presentation. To him will be given "dominion, and glory, and a Kingdom, that all people, nations, and languages, should serve him: his dominion is an everlasting dominion, which shall not pass away, and his Kingdom that which shall not be destroyed" (Daniel 7:13, 14; cf. Zechariah 9:10). In this passage, the bringing of the nations to the Son of Man is seen as a gift which God bestows upon himself, the revelation of his glory in the consummation of all things.

## *THE GOSPEL OF THE KINGDOM*

Jesus ministered in the joyous confidence of this day. The sound of the hosts of heaven praising God about the throne was vibrant in his soul. But he also knew that before it could come to pass, the rebellious world had to be reconciled to God through the sacrificial offering of the Messiah-Son.

To accomplish this mission, he "made himself of no reputation, and took upon him the form of a servant, and was made in the likeness of men" (Philippians 2:7). He carried our griefs; he bore our sorrows; and, finally, in our stead, he offered up himself on the cross. By accepting the judgment of our sins in his own body, he effected once for all the redemption of the world (Isaiah 53:1-12; 1 Peter 2:24; 3:18). Then, witnessing this finished work, after three days in the tomb, he rose from the grave in death-rending triumph.

Before returning to the Father, he carefully instructed his disciples from the Scriptures as to the meaning of the great redemptive events of his life, emphasizing their role in getting out the news. "Thus it behooved Christ to suffer, and to rise from the dead," he explained, "and that repentance and remission of sins should be preached in his name among all nations, beginning in Jerusalem" (Luke 24:46, 47).

This was the gospel of the Kingdom—the good news of God's grace in Christ. It had characterized the preaching of Jesus from the beginning of his ministry. The message found fulfillment in the way he proclaimed release to the captive, recovering of sight to the blind, and freedom to those in bondage, consummating in his conquest of death and hell (Matthew 12:28; Luke 11:20). In him the Kingdom was already present, and all who come to him in true repentance and faith enter into that spiritual reality (Mark 1:14, 15; 18:3; Luke 4:43; John 3:3, 5). Only as people learn of his saving work, and yield themselves to follow him, can they become a part of that Kingdom of which there is no end.

## WITNESSES TO THE WORLD

Partakers of this new creation form a society of "called out ones," the church. Custodians of the gospel, we display to this world the character of the age to come. Though perfect attainment awaits the day when all evil is banished, still the values of heaven establish the ethic of God's people now. Love becomes the rule of conduct. In this devotion, followers of Christ are to govern their lives by the same commitment which constrained the Savior. As he was sent into the world, now he sends us (John 20:21). His instruction was given explicit focus in the commission to "go and make disciples of all nations" (Matthew 28:19).

Jesus was simply asking his disciples to do what he had done with them. While ministering widely to multitudes, he concentrated his efforts upon those who wanted to learn more of him. As they had freely received, they were expected to transmit their knowledge to other seekers of the truth, leading them in turn to do the same. In this manner, through the process of reproduction, the world will be reached with the gospel.

How disciples witness, of course, will vary according to God's gifts and calling. Few will serve in the role of pastor or itinerant evangelist, but all are witnesses to his grace, and can make disciples in their sphere of influence.

Good news by its nature cannot be self-contained, the more so when it means the difference between life and death. Little wonder, then, that the 120 Spirit-filled disciples at Pentecost went out on the thoroughfares of the city and began to speak the wonderful words of God. As Peter observed, referring to the prophecy of Joel, God's people cannot be silent when his Spirit is poured out, nor can those who hear remain unaffected. "Whosoever shall call upon the name of the Lord shall be saved" (Acts 2:17, 21).

The witnessing power of Pentecost becomes increasingly apparent as the disciples scatter through Judea, Samaria, and finally to the ends of the earth. Before the Acts of the Apostles closes, the witness is firmly planted in Rome, and the Kingdom message of the Savior is going out "with all confidence" (Acts 28:31). Indeed, the book has no conclusion, for we are still living in the age of the harvest, and it will continue until the work is finished, the Great Commission fulfilled, and the King returns in glory.

## THE CHALLENGE TODAY

For years I have been intrigued by the testimony of Paul before Agrippa when he affirmed obedience to the "heavenly vision" (Acts 26:19). Was he thinking of the celestial city described in the book of Revelation, or more specifically the celebration of the heavenly host about the throne, where Christ reigns in majesty? While I would not want to exclude these aspects of heaven, I have come to believe that the vision takes in a much wider reference, encompassing the whole process by which disciples are made, including the preaching of the crucified and exalted Christ, with the call for every creature to worship before him. It is as God's gospel is communicated to a lost world, and persons are born from above, that the Kingdom comes to fruition.

This is the vision before us. Men and women who turn from darkness unto light, from the power of Satan unto God, receive forgiveness of sins, and an inheritance among those who are sanctified by faith in Christ (Acts 26:18). With this message in our hands, we dare not withhold it from the perishing souls about us. Jesus saves! And those transformed by his Spirit become a part of that countless throng that will never cease to declare his praise.

Evangelism makes it happen. In fact, apart from bringing people to Christ, there would be no church. That is why we take this task to heart. It is the only hope for mankind. Whatever the means necessary, however costly the involvement, we must be about the Father's business. Time cannot be wasted. As Amy Carmichael reminds us, "We have all eternity to celebrate the victories, but only a few hours before sunset to win them."

The insights of representative leaders contained in this book will help us get our priorities in order. More to the point, sharing out of their own experience, they show us how the work can be done. That is the issue. Finally, it is not what we say, but what we do that makes the difference.

Obedience to the heavenly vision is the challenge before us. In accepting it, we align ourselves with God's triumph for eternity, to which history is moving, when the completed body, the blood-washed Bride of Christ, will be presented a glorious church. Then all creation will worship before him; his judgments will be manifest; the kingdoms of this world shall become the Kingdom of God, and of his Christ, and he shall reign, King of kings and Lord of lords, from hallelujah to hallelujah, forever and forever (Revelation 11:15; 17:14; 19:1, 3, 6).

*—Dr. Robert E. Coleman*

Dr. Robert E. Coleman, now director of Trinity Evangelical Divinity School's Doctor of Missiology Department, has a long record of outstanding scholarship and work in the field of evangelization. He was professor of Evangelism at Asbury Theological Seminary and past president of the Academy for Evangelism in Theological Education. He is a member of the Lausanne Committee for World Evangelization, where he serves as chairman of the North American Section. His books on Bible study and discipleship are read around the world in more than sixty languages. His book, *Dry Bones Can Live Again*, now in its twelfth printing, is one of the most read books on church revival in our generation. He can be reached by writing to: Dr. Robert E. Coleman, Trinity Evangelical Divinity School, Bannockburn, Deerfield, IL 60015.

# Evangelization for Today

# BILLY GRAHAM
## "DO IT AGAIN, LORD!"

THERE seem to be periods of special urgency in history when it can be said with peculiar relevance, "The fields are white unto harvest." I believe that we are now in such a period. Because of technology, this generation is the most critical in modern history—not just for world events, but for the advancement of the Kingdom of God  And that should give us a sense of urgency greater than anything the church has ever experienced before. We stand at the heart of a world revolution. Our world is on fire, and man without God cannot control the flames.

We were in France on July 14 for Bastille Day (which is their Fourth of July). *Le Monde* is one of the most respected newspapers in the world. Here was their editorial as they looked forward to the long weekend:

In France, overheated and overcrowded prisons are about to explode. In Northern Ireland, IRA inmates are dying one after the other. In El Salvador it is murder unlimited. In Chile, disorder reigns. In Asia the refugees keep looking for refuge; Poland fears the summer. Afghanistan resists in silence. Iran rants on. Purges are underway just about everywhere. The South is hungry. The North is afraid. Happy weekend everybody.

In another French newspaper an editorial said, "The possibility of Armageddon before the end of this decade frightens us all."

Not only is there a new urgency, but it also means millions of people are searching for answers to the crushing problems and fears they face every day. There is an openness to the gospel in this generation which we may never see again. Almost every newspaper and every book screams from its pages, "The harvest is ripe." Seldom has the soil of the human heart and mind been better prepared. Never has the grain been thicker. Never have we had more efficient instruments in our hands to gather the harvest. Yet at a time when the harvest is the ripest in history, the church often flounders in confusion—especially concerning evangelization. That is why such a book as this is so important to help clarify our thinking.

At one of the recent Roman Catholic conclaves to choose a new Pope, confusing signals were sent out! The custom is that the secret ballots of the cardinals are burned after each vote, and black smoke comes billowing out. When a new Pope has been elected, a chemical is added so that white smoke comes out to indicate that the decision has been made. At one election, not enough chemical was added and the smoke came out "gray." The "wondering crowds" outside were left in confusion as to whether they had a new Pope or not.

Perhaps this is an illustration of the confusion that exists concerning evangelization today. And yet we cannot risk confusion if we are to make the impact on our generation that God expects of us. "For if the trumpet give an uncertain sound, who shall prepare himself to the battle?" (1 Corinthians 14:8).

## FIRST, LET THERE BE NO CONFUSION ON THE MEANING OF EVANGELISM

Today we have scores of definitions of evangelism. During the early years of my ministry it never occurred to me that I had to have it defined for me. To me it was simply "soul winning." However, I came to realize that it meant a bit more than that. Some think of evangelism simply in terms of getting more people to join the church. Still others, though in diminishing numbers, define evangelism in terms of social action almost exclusively. Or again, there are those who have moved from a belief in man's moral responsibility before God to a concept which declares all men are saved. This "spreading universalism" is deadening the urgency of the church in some quarters.

Evangelism in its biblical sense is concerned with individuals and their relationship to God. It seeks to declare the gospel of Jesus Christ, and urges people to trust Christ as Savior and follow him as Lord—as his disciples.

During the past three or four years I have noticed a new emphasis in my own preaching. The emphasis is on discipleship. In our crusade in Baltimore, I tried to put an emphasis on the "cost" of following Christ, and yet in one week more than 15,000 people responded to receive Christ. I believe that especially young people respond to a hard challenge, and certainly there has never been a challenge harder than that of the Lord Jesus Christ.

## SECOND, LET THERE BE NO CONFUSION ABOUT THE MOTIVE OF EVANGELISM

Our primary motive is "the command" of our Commander-in-chief, the Lord Jesus Christ. To fail to heed this command is deliberate disobedience. If there were no other reason for going to the ends of the earth proclaiming the gospel and winning souls, the command of Christ would be enough. It is not optional—we have no choice. We are ambassadors under authority.

Another motive for evangelism is the example set by the preaching of the apostles.

Another is found in St. Paul's words, "the love of Christ constraineth us" (2 Corinthians 5:14). I am convinced the greatest act of love we can ever perform for another person is to tell him about God's love for him in Christ. John Stott, at the General Assembly of the World Council of Churches in Nairobi, said, "If justice means the securing of people's rights, is not one of their most fundamental rights the right to hear the gospel? If love seeks to serve man's highest welfare, can we leave them alone in their spiritual lostness and still claim to love them?"

Often we are asked what the relationship is between social action and evangelism. We should remember that social concern has a legitimacy of its own, and so does evangelism. Even if there were no connection between the two, both evangelism and social concern would be our concerns, because Christ taught both as our responsibility.

I just mention several examples: First, certainly we must take a strong stand for racial understanding. The racial problem in America has not yet been fully solved. Christians should be taking the lead in helping solve it.

Second, we should take a strong stand on the moral issues of our day. The pendulum of moral permissiveness has swung too far in our country, and we should support those who are calling for a reversal of this trend.

Another example would be the arms race. The world is involved in the greatest arms race in history. We stand on the verge of a manmade Armageddon. I am not a pacifist, nor am I for unilateral disarmament, but I believe that as Christians we need to call for a SALT 10, which is the destruction of all nuclear and biochemical weapons.

Another problem that we not only need to be concerned about, but do something about, is world hunger. I was delighted to read a major article the other day in which it said that evangelicals are playing a major role in helping meet the needs of starving millions.

But remember, some of the greatest social movements in history have been the fruit of true evangelical revivals. However, there is a danger that we can be so preoccupied with social action that we neglect the greater priority—the proclamation of the gospel.

My father-in-law, Dr. Nelson Bell, gave the twenty-five prime years of his life serving the people of China as a missionary surgeon. He helped build and operate one of the largest mission hospitals in the world. It was recognized around the world, and many Americans and European medical students came there to do their internship, including Dr. Ken Gieser, whom many of us know. On his fortieth birthday, Dr. Bell was made a Fellow of the American College of Surgeons. He was firmly convinced that the primary reason for the hospital's existence was the proclamation of the gospel. They had a full-time Bible evangelist, and a full-time Bible woman who witnessed to each patient. Every ambulatory patient, and all accompanying family members, were required to attend daily chapel. Thousands of tracts and Gospel portions were distributed yearly. Late in his life, when he was Moderator of the Presbyterian Church in the United States, someone asked him how many of his former patients were still living. He replied he thought most likely that 98 percent would be dead by now. Then he added, "Which shows what we did for them spiritually was what really mattered."

Evangelism is an act of compassion, as it was for Jesus. We are sent, as he was sent. Matthew 9:36 tells us that "When he saw the crowds, he had compassion on them, because they were harassed and helpless, like sheep without a shepherd" (NIV).

Christ's love for others is also a powerful motive, but so is my own experience of Christ's love for me, which I in turn—out of love for others—want to share.

It could be that one of the greatest hindrances to evangelism today is the poverty of our own spiritual experience. Whether we like to face the reality of it or not, we have become "worldly." We have been told not to love the world, nor the things of the world. And yet how can we have the spiritual experience of some of the giants of the past when we spend so much time watching television, and occupied with the things of this world?

Last week, my friend Gordon MacDonald and I were talking about the need in our busy ministries of getting away for quiet reflection, prayer, and study. I would say that this is one of the greatest needs that pastors have today. And their congregations should understand this, and be willing to urge their pastors to take several periods a year, and to supplement their income so they can do it. It has been my own practice for several years to take two periods a year for prayer, study, recreation, and writing. True evangelism is the spontaneous outflow and overflow of a heart full of Christ.

Another motive for evangelism is the approaching judgment. St. Paul said, "Knowing therefore the terror of the Lord, we persuade men" (2 Corinthians 5:11). When the Apostle Paul preached his great sermon on Mars Hill, he said God "commands all people everywhere to repent. For he has set a day when he will judge the world with justice by the man he has appointed" (Acts 17:30, 31, NIV).

There is a judgment day approaching. The secular world is talking more and more about Armageddon and the end of the world. A newspaper columnist in England wrote last month, "The day of reckoning is near." Another newspaper carries an article entitled "Orwell's *1984* is on schedule." Marshall Shulman, a Carter administration expert on the Soviet Union, said in late 1980, "Sometimes I get the feeling I am sitting on a hilltop watching two trains racing towards each other on the same track." Whether the church does or not—the secular world senses that a gigantic disaster is building up.

It seems to me this is the time for the Christian minister to proclaim "the hope" of the return of Jesus Christ, coupled with a warning of impending judgment. In the terrifying light of that day of judgment, man's greatest need is for reconciliation with God. This brings us back to the urgency of evangelism.

In recent years, many have rejected the biblical doctrine that men are individually sinners before God and will be held responsible to him at the judgment. Instead, they believe in a doctrine of collective sinfulness and of the corporate guilt of society. I accept the fact that sin affects society as a whole, and we must take that seriously. But we are in danger of neglecting the need for personal repentance of sin, and faith in the Lord Jesus Christ. We are forgetting the "must" in "Ye must be born again"—which is where the New Testament places its emphasis. Peter proclaimed, "Neither is there salvation in any other: for there is none other name under heaven given among men, whereby we must be saved" (Acts 4:12).

The great Methodist preacher of London, and a longtime personal friend of mine, Dr. Leslie Weatherhead, once wrote: "We do our generation a great disservice if we make light of sin and pretend that it does not matter and that we are all going to the same place and that God will pat everyone on the head and say: there, there, it doesn't matter, I'm sure you didn't mean it, come now and enjoy yourselves." He went on to point out that there are many things we don't know about hell, but that Jesus used every image in his power to tell us that hell is real, that it is terrible, that it is something to be feared, and that it is something to avoid. The most compassionate person who ever lived—

Jesus—was "the One" who spoke of outer darkness, a closed door, gnashing of teeth, and the lake of fire.

## THIRD, LET THERE BE NO CONFUSION ABOUT THE MESSAGE OF EVANGELISM

Last year at a reception in Osaka, Japan, the governor of Osaka gave a brief address. He turned to me and said, "Dr. Graham, why is it that the church in Japan is still only 1 percent, which is about the same as it was in the seventeenth century?" He said, "I believe it is because the gospel has not been made clear to the Japanese people. I hope that you will make it clear."

There are millions in America for whom the gospel has not been made clear. We have failed in our communication, so that people have only a hazy idea of what it means to be a Christian. Three weeks ago, some English church and parachurch leaders came to see me in France. They were thrilled with the results of the Luis Palau Glasgow Crusade. But they made one startling statement. They said that according to their statistics and surveys, only 15 percent of the people of England have heard the gospel.

At the time of the 1960 Olympics a magazine carried a cartoon showing a runner from Marathon, of the classic story, carrying the message of victory—come stumbling and gasping into the palace, fall prostrate before the king, a puzzled, blank look on his face as he mumbles, "I have forgotten the message."

There are many times when I hear preaching on the radio and even on television, or read religious periodicals—and I sometimes wonder: Have we forgotten the message?

Jesus Christ by his death and resurrection *became* the gospel. It is not just a new set of morals, or a guide for happy living. It is the solemn message that we are alienated from God, and only Christ can save us. In the Old Testament we are promised prosperity and good health for trusting in God. But in the New Testament we are promised suffering, persecution, and death as followers of the Lord Jesus Christ. Any other message than the gospel of Jesus Christ is not evangelism. Paul sums up this message in 1 Corinthians 15:3, 4, "Christ died for our sins according to the scriptures; and that he was buried, and that he rose again the third day according to the scriptures."

# FOURTH, LET THERE BE NO CONFUSION ABOUT THE METHODS OF EVANGELISM

There are one or two things we need to keep in mind as we talk about methods. One, we need to remember that not every method of evangelism is legitimate—"the end" does not justify the means. It is interesting to me that Jesus rejected the testimony of the devil. The devil recognized Jesus' deity, but Jesus refused his testimony. Even the demons would cry out and give testimony concerning Christ. In Matthew 8, the demons cried out, "What have we to do with thee, Jesus, thou Son of God? art thou come hither to torment us before the time?" Jesus cast them into a herd of swine. He rejected their testimony.

Thus, in these days when many voices are being heard, we should ask God for the gift of discernment. The Apostle John warned us, "Believe not every spirit, but try the spirits whether they are of God: because many false prophets are gone out into the world."

Second, we need to explore every legitimate method for reaching our world for Christ. New challenges call for new methods and new strategies. God has raised up parachurch groups because many of our mainline churches have failed. Fortunately, there is a tremendous amount of evidence that mainline churches are now beginning to adopt both "the message" and "the methods" that the parachurch groups have been using so successfully to reach millions of Americans with the gospel. But methods alone are not enough, important as they may be. The reason is that we are involved in a spiritual battle. The evangelist and the work of evangelism are opposed on every hand by Satan and his forces. When the seed of the gospel is being sown, he is always there also sowing the tares and binding the minds of those whom we seek to evangelize. Paul declared, "The god of this world has blinded the minds of the unbelievers, to keep them from seeing the light of the gospel of the glory of Christ, who is the likeness of God" (2 Corinthians 4:4, RSV). Do not underestimate the strategy of Satan. He uses every kind of deception, force, and error to try to destroy the effectiveness of the gospel. But we know greater is he that is in us than he that is in the world. We need to trust the Holy Spirit for results, because he alone can give success. And that is why prayer is such a critical part of evangelism.

But there is one final thing we must say about the method of evangelism. Dr. Oswald Smith said once long ago: God's method is men. There is no doubt that the heart of the method of God is men and women who have been filled and anointed by the Holy Spirit and are in turn witnessing for him wherever God sends them. That is why the greatest need of the hour is the revival of the church of Jesus Christ. We are now living in a generation when nothing will break through the overwhelming power of Satan except the supernatural power of the Holy Spirit.

If the church was supernaturally blessed of God at its birth, who will say that in the closing days of its witness here on earth it will not be blessed in an even mightier way? Our prayer should be, "O Lord, stir the flames of revival."

Alexander Whyte, the great Scottish preacher, in his book *Lord, Teach Us to Pray,* reminds us that our Lord said in John 17:19, "And for their sakes I sanctify myself." This is a startling statement. Jesus, the sinless Son of God, is still sanctifying himself—that is, surrendering himself, dedicating himself, devoting himself, to fulfill and to finish his Father's will and to accomplish the salvation of all whom the Father hath given him. "For their sakes I sanctify myself, that they also might be sanctified through the truth." This would teach us that we must sanctify ourselves for the sake of others. We must first sanctify ourselves and then pray, first for ourselves and then for others. He was saying it to these eleven disciples. They were to be the future preachers of the gospel and pastors of the flocks. That night they did not understand all that Jesus was saying. But after the crucifixion, the resurrection, and the Pentecostal outpouring of the Holy Spirit, it all came back to their understanding. I am sure that nothing he said that evening was remembered more fully than this: "For their sakes, I sanctify myself."

No man or woman deserves to be ordained to the Christian ministry who does not look around on the people and say, "For their sakes, I sanctify myself." "For their sakes I keep myself at peace with God." "For their sakes I practice the presence of God." "For their sakes I am separate from the sins of the world." In every new sermon there should be a new sanctification of the preacher for his people. In every pastoral visit, at every sickbed, or every deathbed, there should be a new sanctification. We are to have meekness and humility in our ministry for the sake of others. We are to endure suffering, misunderstanding, persecution for the sake of others. This Scripture verse should be the law and the rule for your family life. The devil is attacking the families of clergy today more than any other time, I think, in the history of the church. Let every father and mother look upon their families every day and say together, "For their sakes we sanctify ourselves." For the sake of that son and daughter who are giving difficulty, and for whom you shed many a tear—for their sake you sanctify yourself. In trying to solve some family problems, have you ever tried self-sanctification—upon your son, or daughter—upon yourself—upon your husband or wife? I do not believe God can resist a parent's prayer when it is sufficiently backed up with a parent's sanctification.

John Wesley told his co-workers: "You have nothing to do but save souls. Therefore spend and be spent in this work. . . . Observe: It is not your business to preach so many times, and to take care of this or that society; but to save as many souls as you can; to bring as many sinners as you possibly can to repentance; and with all your power to build them up in that holiness without which they cannot see the Lord" (*The Works of John Wesley*, Volume VIII, Zondervan, p. 310).

Both John Wesley and George Whitefield, for great periods of time, were barred from the churches of England. They took to the fields to preach the gospel. Out of it grew the great Methodist movement, and revival in some areas within the Anglican Church. D. L. Moody used to go about the streets of Chicago giving out tracts and talking to everyone he met about Jesus Christ. He was called "Crazy Moody." William Booth, the founder of the Salvation Army, was a wild young lad of seventeen in the town of Nottingham, England. He heard that an American evangelist had come to town. He was eager to hear this stranger from the New World with his funny accent and his great stories. But when he went that night he was transfixed by the message of the gospel. He saw the unholiness and sinfulness of his heart and the demands of God before him. He said that he was almost transported into another world. When the invitation to receive Christ was given, this young boy responded, and out of that conversion came the worldwide ministry of the Salvation Army. An American Black man, a humble preacher of the gospel, went back to that chapel in England where Booth was converted, and when he thought of the souls that had been won and the people who had been blessed by Christ through the ministry of William Booth, he placed his hands on the bronze marker that marked the place of Booth's conversion and prayed aloud, "Do it again, Lord. Lord, do it again."

My prayer for all of you is in the same manner: "Lord, do it again. Do what you did when the apostles were called. Do what you did following Pentecost. Do what you did with Saul of Tarsus, and Augustine, and Luther, and Calvin, and George Whitefield, and D. L. Moody, and William Booth. Lord, do it again, and help us to reach the world for Jesus Christ."

## GOD'S HOLY MOMENT

At the close of every crusade, Dr. Graham considers this "God's Holy Moment." It is the moment of decision, of commitment. Listen to Dr. Graham as he pleads with his hearers to, "Come, follow Christ!"

"It is hard, and it is wonderful. There is a joy and a peace and a satisfaction in living for Christ. There is security. You know what life is all about, you know why you are here, you know where you are going when you die. But you don't have to wait until you die to experience heaven. You can have the peace and joy and happiness of heaven right now—in your heart. You don't have to go on with those terrible loads that you have been carrying, those terrible habits that have a grip on you. Let Christ come in by his Spirit and set you free.

"I am asking you to make that commitment right now. You can say 'yes' to Christ, and a great transformation can take place inside you. You can become a new person.

"You say, 'What do I have to do?' First, be willing to repent of your sins. That means that you say, 'Lord, I am a sinner; I am willing to turn from my sin.' Second, by faith you receive Christ. You don't have to wait till you understand it intellectually. All you have to know is that you have sinned against God, that God loves you and is willing to forgive you because of Christ's death on the cross. *Third,* you receive him personally, openly. Every person Jesus called in the New Testament, he called publicly for a purpose and a reason. He said, 'If you are not willing to openly acknowledge me before men, I will not acknowledge you before my Father which is in Heaven.'

"I am going to ask hundreds of you to get up out of your seats and come and stand on this field and say by coming, 'I am willing to acknowledge that I have sinned—I have broken God's laws. I am ready to change my life and receive Christ and follow him no matter what the cost.'

"You say, 'But, Billy, I am a member of the church—I am a member in good standing,' but you are not really sure that your heart belongs to Christ. You are not really sure your sin is forgiven. You are not sure if you died that you would go to heaven. You want to be sure.

"You may be Catholic, Protestant, or Jewish; you may not have any church relationship. God is speaking to you and you know that you need Christ. You want his forgiveness. You want his love. You want to surrender to him now not only as Savior but as Lord. You come. Now you can say, 'I will receive Christ, I will follow Christ. I will give him all I have. I want to serve him.'"

Beginning in a small stadium in Grand Rapids, Michigan, in October of 1947, people began to come—500 that night, 1,200 a month later, 2,200 the next year, 6,000 the next year, 40,000 the next year—until today several millions of people have gotten up out of their seats and stood before this evangelist of Jesus Christ and dedicated the rest of their lives to Jesus Christ, the Savior of mankind. It will not be until we reach heaven itself that we shall know how many people received Jesus Christ through the evangelistic outreach of this one man, Billy Graham.

# POPE JOHN PAUL II
## "YOU ARE ALL WITNESSES"

MY Brothers and Sisters in Jesus Christ.

The readings of today's celebration place us immediately before the deep mystery of our calling as Christians.

Before Jesus was taken up to heaven, he gathered his disciples around him, and he explained to them once more the meaning of his mission of salvation: "Thus it is written," he said, "that the Messiah must suffer and rise from the dead on the third day. In his name, penance for the remission of sins is to be preached to all nations" (Luke 24:46, 47). At the moment that he took leave of his apostles he commanded them, and through them the whole church, each one of us: to go out and bring the message of redemption to all nations. St. Paul expresses this forcefully in his second letter to the Corinthians: "He makes us ambassadors of Christ. God as it were appealing through us" (2 Corinthians 5:19, 20).

Once again, the Lord places us fully in the mystery of humanity, a humanity that is in need of salvation. And God has willed that the salvation of humanity should take place through the humanity of Christ, who for our sake died and was raised up (cf. 2 Corinthians 5:15), and who also entrusted his redeeming mission to us. Yes, we are truly "ambassadors for Christ," and workers for evangelization.

In the Apostolic Exhortation *Evangelii Nuntiandi* ("The gospel must be proclaimed"), which he wrote at the request of the Third General Assembly of the Synod of Bishops, my predecessor in the See of St. Peter, Paul VI, invited the whole people of God to meditate on their basic duty of evangelization. He invited each one of us to examine in what way we might be true witnesses to the message of redemption, in what way we might communicate to others the Good News that we received from Jesus through his church.

There are certain conditions that are necessary if we are to share in the evangelizing mission of the church. This afternoon, I wish to stress one of these conditions in particular. I am speaking about the unity of the church, our unity in Jesus Christ. Let me repeat what Paul VI said about this unity: "The Lord's spiritual testament tells us that unity among his followers is not only the proof that we are his but also the proof that he is sent by the Father. It is the test of credibility of Christians and of Christ himself. . . . Yes, the destiny of evangelization is certainly bound up with the witness of unity given by the Church" (*Evangelii Nuntiandi*, 77).

I am prompted to choose this particular aspect of evangelization by looking at the thousands of people whom I see gathered around me today. When I lift up my eyes, I see in you the people of God, united to sing the praises of the Lord and to celebrate his eucharist. I see also the whole of America, one nation formed of many people: *E pluribus unum.*

In the first two centuries of your history as a nation, you have traveled a long road, always in search of a better future, in search of a stable employment, in search of a homestead. You have traveled "From sea to shining sea" to find your identity, to discover each other along the way, and to find your own place in this immense country.

Your ancestors came from many different countries across the oceans to meet here with people of different communities that were already established here. In every generation, the process has been repeated: new groups arrive, each one with a different history, to settle here and become part of something new. The same process still goes on when families move from the south to the north, from the east to the west. Each time they come with their own past to a new town or a new city, to become part of a new community. The pattern repeats itself over and over: *E pluribus unum*—the many form a new unity.

Yes, something new was created every time. You brought with you a different culture and you contributed your own distinctive richness to the whole; you had different skills and you put them to work, complementing each other, to create industry, agriculture, and business; each group carried with it different human values and shared them with the others for the enrichment of your nation. *E pluribus unum:* you became a new entity, a new people, the true nature of which cannot be adequately explained as a mere putting together of various communities.

And so, looking at you, I see people who have thrown their destinies together and now write a common history. Different as you are, you have come to accept each other, at times imperfectly and even to the point of subjecting each other to various forms of discrimination; at times only after a long period of mis-understanding and rejection; even now still growing in understanding and appreciation of each other's differences. In expressing gratitude for the many blessings you have received, you also become aware of the duty you have toward the less favored in your own midst and in the rest of the world—a duty of sharing, of loving, of serving. As a people, you recognize God as the source of your many blessings, and you are open to his love and his law.

This is America in her ideal and her resolution: "one nation, under God, indivisible, with liberty and justice for all." This is the way America was conceived; this is what she was called to be. And for all this, we offer thanks to the Lord.

But there is another reality that I see when I look at you. It is even deeper, and more demanding than the common history and union which you built from the richness of your different cultural and ethnic heritages—those heritages that you now rightly want to know and to preserve. History does not exhaust itself in material progress, in technological conquest, or in cultural achievement only. Coming together around the altar of sacrifice to break the bread of the Holy Eucharist with the successor of Peter, you testify to this even deeper reality: to your unity as members of the people of God.

"We, though many, are one people in Christ" (Romans 12:5). The church too is composed of many members and enriched by the diversity of those who make up the one community of faith and baptism, the one body of Christ. What brings us together and makes us one is our faith—the one apostolic faith. We are all one, because we have accepted Jesus Christ as the Son of God, the Redeemer of the human race, the sole Mediator between God and man. By the sacrament of baptism we have been truly incorporated into the crucified and glorified Christ, and through the action of the Holy Spirit we have become living members of his one body. Christ gave us the wonderful sacrament of the Eucharist, by which the unity of the church is both expressed and continually brought about and perfected.

"One Lord, one faith, one baptism" (Ephesians 4:5), thus we are all bound together, as the people of God, the body of Christ, in a unity that transcends the diversity of our origin, culture, education, and personality—in a unity that does not exclude a rich diversity in ministries and services. With St. Paul we proclaim: "Just as each of us has one body with many members, and not all the members have the same function, so too we, though many, are one body in Christ, and individually members one of another" (Romans 12:4, 5).

If then the church, the one body of Christ, is to be a forcefully discernible sign of the gospel message, all her members must show forth in the words of Paul VI, that "harmony and consistency of doctrine, life and worship which marked the first day of her existence" (Apostolic Exhortation on Reconciliation within the Church, 2), when Christians "devoted themselves to the apostles' teaching and fellowship, to the breaking of bread and prayers" (Acts 2:42).

Our unity in faith must be complete, lest we fail to give witness to the gospel, lest we cease to be evangelizing. No local ecclesial community therefore can cut itself off from the treasure of the faith as proclaimed by the church's teaching office, for it is to this teaching office of the church, to this magisterium that the deposit of faith has been especially entrusted by Christ. With

Paul VI I attest to the great truth: "While being translated into all expressions, the content of the faith must neither be impaired nor mutilated. While being clothed with the outward forms proper to people: it must remain the content of the Catholic faith just exactly as the ecclesial Magisterium has received it and transmits it" (*Evangelii Nuntiandi*, 65).

Finally, and above all, the mission of evangelization that is mine, and yours, must be carried out through a constant unselfish witnessing to the unity of love. Love is the force that opens hearts to the word of Jesus and to his redemption: love is the only basis of human relationships that respect in one another the dignity of the children of God created in his image and saved by the death and resurrection of Jesus; love is the only driving force that impels us to share with our brothers and sisters all that we are and have.

Love is the power that gives rise to dialogue, in which we listen to each other and learn from each other. Love gives rise, above all, to the dialogue of prayer in which we listen to God's Word, which is alive in the Holy Bible and alive in the life of the church. Let love then build the bridges across our differences and at times our contrasting positions. Let love for each other and love for truth be the answer to polarization, when factions are formed because of differing views in matters that relate to faith or to priorities for action. No one in the ecclesial community should ever feel alienated or unloved, even when tensions arise in the course of common efforts to bring the fruits of the gospel to society around us. Our unity as Christians, as Catholics, must always be a unity of love in Jesus Christ our Lord.

In a few moments we shall celebrate our unity by renewing the sacrifice of Christ. Each one will bring a different gift to be presented in union with the offering of Jesus: dedication to the betterment of society; efforts to console those who suffer; the desire to give witness for justice; the resolve to work for peace and brotherhood; the joy of a united family; or the suffering in body or mind. Different gifts, yes, but all united in the one great gift of Christ's love for his Father and for us—everything united in the unity of Christ and his sacrifice.

And in strength and power, in the joy and peace of this sacred unity, we pledge ourselves anew—as one people—to fulfill the command of our Lord Jesus Christ: Go and teach all people my gospel. By word and example give witness to my name. And behold, I am with you always, until the end of the world.

This was the Pope's last meeting with the people in the Chicago area and took place in Grant Park, which borders Lake Michigan. To the immense gathering of over one million people, he called the people to be "ambassadors for Christ," to "witness to their faith," to "stand in unity" and "go and teach all people" the gospel of Jesus Christ.

At this occasion, he received into the church hundreds of persons who had prepared for reception into the Christian community from all walks of life.

# DR. D. JAMES KENNEDY
## TRAINING LAYMEN
## FOR THE TASK OF EVANGELISM

## I. SURVEYING THE PROGRAM

This program for training laymen for the task of evangelism grew out of the specific problems and specific situation of the Coral Ridge Church in Fort Lauderdale, Florida, and yet the program contains within it some "readily transferable techniques" which can and have been used by other congregations. We believe that the principles contained in the program represent some of the basic principles of the New Testament concerning the matter of evangelism, though by no means does this program exhaust all of the biblical teaching and possibilities of evangelism. It should be stated here at the outset that this is a program of personal lay evangelism and does not begin to encompass many of the other sound and biblical methods of evangelism, such as mass evangelism or pulpit evangelism.

Realizing that laymen are perhaps the most strategic and also the most unused key to the evangelization of the world, we have endeavored to build a program which will motivate, recruit, and train men and women to do the job of evangelism, and then to keep them doing it. This, of course, is not an easy task, as most every pastor can testify. And yet it would seem that the basic principles of New Testament evangelism would require that this mobilization of the laity take place. Let us look for a minute at some of these principles.

## II. EXAMINING THE PRINCIPLES

Christ's first instructions to his new followers in the first chapter of Mark were, "Come ye after me, and I will make you to become fishers of men." His last words on this earth to his disciples were, "But ye shall receive power, after that the Holy Ghost is come upon you: and ye shall be witnesses unto me both in Jerusalem, and in all Judaea, and Samaria, and unto the utttermost part of the earth." Christ thus began and ended his ministry with the command to be witnesses and fishers of men. This thrust of his teaching is summed up in the Great Commission where Jesus commands his followers to go into all of the world and preach the gospel to every creature. The first and obvious principle then is that *the church is a body under orders by Christ to share the gospel with the whole world.*

But the question then arises, *How is this to be done and by whom?* We believe that one of the greatest victories Satan has ever scored is the idea which he has foisted off on probably 90 percent of the Christian church that it is the task of ministers and evangelists only to share the gospel of Christ and that this is not the job of laymen. So successful has Satan been with this stratagem that it has been estimated that probably 95 percent of our church members never lead anyone to Christ. Thus the army of Christ has been more than decimated and the response from the pew has been, "Let clerical George do it." I am thankful that today there is an obvious trend in the opposite direction, as more and more laymen and churches are realizing and accepting their responsibility to witness. The second important principle then is that the laymen as well as the ministers must be trained to evangelize. Over 99 percent of the church is made up of laymen. Therefore, if they are A.W.O.L. there is little doubt that the battle will be lost.

It was the witness of the entire early Christian church that produced such a tremendous impact upon the world. In Acts 8:4

we read, "Therefore they that were scattered abroad went every where preaching the word." But some have said, "Does not this refer to the apostles? After all, what do laymen know about such things?" A standard exegetical axiom is that "a text without a context is a pretext." Thus, this text has been ripped from its context and used as a pretext for idleness on the part of multitudes of laymen. But let us examine its context. In Acts 8:1 we read, ". . . they were all scattered abroad . . . except the apostles." Therefore we see that according to the emphasis of this passage *those who went everywhere preaching the word were everyone except the apostles.* And the term translated "preaching the word" is from the Greek verb εὐαγγελίζομαι which means, of course, *to evangelize.* Thus we see that in the early church all of the laymen went everywhere "evangelizing." This is the lost ideal that we are striving to regain.

We have seen what needs to be done and by whom; now let us ask, *How are we going to get them to do it?*

There have been hundreds of thousands of messages preached on the responsibility of Christians to witness, and yet there is a striking absence of any formidable army of lay witnesses. Something, therefore, must be missing. This brings us to our next important principle, namely, *evangelism is more caught than taught.* This oft-repeated phrase rather accurately describes what is missing in most attempts at teaching laymen to evangelize, and also describes fairly well the method that Christ used to teach his followers. I have asked thousands of ministers how many of them have preached sermons on the need to witness and have taught classes on this subject. Most of them have raised their hand, but when I have asked how many of them make a habit of taking their people with them when they go out to evangelize, only 3 or 4 percent will usually respond. Just this week I questioned a group of ministers, missionaries, and teachers, and found that only about 1½ percent of their members were regularly engaged in leading people to Christ. Then I discovered that only three of these people took their laymen with them when they went to evangelize. The average person can no more learn to evangelize in a classroom than he can learn to fly an airplane in the living room. The missing link of modern evangelistic training, which was so thoroughly provided by Christ, is *"on-the-job training."*

These are the most basic principles that we feel need to be understood and accepted if a church is to have an effective program of evangelism.

## III. REVIEWING THE HISTORY

This program grew out of the experiences I had in starting this church, which was a home mission project and which is now nine years old. I came directly to this work from seminary, and though I preached evangelistically and had taken all of the courses offered at seminary on the subject of evangelism, and read many books besides, I found that the sophisticated people of Fort Lauderdale did not respond to my message from the pulpit. I was totally lacking in both confidence and know-how as far as confronting individuals face to face where the gospel was concerned. After eight or ten months of preaching, the congregation had gone from forty-five to seventeen people, and I was a most discouraged young minister. About this time I was invited to Decatur, Georgia, to preach ten days of evangelistic services. Happy to get away for a while from my Fort Lauderdale fiasco, I accepted the invitation. When I arrived the pastor told me that I would be preaching each night, but more importantly, he said, we would be visiting in the homes each day—morning, noon, and night—to present the gospel to people individually. I was petrified, for I knew that I had no ability whatsoever to do this. However, the next morning we went out. After about a half hour of my stumbling attempts at evangelism, the pastor took over the conversation, and in about fifteen or twenty minutes led the man to Christ. I was astonished but did not realize even then the impact this was to have on my life. For ten days I watched this pastor lead one person after another to Christ for a total of fifty-four individuals during those ten days. I went back to Fort Lauderdale a new man, and began to do just what I had seen done. People responded. Soon dozens, scores, and then hundreds accepted Christ. The principle of "on-the-job training" had been applied to my life, and had produced its results.

I then realized that there was a definite limit to the number of people that I myself could see, and that what I ought to do was to train others to do the same thing. What I then foolishly did is the same thing that thousands of others no doubt have done: I organized a class on witnessing. I gave them six lessons and sent them out. They all went home terrified! I waited a few months and tried again. This time I gave them twelve lessons—again no success. A few more months and another series, more elaborate, more complex; fifteen weeks—again no results. I do not know of one single adult that was brought to Christ by one of these laymen as a result of these witnessing classes.

Finally it struck me like a bolt of lightning—I had had classes for three years and had not learned how to witness. It was not until someone who knew how had taken me out into people's homes, that I finally got the confidence to do it myself. Thus I began the program which has continued for the past six years. It began by my taking out one individual until he had confidence to witness to others, and then another, and another. And so it has grown. After the people are trained, they in turn can train others.

## IV. MOTIVATING THE CHRISTIANS

Often when an evangelism program is envisioned, a pastor will begin by preaching on the subject and then inviting everybody who is willing to take part to come on some specified night to begin the program. This is the way that we tried at first to motivate people and recruit them, but we found that it was not very successful. The basic motivation will no doubt begin from the pulpit with sermons on the responsibility, privilege, and necessity for witnessing for Christ. The great texts already mentioned, and others, should certainly be preached with clarity and forcefulness. However, our experience would teach us that the actual recruiting should not be done from the pulpit, but rather on an individual, person to person basis.

## V. RECRUITING THE WORKERS

When Christ called his apostles he first prayed all night and then called them specifically by name. Now an apostle (ἀπόστολος) was one sent forth with a commission. The term has both a narrow and a wider meaning. In its narrower sense it refers only to the twelve apostles whom Christ first called. In its broader sense it refers to every Christian who has been sent forth by Christ with a great commission. We would therefore recommend that, after much prayer, the minister select several people whom he would like to take with him to learn how to evangelize. (I might add at this point that we have changed from going out two by two, to going out by threes. The reason for this was that it solved the problem of what to do about women in a program of this sort. To send out two women at night in a large modern city can be quite dangerous; to send out one woman with somebody else's husband can be dangerous in a different way; to send out only husbands and wives defeats the purpose of multiplication.)

We have selected Wednesday morning from 9:00 to 12:00 and Thursday evening from 7:15 to 10:30 as our time of visitation. In each case we have a report back meeting which I feel is quite important to prevent discouragement. On Wednesday noon we have lunch; we provide the coffee and the people bring a bag lunch. On Thursday night we provide Sanka and doughnuts. At these times we hear the reports of the work of the day. These report sessions help reduce dropouts due to discouragement, as they have an opportunity to have their spirits lifted by others whom God has blessed that night or morning. I would suggest then that the pastor select two people for Wednesday and two others for Thursday night. As long as we do not have three men together, which seems a bit heavy, we have not found that the three individuals constitute much of a problem.

We have two training programs a year, the first beginning early in October and running about four and a half months until the middle of February. At this time we hold our clinic for ministers for a week. Then we begin our next training class, which runs till the beginning of summer. Again, all of these details will vary according to local customs and circumstances.

I did not want to begin a program in this small way with only one or two individuals, but wanted rather to train a whole class of evangelists at one time. The result was that I ended up with none. However, if you begin with a few, you can grow in not too much time into a large body of witnesses. At the end of the four-and-a-half-month training program each of these four trained individuals would recruit two more workers and the minister also would recruit four more. Now there would be the original four plus their eight, making twelve, plus the minister's new four, making sixteen, plus the minister, or a total of seventeen. After the next class the sixteen laymen would get thirty-two more, making forty-eight, plus the minister's four, which makes fifty-two, plus the minister, making fifty-three. And soon it could grow to a hundred, then two hundred. The people are recruited by personal visits at which time the program is explained in detail by the trained individual. The people are then invited to a dinner which will consist of a greater explanation of the goals and principles and reasons for the program, plus testimonies of what has been accomplished. Then they are asked to commit themselves to the entire four-and-a-half-month training program *or else not to start*. Paul said, "I am afraid of you, lest I have bestowed on you labor in vain."

## VI. TRAINING THE EVANGELISTS

Our program consists of three types of training.

1. CLASS INSTRUCTION
These classes, lasting about a half hour each, are held once a week on the day the people come to the church for visitation. They meet together for class instruction for a half hour and then go out into the field. During this class instruction there is a brief lecture on the topic of the week, assignments are given for study during the following week, and the class is divided into twos where they practice what has been learned during the previous week.

2. HOMEWORK ASSIGNMENTS
A detailed notebook has been prepared containing instructions in how to present the gospel logically and interestingly. Assignments are given each week, consisting of portions of the gospel to be learned. These are checked and recited each week at the class.

3. ON-THE-JOB TRAINING
The third and most important part of the training is the "on-the-job training." Here each trainee goes out with a trained individual and listens as this trained person endeavors to lead someone to Christ. *This is the vital, almost indispensable, element of training.*

# VII. PRESENTING THE GOSPEL

Our basic approach is neither apologetic, defensive, nor negative. It is a simple, positive statement of the *Good News of the gospel*. We have found that most Christians do not know how to make an intelligible, forceful, and interesting presentation of the gospel. This is basically what we are trying to teach them to do.

We feel that a very useful tool, which is often omitted from texts on evangelism, is an actual presentation of the gospel itself. Such a presentation is included in the training materials and the people are encouraged to learn it and use it as a guide as they begin to present the gospel of Christ. Later it is no doubt adapted to the individual personality, to which many additions or subtractions are made, as the case may require. But most people need something to start with.

The essential things which we are trying to teach our people are: how to get into the gospel and find out where the person is spiritually, how to present the gospel itself, and how to bring the person to a commitment to Jesus Christ at the conclusion.

In teaching the trainees the presentation of the gospel itself (II in the outline), we proceed in the following manner. First we have them learn the outline of the gospel, which might be considered as the *skeleton*. Second, we have them learn *Scripture verses* which give muscle, so to speak, to the outline. Third, we have them learn *illustrations* which *flesh out* and make clear and understandable the outline of the gospel.

In having the trainees learn the gospel we do not have them memorize the entire presentation but rather have them first learn the outline and then gradually *build on it*. First we have them add just enough so that the bones of the outline don't rattle. Then we have them give a three-minute presentation of the gospel. And then we enlarge it to five minutes, and then to eight. We continue to enlarge the presentation until they are able to present the gospel in anywhere from one minute to one hour, depending on what the particular situation warrants. We provide them with the long presentation of the gospel, as well as a shorter one, which are used as resource materials from which they can build their presentation, based on the outline. In this way it becomes their own. We encourage them to work on it, practice it, give it, until indeed *they own it* and can give it with authority.

## VIII. PRESERVING THE FRUIT

A program of evangelism such as this generates a tremendous need for *followup*. It has produced a need for a followup secretary and also a followup minister on our staff; but the main responsibility for followup rests with the individual who has led the person to Christ. In our training notebook we have a rather elaborate section on followup principles and procedures. In essence the followup procedure involves several individual return visits wherein the new convert is established in the Scriptures and assured of his salvation. We use a variety of materials and recommend highly the Navigator followup materials. After several personal visits we then endeavor to get the people into a small Bible study group which will consist of several more mature Christians, plus four or five newer Christians. These classes of six or eight people then provide the *spiritual incubator* in which the newborn babe will live out the first few months of his Christian life.

Followup procedures are not completed until the convert has been taught to study God's Word, to pray, to live the Christian life, and to walk with Christ. Then he is encouraged to come into the evangelism program to learn how to win others to Christ. Yet at this point the followup still is not complete, for he must be taught not only *how to reproduce* but also *how to disciple* his new convert until he has matured to the point that he also is able to bring someone else to Christ. This emphasis of *spiritual multiplication*, looking past the first generation to the second, third, and fourth, is the secret of an expanding and multiplying evangelistic ministry. In just a few years this has produced instances of great, great, great, great, great, great, great grandchildren in the faith. The acid test of any followup procedure ultimately will be: *Is it producing spiritual grandchildren and great grandchildren?* If not, then something is amiss and somewhere the process is breaking down.

## IX. MULTIPLYING THE RESULTS

Christ said, "The field is the world." I believe that *our field should be the world;* that every church, every individual, has a worldwide responsibility. I do not believe that any church can settle for anything less than worldwide evangelism as its own responsibility. Is it utterly unrealistic? I think not. Eleven men, indeed a very small church, have succeeded in carrying the gospel to almost every nation on earth. And the march of those eleven men goes on today. I do not believe, however, that it necessarily must take hundreds or thousands of years for the impact of the gospel to spread around the world. *The process of spiritual multiplication can grow with the rapidity of the physical population explosion that we are seeing today.* Our goal then is to reach the world for Christ. *How can this be done?*

First we must realize that *our responsibility extends beyond our own church, our state, and even the United States.* But how are we to meet this responsibility? We have proceeded in this manner. In addition to training an increasing number of people in our own country (in our last class we hade 298 individuals), we have also trained a good many other churches in the city and the immediate area. In addition to this we have an annual clinic in February when we have been bringing down almost a hundred ministers for five days of intense training, both in classroom instruction and on-the-job training, going out with our trained laymen. This has proved very successful and hundreds of ministers have gone back to their churches with a new vision for evangelism and a new zeal for training their people to do the work of ministry.

There are now churches all over the United States which are building programs of lay evangelism as a result of these clinics. But this does not yet meet the need. After these ministers have trained their people to become evangelists *we encourage them to have their own clinics,* inviting ministers of other churches in their sphere of influence to come and learn from their people. Then they may go back and train their members, and, even further, hold clinics and invite other ministers, so that the multiplication procedure may continue.

Our first daughter clinic was held this spring with forty ministers involved in a church in Michigan. A second and third clinic are planned for this summer and fall, and so the process continues. This program has already jumped the boundaries of the United States, and such programs are being conducted in a number of other nations. As this is being written, the program is being introduced in Japan. We hope that in the not too distant future there will be churches in every nation training their laymen and then training other ministers to teach their people, until a vast army of tens of millions of Christian lay evangelists has been raised up. *This is our goal.* This is our challenge. And by the continual supply of the Spirit of Christ, we trust that it shall be done.

*Soli deo Gloria.*

# JOSEPH CARDINAL BERNARDIN
## EVANGELIZATION: FOCUS OF ALL MINISTRY

CHAPTER

4

EVANGELIZATION. What has been happening to that word in the years since Pope Paul VI's *Evangelii Nuntiandi?* For many, it is a buzz word that describes anything from a parish's social affairs to its outreach to the unchurched. For some, it remains a somewhat disturbing or frightening word, one that does not belong to Catholics. So often, evangelization seems to have the connotation of hitting people over the head, or asking them questions, in a coercive way, about the quality of their spiritual lives. For others, it has become a kind of automatic, mechanistic way of achieving a "born again" experience. Such approaches to evangelization leave a bad taste in our mouths. We know life's ambiguities and the mysterious nature of things. We know how faith often involves risk, surrender, trust in the face of that ambiguity and mystery. Evangelization efforts that smack of superficiality, coercion, easy answers, or cheap grace—that is, evangelizing that is not rooted in the human experience and does not try, through faith, to make sense out of daily living—will ultimately turn people off to the whole notion of evangelization.

"Evangelization" must not become just another term in our ministerial jargon, one whose meaning is diffuse. Neither can it be, in the Catholic perspective, a ministerial strategy that plays on people's vulnerabilities, offering them a world of easy answers, a world of black and white, one that is mystery free. And it certainly is not a continuation of the evangelization of Jesus, if it reinforces some of the values present in our culture. By that I mean ministry or evangelizing styles or ways of doing church that allow godless people to pursue godless ways, all the while feeling religious about it.

## WHAT IS EVANGELIZATION?

So as not to spend all my time explaining what evangelization is not, allow me to make a few positive statements about what I believe it to be. In the Scriptures, Jesus never evangelized through coercion. Rather, he did it by invitation. Jesus evangelized by inviting people to embrace several realities . . . all of which are connected and interrelated.

First, Jesus invited people to the Kingdom of God. This is the essence of his evangelization. What did he mean by this term, "the Kingdom of God," which he uses so often in the Scriptures, sometimes referring also to the reign of God? The Kingdom or reign that Jesus preached was at once a new vision of life and a task or responsibility for his followers to achieve. The Kingdom was and is a vision or a dream, a reality yet to be fully realized. Jesus knew that the human heart hungers and thirsts for something beyond itself. He also knew the human tendency to try to satisfy our growling spirits with illusions, with what I would call spiritual junk food. In inviting people to the Kingdom of God, Jesus was revealing the reality—and the only one—that satisfies the heart's deepest hunger and thirst, namely the presence and love of God in our lives. The evangelizing of Jesus offered people a new foundation for their lives, a new filter through which life could be experienced. So Jesus' encouragement and invitation to the Kingdom is a beckoning: (1) to build our lives on God's love; (2) to live a spirit of trust and surrender; (3) to believe in the paschal nature of daily living; (4) to hope in his promise of eternal life; (5) to relate to each other as brothers and sisters who have a common Father; (6) to redeem society and culture. The Kingdom is both a new consciousness and a task, a quest.

Second, Jesus invited people to conversion. Conversion is the rite of passage into the Kingdom. Conversion now, as then, is a turning, a turning from something to something else. Generally, conversion is a turning from sin to grace. To use our previous terminology, conversion is a turning from illusions about life to the Kingdom, that is, the truth about life. As we try to continue the conversion ministry of Jesus, his evangelizing, we need to be more and more attuned to the thresholds for conversion in people's lives.

The life cycle itself is a threshold for conversion. As we grow older, the life questions we thought we had already answered satisfactorily present themselves to us again.

Evangelization is an invitation to conversion. Like Jesus, we must be sensitive to the thresholds or opportunities in people's lives when the potential for conversion is most alive.

Third, the evangelizing of Jesus was also an invitation to discipleship. In a recent book, *A Church to Believe In,* Father Avery Dulles encouraged us to begin seeing the church in the way Pope John Paul II saw it in his encyclical *Redemptor Hominis.* In that letter, the Holy Father referred to the church as a community of disciples. When Jesus evangelized, he invited people to develop a consciousness of the Kingdom which calls us to a totally new vision and way of life. The process of growing in this new consciousness is discipleship.

The Scriptures tell us a great deal about the disciples. Disciples are on a journey, the journey of life. On that journey they are following the teacher, the rabbi, Jesus. Most important in the discipling process is the personal relationship they have with the Master. As that relationship grows, they grow, however imperfectly, in appreciation of his vision, his values. Finally, this new vision or consciousness is shared with others. Conversion and discipleship constitute the experience of a transforming relationship with Jesus the Master. Evangelization is an invitation to that relationship.

Let me summarize. Evangelization is always an invitation—to the Kingdom, to conversion, to discipleship. Jesus evangelized through word and deed. At times, his very presence evangelized.

When Jesus evangelized, he offered meaning to people. He joined words and meanings to gestures of healing. For so many people today, the most effective evangelizing can be done through ministries of caring, healing, and helping. Evangelization is not just a piece of the church's educational ministries. It is surely that, but it is more, much more. It is the integrating force and thrust of all the church's ministries.

The church exists to teach the Lord's meaning and extend his healing.

## EVANGELIZATION IN CULTURAL AND ECCLESIAL CONTEXTS

One of the dangers in talking about evangelization and conversion in this way is the tendency to think in overly narrow categories, or to focus too much on personal salvation. In the Catholic tradition evangelization is also an invitation to become part of that community of believers we call the church. There can be no closet Christians. Our call to conversion is to become part of a redeemed people. In the body of Christ, believers become agents of conversion to one another. We become sacraments of God's presence for one another. The Kingdom happens for us in relationship, dialogically. We are a converting church, and the church (whether the parish, or some other ecclesial body) is the organism that nurtures the ongoing conversion of its members.

## THE CHURCH EXISTS TO TEACH THE LORD'S MEANING AND EXTEND HIS HEALING

Along the same relational line, evangelization must involve a confrontation with the values of the culture around us. In *Evangelii Nuntiandi*, Pope Paul VI spoke of evangelization as the transformation of culture. The loudest and most effective evangelizing force in our midst today is the media. Movies, television, and radio speak to our people's hungers and thirsts, our collective search for meaning, but the gospel they preach does not touch the mind and heart. Their gospel is about things. There are things outside of you; only achieving them, they say, will make you happy. Things are offered as satisfaction for our need for love, belonging, and meaning. In its proclamation of truth and meaning, evangelization must address this consumer culture, in which human beings and human nature are treated as commodities.

Paul VI also stated in *Evangelii Nuntiandi* that authentic evangelization leads to the development of people. Our evangelization, in other words, must lead us toward justice and peace. While the bishops' pastoral letter on nuclear arms addressed one demonic force in our day—the threat of a nuclear holocaust—there are many more that cry out for attention and evangelizing. Poverty, racism, sexism—indeed, all the paralyzing "isms" of institutionalized living are in need of the Good News. Our evangelizing efforts will not be authentic if they do not create a greater awareness of and a more intense determination to promote justice and peace in every sphere of life.

## EVANGELII NUNTIANDI: A BLUEPRINT FOR THE EVANGELIZING CHURCH

In *Evangelii Nuntiandi,* Pope Paul VI weaves a beautiful description of evangelization. He also issues a challenge: that evangelization indeed be seen as the central mission of the church in the third millennium of Christianity. He attaches to the challenge a hint about the future of ministry in the church. He speaks of the beneficiaries or the target groups of our evangelizing. In sum, Pope Paul VI's blueprint for an evangelizing church calls us to evangelize the churched, and the unchurched, the alienated, the young, and to join hands with our Protestant brothers and sisters.

## MEANING OF THE WORD OR ENERGIZING CENTER OF ALL MINISTRIES

As I conclude, I would like to emphasize again the point I have tried to make in this presentation. The popular understanding of evangelization as the primary step in the process of ministry of the Word, followed by catechists and theology, is indeed a proper understanding of the term. But the term is broader than that. Evangelization is the meeting ground where the ministries of the

Word, worship, youth, pastoral care, and other areas of the church's work all converge. The church's central mission is to evangelize, that is, to invite everyone to the Kingdom, to conversion, to discipleship. The church's central mission is to evangelize, that is, to proclaim the Lord's meaning of life, offer and extend his healing, transform culture, promote justice and peace. The church's central mission is to have an expansive notion of evangelizing, one that includes the many kinds of people hungering and thirsting for the Kingdom. For such an expanded notion of evangelization, the church needs a broad range of strategies and skills if it is to minister successfully in a culturally pluralistic society.

## CONCLUSION

I would like to close by again encouraging us, as ministers, to open ourselves to wisdom and richness of the Rite of Christian Initiation of Adults. In the third century, the golden age of the catechumenate, evangelization always had two characteristics: (1) it was not so much programmatic as it was relational; the Lord, his vision, and his Kingdom life style were transmitted initially through primary relationship in which people witnessed in word and deed to their newfound life; (2) it was not so much cerebral as it was experiential; the Kerygma became a life-changing event. In other words, conversion was always involved. In the fourth and fifth centuries, however, the relational, experiential tone of evangelization began to be minimized.

To be effective, evangelists need to recapture that earlier, twofold approach. An ecclesial conversion needs to take place, wherein Catholics sense the power and responsibility invested in them through the sacraments of initiation. No longer can the cleric or the religious be looked on as the ones entrusted with the mission to evangelize. All are called to evangelize by who they are, what they say, how they live. All are called to give witness to that transforming relationship present in their lives.

My fellow evangelists, to evangelize we need not hit anyone over the head with anything. We need only to speak the Lord's Word of meaning and extend his healing touch. Then we will change lives and transform hearts.

Joseph Cardinal Bernardin is the Archbishop of the largest diocese in the Catholic Church. With over three million members, the Archdiocese of Chicago serves almost every national group, every ethnic group, every social strata to be found anywhere in the United States. While Archbishop of Cincinnati, he established one of the most active and effective offices of evangelization to be found in the United States.

This address was given at the opening session of the newly founded National Council for Catholic Evangelization held in Chicago on June 12, 1983.

# THE REV. DR. ROBERT J. HATER
## EVANGELIZATION AND THE PRIESTHOOD OF ALL BELIEVERS

CHAPTER

5

## INTRODUCTION

Evangelization is rooted in the ways God communicates with people. The Good News which the Scriptures proclaim draws motivation and purpose from life itself. Life grounds the proclamation of God's Word. Hence, the universe, all living creatures, human love, and other life experiences communicate God's presence. Christians believe, however, in a unique revelation manifested through the Judeo-Christian Scriptures.

To evangelize means to proclaim this unique revelation, culminated in Jesus Christ, but rooted in life itself. In this paper we will look at evangelization in the Christian community, with special emphasis on its relationship to the priesthood of all believers. We will do this in three major parts: (1) evangelization and the communication/revelation of God's presence; (2) evangelization and the priesthood of all believers; and (3) evangelization, the family, and the world.

# I. EVANGELIZATION AND THE COMMUNICATION/ REVELATION OF GOD'S PRESENCE[1]

Catholic theology grounds creation in God's gracious designs. All creation is graced, yet imperfect, in the process of coming to fulfillment. Consequently, all creation can communicate, even though imperfectly, aspects of God's presence. This communication/revelation of God is in process, as the world continues to move toward completion. We see God's communication taking different forms and employing fresh symbols in changing historical periods.

In the beginning of recorded history, God communicated through nature, holy people, and communal celebrations. Christians believe that Jesus proclaimed a message that grounds all religious communications and reveals a once-for-all insight about God and life that focuses all religious symbol systems into a meaningful synthesis of the divine and human.

This synthesis effected in the life/teachings of Jesus Christ focuses on the unique way God is present in the world. The goal of this presence is described in terms of the "Kingdom of God." For our purposes we shall translate the "Kingdom of God" as equivalent to the "presence of God." What does Jesus teach us about the Kingdom/presence of God?

The Hebrew/Christian Scriptures teach that this Kingdom/presence is already here, but still to come. In other words, God is present "now," but since creation is incomplete and in process, we have "not yet" experienced the fullness of God's Kingdom/presence. The Scriptures teach us, however, important aspects of God's presence which form the basis for the Good News that evangelization proclaims. In particular, the Gospels of Matthew and Luke offer important insights about the way God's Kingdom/presence is in the world. Here we learn that:

1. Jesus' birth announces God's Kingdom. We notice how God's Son accepts the vulnerable, hurting condition of people from the first moment of his conception. This says much about the subsequent Kingdom theme of the synoptic Gospels.[2]
2. The Kingdom theme emphasizes the call to service—how the Christian God dwells with humans as one who serves.
3. The poor are God's special concern. "Poor" is to be

understood in terms of physical (economic), psychological, and spiritual poverty. The Gospels promise blessing for the poor, but imply that poverty is an evil to be overcome.[3]

4. Jesus' suffering and death attested to the message of the Kingdom, and his being raised up confirmed the authenticity of his person and teaching.

Jesus' first followers understood the message of the Kingdom/presence after the Pentecost experience. The latter illuminated the early Christians to see that Jesus continues to live and evangelize through them. The Kingdom/presence of God was communicated to the degree that they lived and taught as Jesus did. They saw that central to Jesus' life and teaching was the need to confess one's sins and be reconciled to God and one another. Consequently, forgiveness became the test of the presence of the Kingdom in the Christian community. Reconciliation had to happen before the Spirit of the risen Lord could effectively proclaim the Good News of God's love and forgiveness.

## II. EVANGELIZATION AND THE PRIESTHOOD OF ALL BELIEVERS

A priest is one who mediates between God and people. Most religions have their priests, who serve as a communication channel linking the human and divine.[4] In the Hebrew Scriptures the entire Jewish nation was described as a "priestly people"; in particular, the official priesthood was exercised by members of the tribe of Aaron—the Levitical priesthood.[5]

The epistle to the Hebrews describes Jesus as the one, supreme high priest.[6] Here Paul develops the underlying Christian belief about priesthood. For Christians there is only one priesthood, the priesthood of Jesus Christ. The Christian church is called a "priestly people" because all baptized members share in Jesus' priesthood.[7] Consequently, every baptized person is called to mediate or proclaim the Good News of the Kingdom of God.

### DIFFERENT RESPONSIBILITIES

Catholic theology since Vatican II stresses that the entire Christian community is a priestly people. This puts added emphasis on the unique gifts of each person and the community as a whole. The focus of mediation has shifted from the ordained priest to the entire community and individual members who mediate in different ways the one priesthood of Jesus Christ.

The Catholic Church distinguishes, however, between the common priesthood that all Christians share by virtue of baptism and the ministerial priesthood that is shared by the presbytery by virtue of ordination. This distinction is not of inferior versus superior, but one emphasizing different gifts. The ordained priest is the symbol/sign that the priesthood of Jesus Christ is present in the entire community, which mediates the Good News of God's love and forgiveness. The common priesthood of all baptized people focuses on the family and world. Here, the manifestation of God is already present through life itself. The Christian brings to life the new revelation of Jesus, thereby illuminating life in virtue of the salvation promised by Jesus Christ.

GROWING APPRECIATION[8]
Catholics often fail to appreciate that all Christians share in the one priesthood of Jesus Christ, with its accompanying responsibility to communicate the Good News through evangelization, catechesis, service, witness to the world, and liturgical celebrations.[9] Catholics will find it difficult to understand the implications of their priesthood, until they see that the call to minister belongs to the entire community, not only to ordained or institutionally appointed ministers.

The entire Christian community needs to view itself as a people engaged in the evangelization/conversion process.[10] The success of evangelization and catechesis within and beyond the community will be influenced by the degree to which all church members accept their responsibilities.

The Christian community calls forth ministers to take leadership roles in evangelization and catechesis. Parents, catechists, other pastoral ministers, priests, and bishops have special responsibilities.[11] To be most effective, these special ministries need to be understood and supported by the rest of the community. In addition, evangelizers and catechists must work in harmony within the church community, especially with the pastor and bishop.[12] These ordained ministers should serve as a sign that the ongoing mediation between God and the world is being carried out by the risen Lord ministering through the entire priestly people.

## APPROACHES TO EVANGELIZATION[13]

The church exists to carry on the mission of Jesus, who proclaims the Good News of God's Kingdom.[14] This Good News is rooted in the Christian community where the risen Lord continues to proclaim the message of Jesus' love.

1. *Jesus the evangelizer.* Following the tradition of the Jewish prophets, especially Isaiah, Jesus focused on hope as central to his evangelical activity. He holds out the hope of peace in this life and blessedness in the next for those who believe and respond in love. In so doing, Jesus becomes the model of all future evangelization. His message of hope becomes our message also if we share the Good News. We are empowered to hope because the Father raised Jesus from the dead. The paschal mystery is the heart of why we teach as he did.

We believe that Jesus is the fulfillment of the covenant between God and the Hebrew nation. Therefore, we look to him for direction as the church seeks new ways to proclaim the Good News. In the Christian Scriptures, we discover many components of Jesus' evangelizing activities. Pope Paul VI lists them as: (1) Jesus' incarnation, (2) his miracles, (3) his teaching, (4) the gathering of the disciples, (5) sending out of the twelve, (6) the cross and resurrection, and (7) the permanence of his presence in the Christian community.[15] These components remind us that evangelization is much more than teaching—it presupposes the witness of a life filled with hope and love.

2. *The church continues Jesus' evangelizing mission.* Pope Paul VI says, "We wish to confirm once more that the task of evangelizing all people constitutes the essential mission of the Church."[16] The Christian community carries on Jesus' mission— priest, prophet, and servant-king.

All Christians share in the one priesthood of Jesus Christ. This means that we incarnate his presence in the marketplace, at home, or in church. Together we are the body of Christ; separately we possess unique gifts for ministry. To accomplish our priestly mission, various ministries exist in the church. Their chief focus is evangelization or proclamation of the Good News. "Thus it is the whole Church," Pope Paul VI says, "that receives the mission to evangelize."[17]

To evangelize others the Christian community must constantly be evangelized, for the gospel message needs to be heard anew in the many circumstances of life. Without ongoing evangelization, the teachings of Jesus become lifeless, ministries become jobs, and church structures become ossified. In other words, the Christian community "has a constant need of being evangelized, if she wants to retain freshness, vigor, and strength in order to proclaim the gospel."[18]

*3. What is evangelization?* Evangelization is the activity whereby the church proclaims the gospel, so that faith may be aroused, may unfold, and may grow.[19] Evangelization is an ongoing process within the Christian community that seeks to initiate people ever more deeply into the mystery of God's love as it is manifested most fully in the dying and rising of Jesus.[20] This process inspired by the Spirit is a response to God's call to proclaim the Good News of the Kingdom in word and deed. It is not a separate ministry but is central to all ministries. It creates the climate for the ministries of Word, worship, and service.[21]

*4. Evangelization, the energizing center for ministry.* Jesus came to proclaim the Kingdom of God, a kingdom of love and service. This was his essential mission. Jesus' ministry, culminating in his dying, rising, and sending the Spirit, was the response to his mission. The church exists to continue the mission and ministry of the risen Lord. Consequently, ministry is the continued communication by Christians of God's love for all peoples as this love is forever shared in the real presence of the dying and rising of Jesus among us. Evangelization is the witness in deed and word that this is happening. Consequently, the content/process of evangelization and the paschal mystery are the same—the living Lord as he continually invites us to transform our lives and follow him.

All Christians share in Jesus' mission and ministry. *Sharing the Light of Faith* says that this mission is essentially one, namely, to bring about God's Kingdom. This mission has three aspects: to proclaim and teach God's Word, to celebrate the sacred mysteries, and to serve the people of the world. Then, *Sharing the Light of Faith* says that three ministries serve this mission, namely, the ministry of the Word, the ministry of worship, and the ministry of service. These are inseparably linked. Each includes and implies the others, even though we can discuss them separately.[22] Evangelization gives these ministries a reason and purpose. In proclaiming the dying and rising of Jesus which continues in all communal ministry, evangelization energizes Christian endeavors, thereby reminding us of our mission to hasten God's Kingdom. All ministry needs to be rooted in the life-blood of evangelization. Without it, individual or institutional efforts to proclaim the Word, celebrate it, or serve others will lack the dynamism promised by the Good News. In a pictorial way, we can illustrate the relationship between evangelization and the chief ministries that serve the mission of Christ and the church.

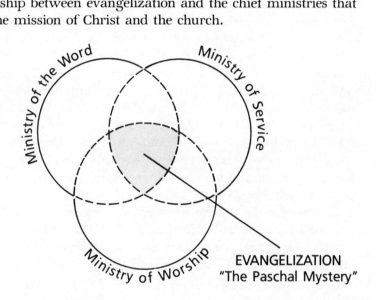

EVANGELIZATION
"The Paschal Mystery"

1. Evangelization, or the lived and proclaimed reality of Jesus' dying and rising, is the energizing center of all Christian ministry. It provides the dynamism for the ministries of Word, worship, and service.

2. The ministries of Word, worship, and service are inseparably linked. In reality, they never exist in isolation, but constantly interpenetrate one another, even though in various church ministries, or at a given time or place, one or the other may predominate. Their effectiveness depends upon whether or not they are enlivened by the lived reality of an evangelized and evangelizing community.

3. Evangelization and its lived reality in a community of Word, worship, and service, constitutes the heart of the church's witness to the presence of Jesus among us, especially manifested in his ongoing dying and rising in the Christian community.

4. All church organizations, structures, and programs exist to help the Christian community evangelize through the ministry of the entire church.

## EVANGELIZATION AND CATECHESIS[23]

Catechesis further specifies evangelization. It is an element or moment in the evangelization/conversion process. Being a form of the ministry of the Word, catechesis "aims at developing understanding of the mystery of Christ in the light of God's Word. . . ."[24] Consequently, catechesis can be described as a process which invites a person to hear, understand, interiorize, and respond to God's Word in acts of service and celebration. Catechesis simultaneously firms up individual faith and initiates into community. If either of these is deficient, catechesis will not accomplish its full purpose. Catechesis helps adults, adolescents, and children—individually and communally—to better appreciate and respond to the living Lord. He personally manifests himself in individual and communal experiences as his presence is discerned in light of the Scriptures and in solidarity with the believing church. Thereby, the content of catechesis becomes the lived reality of the risen Word as he discloses himself to Christians.

Catechesis is a very important element in the evangelization process.[25] Pope Paul VI calls catechetical instruction a means of evangelization.[26] *Catechesi Tradendae* relates catechesis to evangelization in the words:

> . . . evangelization—which has the aim of bringing the good news to the whole of humanity, so that all may live by it—is a rich, complex, and dynamic reality, made up of elements, or one could say moments, that are essential and different from each other, and that must all be kept in view simultaneously. Catechesis is one of these moments—a very remarkable one—in the whole process of evangelization.[27]

These words focus catechesis within the dynamic process of evangelization. To specify its proper role, catechesis must be seen as an aspect of the ministry of the Word. Following upon our previous diagram, we can illustrate this relationship.

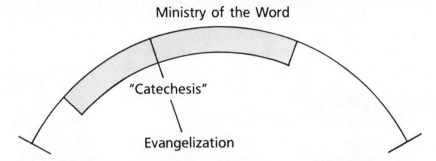

Ministry of the Word

"Catechesis"

Evangelization

1. All church ministries, including the ministry of the Word, are elements in the evangelization/conversion process.[28]

2. Catechesis is one form of the ministry of the Word, which includes, among others, liturgy and theology.[29]

Evangelization and catechesis are closely related. Although we can describe them separately, catechesis cannot exist without evangelization, for its content is the same as the content of evangelization, namely, the person and gospel of Jesus Christ.[30] Consequently, "Within the whole process of evangelization, the aim of catechesis is to be the teaching and maturation stage, that is to say, the period in which the Christian, having accepted by faith the person of Jesus Christ as the one Lord and having given him complete adherence by sincere conversion of heart, endeavors to know better this Jesus to whom he has entrusted himself: to know his 'mystery,' the kingdom of God proclaimed by him, the requirements and promises contained in his Gospel message and the paths that he has laid down for anyone who wishes to follow him."[31]

As a moment in the evangelization process, catechesis presumes that initial evangelization/conversion has taken place.[32] In other words, it presupposes that an individual has accepted Jesus Christ as Lord in accordance with his or her age or state in life. The person, so converted, now desires to know better Jesus Christ—his message and person—as these are believed, taught, and practiced in the Christian community. Seen in this way, the specific aim of catechesis is "to develop, with God's help, an as yet initial faith, and to advance in fullness and to nourish day by day the Christian life of the faithful, young and old. . . . Catechesis aims therefore at developing an understanding of the mystery of Christ in light of God's Word, so that the whole of a person's humanity is impregnated by that word."[33]

All members of the Christian community are called to evangelize through word and deed. Each person mediates the priesthood of Jesus Christ in a unique way. As a community all share Jesus' Good News and become a sacrament to the world.[34]

## III. EVANGELIZATION, THE FAMILY, AND THE WORLD

The Good News should be proclaimed as Jesus did—simply and honestly. Before complex applications make sense to people, they need to understand the simple message of the Gospels, which revolves around love and forgiveness. The failure to proclaim this simple message has led many to leave institutional churches. This is especially significant in today's Catholic community.

PROCLAIM THE SIMPLE MESSAGE OF THE GOSPELS
The number of Catholics, especially youth, who regularly attend or join fundamentalist Christian churches is a cause of concern for sensitive Catholic ministers and parents. Those who leave often claim that the Catholic Church's message and structure are too complicated to meet their needs. On the other hand, they speak of discovering the simplicity of Jesus' message in fundamentalist churches.

While some may be making excuses, others feel it is necessary to leave the Catholic Church to discover Jesus. Whatever their reasons for leaving, the fact remains that their exodus presents a challenge to the church. Their response points to the need for the Catholic community to take a look at the way we convey Jesus' message.

Complex doctrines and structures may be useful for theological clarification and church management, but they do little to move hearts toward conversion. Unless the church relates all doctrines and structures to the goal of proclaiming the simple message of the gospel, these doctrines and structures will have little impact on people's lives. Consequently, the church must maintain a proper balance in its doctrines and structures, never forgetting that it exists to be an evangelical community.

We can receive help from Jesus himself in simplifying our

message and in revitalizing our Christian communities. He emphasized ministry to the poor, alienated, and sinners. Jesus found fault with those aspects of his Jewish tradition which had become too complex. But he never condemned or abandoned Judaism itself. Jesus' example teaches us an important lesson.

The Christian community must always focus on the simple message of Jesus and allow it to speak.[35] No degree of theologizing can substitute for it. We must also examine the witness that our church structures give to members and outsiders. All church structures need to be continually evangelized in one way or another in order to reflect the message of Christ.

Applying the evangelization/conversion process to church organizations is difficult. It will be a tremendous challenge for the Catholic Church—universal, national, diocesan, or parish—to put into institutional practice the challenges Pope Paul VI presents in *On Evangelization in the Modern World*.[36] The degree to which we evangelize our institutions will be a positive indication of the seriousness with which we, as a church, take Pope Paul's words.

The need to simplify applies also to catechesis. Jesus' message is simple. The catechist is not primarily a theologian. To catechize as if catechesis means teaching a mini-theology course will not accomplish the aims of catechesis. Catechesis speaks of the relationship between the Good News and life. When we hear people claim that our teaching is too complex, boring, or uninspiring, we should question what is going on. The Word of God is alive and speaks to all times and experiences. The truths of our faith, when taught simply and presented in a vibrant way, have the power to evangelize and catechize. It is tragic to hear people say they did not hear the Good News in the Catholic Church because the teaching was too complex.

EVANGELIZATION IN DIALOGUE: FAMILY, WORLD, CHURCH
The Good News that evangelization proclaims is rooted in life itself. From the Christian perspective the evangelization process involves a constant relationship between three sources of God's revelation/manifestation: world, family, church. These must be kept in dialectical relationship/tension, and failure to perceive the significance of any of the three poles will bring an incomplete understanding of the evangelization process. Their relationship can be viewed in a schematic way.

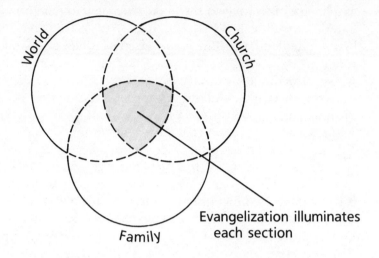

Evangelization illuminates
each section

Family

1. The expression "world" in this schema includes all in life
that sets the stage for family and church. It includes:
relationships of friends, singles, work, science/tele-
communications, human labor, and beauties of nature. By
"family" we mean integral/nuclear/divorced, single
parent, friends living in familial setting, and other family
configurations.

2. God's presence is manifested differently in each sector.
Family and world have a relative autonomy, and
God's Word is often communicated in these sectors
independently of church through nature, human love,
science, labor, art, and community support.

3. "Church" must relate to world and family to proclaim
most effectively the Good News of Jesus Christ.
Consequently, the shape this message takes will be
influenced by different cultures and world/family
situations.

4. Evangelization, from a Christian perspective, happens
when the Christian community addresses the Good News
to world and family in order to illuminate more clearly
God's presence that at times may seem absent or maybe
only vaguely appreciated.

5. The "priesthood of all believers" becomes the link that
unifies world, family, and church through proclaiming the

Word, celebrating the sacred mysteries of Jesus' dying, rising, and continued presence, and serving the family and world.

Seen in this perspective, world, family, and church relate as "subjects," not "objects." The world and family do not exist "out there" to be evangelized like an object that has little to contribute to the dialogue. The relationship is not one way, as it would seem to be in the following diagram.

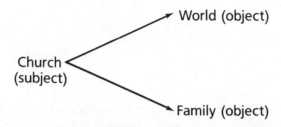

In this case evangelization would take the form of "speaking at" rather than "dialoguing with" life. This approach can too easily see world and family as "objects" to be evangelized.

On the other hand, evangelization must be seen as a relationship between subjects, each manifesting a different face of God.

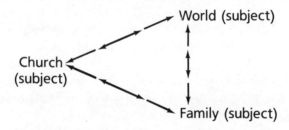

Here the relationship is reciprocal, with each subject-pole seen as a "subject," proclaiming in its own way the communication of God's presence. This perspective allows for the dynamic process of creation and revelation/communication of God's presence to continue in a holistic manner. Only when world, church, and family are in dialogical relationship can God's presence be fully appreciated in all three sectors.

## IMPLICATIONS FOR CHRISTIAN CHURCHES[37]

Evangelization will be a vibrant expression of the Good News as long as the Spirit is not stifled. This stifling happens when the simple message is not proclaimed, Christians are not faithful witnesses, or the relationships between world, family, and church are not maintained. In order to prevent this from happening, we need to:

1. Be evangelized and evangelizing people.
2. Proclaim the simple message of the Gospels.
3. Develop an evangelical thrust in all church personnel, programs, and organizations.
4. Base our evangelical efforts on peoples'/societies' needs. We do this by recognizing various faith levels and cultural differences.
5. Listen, forgive, and learn together as the body of Christ.
6. Dialogue with other Christian churches, basing our discussions on the common evangelical mission which we share.
7. Call forth Christians to bring the heart of the gospel into the heart of society.
8. Consider the world, family, and church as subjects of evangelization, each having a unique contribution to make.
9. Evaluate pastoral/administrative decisions in light of the simple message of the gospel—the message that God loves/forgives us and that we must love/forgive one another.
10. Admit that the Spirit does not effect any significant evangelization in a community unless church people are first converted.
11. Appreciate the common priesthood of all baptized Christians as the ground for the evangelization/conversion process.

These implications offer new challenges to the church. To meet these challenges we must appreciate the power of evangelization in the overall renewal of church life.

## CONCLUSION[38]

Recent church documents have spoken forcefully about evangelization. But words are not enough. Today the church is at a turning point; either we live what we profess or we fall into lethargy.

We should not wait for someone else to take responsibility. This may have been the style before Vatican II, when most decisions in the church came from the hierarchy. The Council changed this. Today the future of the Catholic Church is the responsibility of the entire community. If we like what is happening, the Spirit may inspire us to say, "Amen." If we do not, the same Spirit may urge us to say "no," and to take action. For, in the final analysis, the Holy Spirit is the principal agent of evangelization. This same Spirit, working in the entire community, "impels each individual to proclaim the gospel, and it is he who in the depths of consciences causes the word of salvation to be accepted and understood."[39]

Evangelization needs a new life in the Catholic community. We will say "Amen" to this need if we follow the Spirit and become that community of which St. Paul speaks: "Now you too, in him, have heard the message of truth and the good news of your salvation, and have believed it; and you too have been stamped with the seal of the Holy Spirit of the Promise; the pledge of our inheritance which brings freedom for those whom God has taken for his own, to make his glory praised" (Ephesians 1:13, 14, JB).

When this happens, evangelization will truly proclaim Good News, and people will understand more clearly the love of our Father.

The Rev. Dr. Robert J. Hater is Associate Professor of Religious Studies at the University of Dayton. He is a priest of the Archdiocese of Cincinnati and holds a Ph.D. in philosophy from St. John's University, New York. He has served as a professor of philosophy and director of the Graduate Department of Philosophy at the Athenaeum of Ohio, as well as adjunct professor of theology at universities throughout the country. He initiated the Lay Pastoral Ministry Program in Cincinnati.

He has also served pastorally in parishes throughout his diocese and was the Archdiocesan Director of Religious Education for six years. He is author of *The Ministry Explosion, Ministry in Catholic High Schools*, and many articles in catechetical periodicals. He is a noted lecturer in the fields of ministry and catechetics. He resides at Holy Family Parish in Cincinnati and is the resource theologian for the National Conference of Diocesan Directors of Religious Education—CCD (NCCD). He may be reached by writing to Holy Family Church, 814 Hawthorne Avenue, Cincinnati, OH 45205.

# FOOTNOTES

1. "Revelation" has been used here in a strict sense to refer to the unique communication of God to humans, disclosed through the Hebrew/Christian Scriptures as this revelation was interpreted by the Jewish and Christian communities that formulated them. The term "manifestation" or "communication" is used to refer to what is often called revelation in a wide sense—revelations of God in human life through nature, arts/sciences, human love, the world's other great religions. Although the author believes in the specialness of the communication of God in the other great world religions, the term "revelation" is restricted to Judeo-Christian revelation in this study, since the aim of the author is to limit the discussion to "evangelization" within the Judeo-Christian context.

2. See Matthew, 1:1 seq.

3. See Matthew, 5:1-10.

4. The notion of "priest," although sometimes described in different language, is an almost universal phenomenon. This is true in the world's great religions as well as other nature religions.

5. See Exodus, 6:14-27.

6. See Paul to Hebrews, Ch. 3 seq.

7. See Vatican II, *Lumen Gentium*, Chapter II.

8. This section is taken from my book, *The Relationship Between Evangelization and Catechesis*, p. 21. All sections used with permission of the N.C.D.D.

9. *Lumen Gentium*, 10; E.N., 6, 14, 15, 16, 59, 60, 61; C.T., 16; N.C.D., 30, 93.

10. E.N., 6, 14, 15, 16, 59, 60, 61.

11. C.T., 64 seq. Here, there is a particularly strong emphasis on family catechesis summarized in the words, "Family catechesis, therefore, precedes, accompanies, and enriches all other forms of catechesis"; #68.

12. C.T., 63, 64; E.N., 66, 68, 70, 73. For the central role that the bishop and priest play in evangelization and catechesis, cf. E.N., 68; C.T., 63, 64; R.C.I.A., 11, 44-46; N.C.D., 217, 218.

13. This section is taken from *The Relationship Between Evangelization and Catechesis*, pp. 5, 6, 2, 8-10, respectively.

14. E.N., 14.

15. E.N., 6 seq.

16. E.N., 14.

17. E.N., 15.

18. E.N., 15.

19. *The Evangelization of the Modern World*, U.S.C.C., 1973, 1, 2. This was the working paper for the International Synod on Evangelization. The Synod itself reflected this description of evangelization. In E.N., Pope Paul VI states: "For the Church, evangelizing means bringing the Good News into all strata of humanity, and through its influence, transforming humanity from within and making it new . . ."(18).

20. E.N., 17-24; C.T., 18. This approach sees evangelization as part of a lifelong process of conversion in which God's Word is heard again and again. This view differs from a fundamentalist kind of evangelization which emphasizes hearing the Word of God and accepting Jesus Christ, once and for all, in a definitive moment of "being converted or saved."

21. In using the term "evangelization," there are two tendencies in recent ecclesiastical documents. The first describes evangelization (including pre-evangelization) as operative before a person makes a commitment of faith. Here, evangelization is seen in terms of the initial proclamation of the gospel which is directed toward conversion and is followed by catechesis. This usage has missionary connotations, as well as other ramifications for pastoral practice. Although not used exclusively in this sense, the G.C.D. and N.C.D. tend to use the term "evangelization" in this way (cf. G.C.D., 17 and N.C.D., 31, 34, and 35). This first tendency is also implied in the R.C.I.A. although this document is not limited to this approach (7).

  The second tendency is to describe evangelization in a broader sense as an ongoing activity of the Christian community which includes the initial proclamation of the

Word (the first tendency mentioned above) as well as various pastoral ministries which nourish this initial proclamation. Cf. *Evangelization of the Modern World*, 1-2. E.N. and C.T. tend to use "evangelization" in this broader sense as the constant and necessary driving force of all pastoral ministry. (E.N. 6-24, 44; C.T. 25-28.)

22. N.C.D., 30. The N.C.D uses theological models to describe the mission and ministry of Jesus and the church when it describes this mission and ministry in terms of Word, worship, and service. These cannot exist in isolation. Neither can catechesis, liturgy, or service projects be classified exclusively and respectively into the categories of Word (catechesis), worship (liturgy), and service (service projects). These ministries interpenetrate each other, although catechesis, liturgy, and service projects may often tend to focus respectively within the general context of the ministries of Word, worship, and service. Although these models have limits, the N.C.D. recognizes their utility in clarifying aspects of God's revelation and continued communication with people through the mission and ministry of Jesus and the church.

23. The next two sections are largely taken from *The Relationship Between Evangelization and Catechesis*, pp. 2, 3, 11, 12, 22, 23.

24. C.T., 20.

25. See footnote 21. For the number of elements in the evangelization process which Pope Paul VI lists in E.N. #24, see page 5. It is within this context that C.T. describes catechesis as an element in the evangelizaton process.

26. E.N., 44.

27. C.T., 18. To emphasize the ongoing nature of evangelization in its relationship to catechesis, some use the expression "evangelizing catechesis." Cf. *Metodología y Temas para una Catequesis Hispana* ("Methodology and Themes for Hispanic Catechesis"), U.S.C.C., 1979, page 9 seq.

28. See page 7. Pope John Paul II describes catechesis as an element or moment in the evangelization process. Cf. C.T., 18. "Element" or "moment" is to be understood not sequentially as if these moments were on a continuum, but more like moments in a process to which one can return and reflect on the Word of God time and time again.

29. The N.C.D., following the G.C.D., emphasizes how the ministry of the Word takes different forms, depending upon the circumstances and the end intended. In indicating that the ministry of the Word is present in the liturgy, these documents illustrate how the ministries of Word, worship, and service are intimately linked (N.C.D., 31).

30. C.T., 18.

31. C.T., 20.

32. C.T., 19, 20.

33. C.T., 20.

34. See page 3.

35. E.N. stresses the importance of clearly stating the message in a simple way when referring to the homily (#43). Cf. also #21 and 26. But to relate the church's message and organizational structures to the simple message of the gospel is not to disparage theology or minimize the need for organization. Solid pastoral theology and catechesis, however, should be readily understandable; otherwise, the message that Jesus teaches us in his life of love will too easily be clouded in the complexities of rhetoric. The professional theologian exercises a valuable ministry by building upon the pastoral experience of today and relating the church's great theological systems, magisterial statements, and history of doctrines to the present scene. As far as church structures are concerned, Jesus' teaching invites us to be constantly on guard, lest the evangelical spirit of the Gospels is lost in a maze of bureaucracy. When church structures get too complex, the Christian community is challenged to clarify to what degree the spirit of the Gospels permeates them.

36. E.N., 41 seq. Practical ways to put the challenges of Pope Paul VI into institutional practice might include: 1) studying thoroughly E.N. with groups of parishioners in order to see the practical implications contained here for ministry in all segments of parish life; 2) developing a pastoral plan for evangelization in the parish or institution in question; 3) developing a way to assess how parishioners—regular churchgoers and alienated Catholics—consider the church; 4) looking at the parish or institutional

priorities to see what are the real priorities of the institution; 5) asking whether current managerial and church organizations further or stifle the spirit of evangelization; 6) looking at the degree to which the simple message of the gospel is proclaimed in a challenging and attractive way; 7) evaluating every form of institutional life by using the principles of E.N., especially its call to minister to the poor, as criteria of assessment; 8) incorporating the evangelical conclusions contained in E.N. into a vibrant celebration of God's presence in liturgical worship.

37. Most of these implications are taken from *The Relationship Between Evangelization and Catechesis*, p. 21 seq.
38. This "Conclusion" is taken largely from *The Relationship Between Evangelization and Catechesis*, p. 26.
39. E.N., 75.

# DR. LEIGHTON FORD
## THE SCOPE OF MASS EVANGELISM

### FUNCTION OF MASS EVANGELISM

These words are written on the refectory wall in a theological seminary for home mission priests at Lisieux, France: "I have not to search for the subject of my meditation. It is always the same. There is a wall which separates the church from the masses; the wall must be broken down at whatever cost to give back to Christ the crowds who are lost to him."

Mass evangelism aims to do just that—break down the wall which separates the church from the masses. It seeks to give back to Christ the crowds who are lost to him. In this sense, the term "mass evangelism"—the gathering together of people for the purpose of proclaiming the gospel—is not a misnomer. The term may be misunderstood, however, unless we point out that we engage in mass evangelism so that people may come into the Kingdom of God.

# PHILOSOPHICAL BASIS FOR MASS EVANGELISM

The objection is sometimes raised that a large percentage of those who attend evangelistic meetings are already churchgoing people. How does this relate to the goal of reaching those who are separated from the church? Several aspects of the question need to be examined.

1. Far more people come to a commitment to Christ from outside the church, even when the audience for the most part comprises church-attending people, than is generally appreciated. Dr. Robert Ferm found in his study of 14,000 Graham Crusade converts living on four continents, that 46 percent were unchurched prior to their decisions.

2. Some time ago Archbishop William Temple stated, "We cannot separate the evangelization of those without from the rekindling of devotion of those within." It is obvious to the objective mind that evangelism must begin among those within the framework of the church before it can have a significant impact on those outside. In a mass evangelistic meeting, there is unparalleled potential for communication to both groups.

3. The number of people separated from the church who are present at a mass evangelistic meeting is ultimately the responsibility of the local congregation. If the participating churches have motivated and mobilized their congregations effectively, large numbers of unchurched people will be present.

4. The impact of a series of mass evangelistic meetings is not confined to the meeting time. Such meetings open the way for the gospel to be communicated by radio, television, and newspaper to every possible area of the city and surrounding communities. The evangelistic team and other Christian workers take the message to schools, service clubs, offices, factories, and other strategic social structures not normally open to such a witness. In other words, the venture should be seen not as people attending a series of meetings for a set time, but as the whole people of God penetrating every possible sphere of life that

may be opened to receive the witness of the gospel during the designated period.

## THEOLOGICAL BASIS FOR MASS EVANGELISM

Mass evangelism finds its source in the Great Commission of Matthew 28:19, 20, NIV: "Go and make disciples of all nations." The population explosion means that in the world today there are more people than ever before who know nothing of Jesus Christ.

Yet the Lord Jesus never gave a command that could not be fulfilled. His Great Commission can be achieved, but only if the body of Christ functions as its Lord intended (cf. Ephesians 4:1; 1 Corinthians 12-14; Colossians 1:24 to 2:7).

Ken Strachan of the Latin America Mission made a study of the fastest-growing movements in their field: the Communists, the Jehovah's Witnesses, and the Pentecostal churches. Their common denominator was obviously not their message. The three groups are respectively an anti-Christian ideology, a heretical cult, and a Christian fellowship. Strachan concluded that the growth of any movement is in direct proportion to its ability to mobilize its entire membership for continuous evangelistic action.

Mass evangelism provides a basis for the mobilization of the whole church. It calls all believers to rediscover the power of personal and group prayer. Prayer cells are multiplied in churches and homes across the area while Christians are equipped to share their faith. Contacts with non-Christians are encouraged as believers try to build bridges of friendship to those who are separated from the church. People are enlisted to sing in the choir, usher, or serve in a variety of ways that relate to their particular gifts.

For the first time in many congregations, Christian leaders learn that the church is a body of related believers called to achieve God's purpose through discipleship and witnessing. The church is summoned to action—to advance against the enemy, tear down Satan's strongholds, and establish the Kingdom of God.

When the body of Christ rises to its true calling, the oneness of the church is demonstrated by the believers' love for each other (cf. John 13:34, 35.) In other words, Christians best express the nature of the church when they work together in evangelism.

Mass evangelism provides an excellent basis for a demonstration of Christian love and unity.

## THE MASS EVANGELISM MODEL

When the Leighton Ford crusade team works with local churches in a given city or area, the two basic objectives of a crusade are to evangelize the community and to strengthen the local churches. The four phases in this method of mass evangelism are labeled preliminary, preparation, penetration, and preservation.

In the preliminary stage, churches which desire to cooperate in a given city or area are drawn together to communicate the good news of Jesus Christ to as many people as possible through a corporate witness. At this point a crusade committee may be formed, agreement reached concerning the evangelist to be invited, the location and dates for the crusade decided, and responsible working committees established (prayer, finance, counseling and followup, visitation, Operation Andrew, youth, publicity, ushers, choir, etc.).

Next follows the preparation period designed to lay a foundation for the whole crusade effort. A network of prayer cells is established. Plans are implemented to raise the budget. People are trained in special classes to share their faith and counsel inquirers who will respond in the crusade meetings. Visitation of the total area is organized to invite people to attend the crusade. Believers are encouraged to follow the example of Andrew, who brought Simon Peter to Jesus, and to invite their friends to attend. Young people are urged to bring their peers. Ushers are recruited for the meetings. Practical details of the auditorium setting are given proper attention. Publicity and advertising to promote interest in the witness is planned and developed with special attention given to mass media communication.

When the crusade starts, the penetration phase begins. The focus centers on the evangelist's message. It also opens other areas of opportunity for the gospel to penetrate the life of a city. Doors are opened to the evangelist and his team which are not normally open to local believers. High schools, college campuses, service clubs, factories, office canteens, and homes provide a basis for community penetration because interest has been aroused by the crusade event.

As Christian people work together, the media take notice. Access to radio, television, and newspapers normally generated by a crusade provides an excellent forum for bringing the gospel to people who have not planned to attend the crusade.

The preservation phase begins when the first inquirer indicates an interest in making a commitment to Christ. This person is counseled personally so the way of salvation is clear. The counselor also takes the person's name, address, and other pertinent information to aid a local congregation in their followup. The new Christian then is usually guided into a neighborhood Bible study or local church. Because the goal of evangelism is the formation of mature Christians (cf. Colossians 1:28), the work of the crusade begins with a person's commitment to Christ.

## THE LEIGHTON FORD CRUSADES

Leighton Ford and his team have recently developed a model which seeks to enable the local congregation to develop a life style of reaching out. In this concept the crusade phase becomes a catalyst to inspire continuing evangelism rather than the climax of efforts.

The theme of this reachout process is "Reach Out Now" (cf. John 4:35), and all activity points to that end. It is hoped that this life style may be achieved by a local congregation prior to the celebration or crusade phase. The crusade then becomes one more way for the local church to reach out to others rather than the expression of the sum total of the church's evangelistic endeavor over a period of time.

Principles of the reachout process are based on the under-standing that the church is the extension of the incarnation. It must therefore embody in its life and ministry the principles of the ministry of Jesus (cf. Matthew 9:35—10:7; Luke 10:17-22).

These principles have been defined as:

1. Establishing specific objectives. Helping the local congregation (not just leadership) to discover together what specific goals the Lord is calling them to achieve in the Kingdom of God.
2. Identifying people's needs. Assisting the local congregation to break through the barriers which isolate the church

from people in the community and enable Christians to "build bridges of friendship" to people.

3. Equipping the people of God. Motivating the entire congregation to be the people of God and enabling them with confidence to share their faith.

4. Reaching out and discipling. Encouraging Christians to relate to people in their life situation with special emphasis on the use of the Christian home in this connection, sharing their friendship and faith in a way that will stimulate spiritual growth.

5. Celebrating and evaluating. Joining together in worship and thanksgiving to celebrate God's working in his world and to reach out to others in the context of praise and fellowship.

Reachout resources have been developed which are offered to enable churches to implement the principles outlined.

The effect of these concepts upon the crusade is to provide Christians with a keen sense of participation arising from their prior involvement at the congregational level. They are less inclined to come to the crusade as "spectators" of what others are doing, having already experienced the joy of reaching out to others.

## *THE QUALITY OF THE EVANGELIST*

As a communicator of the Christian gospel, Leighton Ford possesses unusual gifts which make his ministry particularly suited for preaching to contemporary society.

The content of his addresses has a wide appeal to people of all ages and backgrounds. It embraces those who have an academic and intellectual approach to life as well as people whose educational experience is more limited. Its focus is always to the whole man, his intellect, conscience, emotions, and will.

Factors inherent in this popular response to his preaching are:

1. Leighton Ford's subjects and starting point are at a significant level of interest on probable felt-need of a cross-section of his audience, e.g., "Loneliness," "Youth's Questions," "Love, Sex, and Marriage," "Happiness."

He is able to sustain interest in his topic with a local development of the theme, illustrations which are relevant to life today, and appropriate humor.

2. Another quality of his preaching is in the choice of language. Words are used which are easily understood by the total audience. Evangelical cliches are avoided. When an occasional doctrinal or scriptural phrase is used which may not be understood by some of the audience, he clearly explains the meaning by the use of an apt illustration.

3. The style of his preaching is also different from that of the generally accepted stereotype of evangelistic preaching. It is compellingly authentic without being dogmatically authoritarian. With a strong biblical emphasis throughout, Leighton Ford elucidates the truth in a way that carries his audience along with him. It is frequently affirmed in the evangelist's own personal experience, in a way that enables him to maintain empathy with the people to whom he is speaking.

4. Leighton Ford has also impressed vast crowds around the world by the clarity and restraint of his evangelistic invitation. Often at the outset of a message, Leighton Ford will explain why at the end he will give an opportunity for people to make a public response. The invitation is always expressed in terms which clearly establish to whom it is addressed. It is never prolonged nor emotionally manipulative.

Another area in which the evangelist excels is in TV and radio interview programs. Often people are invited to phone in their questions and Leighton Ford responds. In both of these situations, the evangelist not only gives convincing answers to the questions raised, but at the same time disarms any antagonistic attitudes by warmly identifying with the questioner.

This gift of responding to people against the background of their life's experience is never more evident than when Leighton Ford is asked to address special groups such as teachers, doctors, university students, civic clubs, and insurance groups. His ability to relate the Christian faith to the particular background and understanding of the group he is addressing is exceptional. A typical comment was once made following a luncheon of insurance men at which Leighton Ford was the guest speaker: "Before Leighton Ford went into the ministry, was he in the insurance field?"

Leighton Ford's special gifts and calling as an evangelist place him in the tradition of another of whom it was said, "They heard him [John] speak and followed Jesus."

## CRITICISM OF MASS EVANGELISM

1. Concerning the method. Despite its use by our Lord and by great evangelists of the past, there are some critics of mass evangelism who would describe it as a social anachronism with limited appeal in the contemporary world.

   While mass evangelism will not appeal to every person, it does provide an opportunity for non-Christians to hear an explanation of the gospel within the context of a crowd and without becoming self-conscious. Rarely does another opportunity exist to do this in today's society.

   The appeal of mass evangelism to a wide cross-section of the community, including young people, depends largely upon those planning each program. It must relate to each subculture it seeks to reach.

2. Concerning the messenger. There are those who claim that mass evangelism fosters a personality cult which many people find distasteful. Let us agree that mass evangelism at this point is open to the obnoxious self-promotion of the charlatan. But if an evangelist is carefully chosen whose authenticity and integrity are above question, there is no reason why the New Testament formula cannot be repeated. "They heard John speak and followed Jesus" (John 1:37).

   Some claim that apart from Billy Graham very few evangelists have sufficient charisma and drawing power to attract whole communities to mass meetings. But is personal charisma an essential qualification of an evangelist? Surely the response in attendance should arise basically from the action taken by the Christians in the churches sponsoring the evangelistic witness. Any added contribution made by the personality of the evangelist is a plus factor.

3. Concerning the message. Critics of mass evangelism often state that the evangelist's message is too simplistic and void of social relevance. The question is, "What is the gospel?" The Lausanne Covenant described this "objective thrust of the Gospel," this "good news," this way: "that Jesus Christ died for our sins and was raised from the dead according to the Scriptures and that as the reigning Lord he now offers the forgiveness of sins and the liberating gift of the Spirit to all who repent and believe."

The Lausanne Covenant goes on to state: ". . . We affirm that evangelism and sociopolitical involvement are both part of our Christian duty. . . . The salvation we claim should be transforming us in the totality of our personal and social responsibilities. Faith without works is dead."

A basic premise is, then, that the central message of evangelism is personal as it relates to the individual. The outworking of the response to this message must be seen in society as obedience to Christ, incorporation into the church, and responsible service in the world. These three emphases should find expression in evangelistic preaching as they highlight the nature of Christian discipleship; otherwise, the evangelist's preaching may produce decisions but not disciples.

This brief survey has highlighted one factor above others: that the effectiveness of any mass evangelism model is ultimately measured under the blessing of the Holy Spirit by the extent to which Christians in local congregations can be motivated and mobilized to be the people of God and achieve established objectives.

# THE REV. JOHN E. FORLITI
## ALIENATED CATHOLICS ANONYMOUS

*A ministry to Catholic "dropouts" who want
to take another look at their experience and
relationship with the church*

## PART I: BEGINNINGS

In November of 1976, I believed the time had come to develop
and expand the Catholic Church's ministry to its dropouts. It
seemed to be the right time to make special efforts to open its
doors, welcome home, and search out its alienated members.

The 1960s had passed. Some breathing space had settled nerves.
The waters were more calm following the post-conciliar storm.

It appeared to be an appropriate time for many Catholics to
review their faith journeys and take another look at their
religious roots. It seemed that I was meeting more and more
young adults, even some older persons, who were manifesting
renewed interest in their Catholic roots. They were alienated, but
were expressing interest in taking another look at the church.

How many dropout Catholics belong to this "alienated but
interested" category? My guess is that every diocese would have a
significant percentage, and every parish, from the largest to the
smallest, would surely have some. For my own diocese, the
Archdiocese of St. Paul and Minneapolis, I estimated that the

number of "alienated but interested" baptized Catholics aged eighteen to thirty-two, who had currently "dropped out" would be from 7,500 (this is 5 percent of the estimated 150,000 Catholics in that age group) to as high as 15,000 or 10 percent. The diocesan newspaper published an article I wrote entitled "Catholic Dropouts Should Take Another Look." I received a gratifying response—nearly 200 names came in the mail and over the telephone. (I believe that a more extensive effort at publicity would have turned up at least a thousand letters!)

After much pondering I decided to call the group Alienated Catholics Anonymous. "Alienated" seemed appropriate because it was a current and common term, relatively neutral, a fitting and fair description of the actual situation, and it didn't cast a judgment. It means: to feel like a stranger, to have drifted away from home and family, to feel cut off, no longer belonging. The word describes a condition that exists without positing the cause or limiting the experience. "Catholics" was obviously needed to identify the group. "Anonymous" suggested the process. Like other anonymous groups, this one would gather together people who have a *common need,* and who *want to talk about it with others* who will understand, and who will support them as they struggle with the pain their alienated condition causes.

As the names of interested people were coming in, I was trying to get a more firm grasp on the needs of the people I would bring together. My first conceptualization envisioned five sessions. The first session would enable the participants to get acquainted, establish some goals and purposes, and share an aspect of their personal faith journeys. The second would delve into their experience of church as a faith community. The third would identify doctrinal difficulties. The fourth would concentrate on the problem of Catholic identity. And the last session would attempt some resolution and chart some possibilities for the future.

The more I thought about this, the more I realized it was too much like a prayer group, a design for committed Christians, and was therefore unlikely to succeed. So I started over.

I decided to explore Alcoholics Anonymous for some insights and clarification. They have twelve steps. Their statement of each step is unambiguous, challenging, and obviously directed at a particular need crying for a personal decision. I began to construct the steps that I felt an alienated Catholic who wanted to "get back in" would have to go through to accomplish this.

This is what I developed:

| | |
|---|---|
| Admit the problem | 1. I admit to myself and to others that I must thoroughly review my relationship with God and my past experiences with the church. |
| Identify specific hurts | 2. I realize the importance of understanding my likes and dislikes about the church, and I will search out, with at least one other person, my present feelings, both positive and negative. |
| Commit to prayer | 3. I agree that daily prayer and Scripture reading are very important and I commit myself to them. |
| Review positive side | 4. I acknowledge that I want to take a fresh look at the Catholic Church, especially its positive side. |
| Place trust in God | 5. I will place my trust in God and hand over my life to him, desiring in all things to discover his will and do it. |
| Attain peaceful conscience | 6. After an honest appraisal of myself, I will be true to my conscience and respect the conscience of others. |
| Commit to Jesus | 7. I believe that Jesus Christ is the Lord of my life, and I will commit myself to be his disciple and follower. |
| Celebrate sacrament of penance | 8. I will thoroughly review the moral quality of my life and celebrate the Lord's forgiveness of my sins in the sacrament of penance. |

| | |
|---|---|
| Be reconciled to family | 9. I know that since others (family and friends) share a concern about my religious beliefs and practices, I will work toward mutual understanding as much as possible. |
| Tolerate others' beliefs | 10. I will strive always to be an instrument of peace by encouraging all Christians, Catholic and Protestant, to strengthen their religious commitments. |
| Return to eucharist | 11. I will look into active membership in a local parish community, and begin to worship God with that community in the regular celebration of the eucharist. |
| Provide for future | 12. I will continue to call upon other Christian friends to share my joys as well as struggles with my religious faith. |

The first group of Alienated Catholics Anonymous met February 20, 1977, a Sunday evening, at 7:30 P.M. Twenty people came. Their average age was about twenty-seven. The group included a mother over forty-five who came with her son and his girl friend. Overall, it was a real mixture of conservatives and liberals. About an even number of men and women came. Approximately half had Catholic grade and high school backgrounds, and half came with public school-CCD backgrounds. A few were not really alienated, but just interested in finding out more about the church today. One was a Jesus-people convert, Catholic in name, but recently converted to a fundamentalist Christian group located at the University of Minnesota. He was more interested in converting the rest of the group.

After a welcome and some time for introductions, I explained the origin of the idea of A.C.A. and revealed my masterpiece version of the Twelve Steps. I handed out the twelve. They read them, and the response was mixed. A few felt angry—"the same old approach, laying on the answers before we ask the questions!"

Some felt relief—"This is exactly where we're at." And the discussion began. We filled several newsprint sheets with the sources of their alienation, and their dislikes about the church. It was a good evening. I had made two points: (1) I wasn't out to convert them or impinge on their freedom, and (2) I would do my best to clear up their questions and misinformation.

Among the responses at the end of this opening session were:

"I liked tonight. I could say what I wanted to say."

"For fifteen years I have wanted to discuss some of this stuff. Tonight I felt I could do it without getting knocked down."

"I want to come back next time."

"We really got the things on our mind onto paper. Now maybe we can deal with them."

"I wish some of my friends could have been part of tonight's discussion."

"I don't know whether I'll ever join the church again, but at least I'll make a more informed decision."

"Not sure I belong. Everybody else is so much more educated and at a different place than I am. I'm older. I'm not angry at the church. I wanted to find out how I could better take care of my own failures."

"I'm not feeling everything that was brought up, but a lot of it. I need to come back."

The second meeting was held on March 6. We took turns at a timeline and shared our personal faith-journeys, selecting the highs and lows in past experiences and briefly describing them. On March 20, we met to discuss Avery Dulles' five models of the church, namely, organization, community, sacrament, proclamation of the Word, and servant. We also brainstormed their expectations of the church. The next meeting explored current moral issues, church teachings, and the role of conscience in morality. The fifth meeting centered around the question: Who is Jesus Christ for you? Our sixth session explored the meaning of church membership, and the last session was an informal sharing of their A.C.A. experience.

One member's comments were probably not typical, but this is how she painted its meaning for her. She had felt hostile to the church because of its failure to speak out against the Vietnam war, and she also directed some hostility toward it because of family members who are gay and feel hostility toward the church. She said that A.C.A. gave her an opportunity to express her feelings, be heard and listened to, and share with other dropouts similar feelings. She described how her hostility just seemed to disappear as she got involved in A.C.A., how she began to feel better about herself, how her relationship with people at work and other places improved, how she began to pray again, and now was getting something out of Mass. Especially helpful, she said, was the attitude of the leaders of the group. It was OK to speak honestly about your feelings, and the official church was listening.

When this first series ended, I attempted to sort out the causes for the feelings of alienation. They seemed to cluster around five main categories. The first was the *pace of change* in the church. For some it was too much and too fast; they felt they were left behind. For others it was too little and too late; they had given up on renewal.

A second main category was *Catholic belief and practice*. The topics specifically mentioned as troublesome were:

- birth control with the publication of *Human Vitae, 1968*
- marriage, divorce, and remarriage
- confession, and why the insistence upon a priest's absolution
- infallibility of the Pope
- infant baptism; resentment of being baptized without having asked for it; "baptized without consent"
- sexual ethics; "The church's teaching is too tough to accept"
- apathy of church people in the face of social justice needs
- St. Christopher medals; use of statues; teaching on indulgences
- mission theology and attempts to destroy non-Christian religions through conversion efforts
- teaching about hell; mortal sin; missing Mass on Sundays

In a third category I gathered the complaints that came under the humanness of the church—"people problems." Some harbored anger and resentment over an unhappy experience with a priest or sister, e.g., a traumatic confession experience, a refusal of baptism for a child, a refusal of a marriage request, and the usual complaints about dull sermons, liturgies without meaning, and church gatherings which failed to touch hearts. Some felt bad about "distances" of one kind or another between the bishop and the people.

The fourth category of alienation might be called "Vatican II fallout." These were areas of anxiety or anger triggered by the Council. For example:

- the role of women in the church, and the question of the ordination of women
- the search for real person-centered community, and the personalist approach
- lack of instruction in the meaning of the changes (dropouts don't hear the instruction because "they're not there")
- tension of living in a pluralistic church, in a pluralistic world ("How do I know what to believe anymore; how do I know what's right and wrong? One priest tells you one thing, another tells you the opposite."); the church has lost its moorings, some felt
- the priests who have left the active ministry; the sisters and brothers who have left the vowed life

A fifth category simply recognized the fact that young adulthood is a natural time to question life values and religious beliefs in the effort to mature, internalize, and believe "from the inside." It's normal to have some alienated feelings at this age. A valid insight one person had was this question: Can the Catholic Church tolerate questioners, searchers, doubters?

Three principal needs explained why they came and what they liked about their A.C.A. experience.

First, they needed an excuse to come together and talk. Their Catholic roots still had a great deal of meaning for them, but their deep feelings about past experiences and relationships within their church cried out for release. They simply needed an opportunity to ventilate their feelings.

Second, they needed up-to-date information about the church. Most of them lacked meaningful contact with the church since the Vatican Council and were laboring under false information and narrow conceptions of church teachings. Being out of the church the last ten or fifteen years prevented any resolution of this problem, obviously. Recognizing that perhaps the church was no longer what they had thought it was (if indeed it ever had been), they appreciated the chance to take a fresh look.

Third, they needed a warm experience with church people and the experience of a caring Christian community, one which would respect their freedom and their right to search.

## PART II: SHAPING A MINISTRY

Subsequent groups saw the shaping of this ministry into several essential components. We learned that it was better to operate from general principles in a dynamic process rather than from a rigid and detailed outline, or a highly structured plan. The essentials were simple: a small group experience, an opportunity to talk and to be listened to, to be brought up to date on church teachings, to pray, socialize, and search.

It takes about ten two-hour sessions to accomplish significant outcomes. And they have been significant. It seemed that at least one miracle of grace took place each meeting: genuine and deep healing, radical renewal of perspectives and values, significant change in attitudes and feelings, substantive steps in reentering church life, and authentic reincorporation into the body of Christ.

The experience seemed to depend upon several interrelated factors, weaving in and out, in flexible fashion, far from static, occasionally hesitant, but never dull. The key factor is the facilitator of the group. It's important that this person represent the church. His or her style must be reverent and accepting, patient with the process, and trusting that it is God's work. It must be perfectly clear from the start that the participants' freedom will not be violated. They must know that we are not out to bring them back or convert them. No pressure! The facilitator is there to serve, simply and with no other agenda than to help them deal in constructive ways with their own alienation. The participants are not presumed to be sick, and you, as facilitator, there to fix them up! On the contrary, facilitator and dropouts are on a journey together!

Other elements involved in the process were: time to ventilate, time to share the journey of faith, time to learn present teaching and customs of the church, time to pray, and hospitality. We met in my living room. I always provided home-baked cookies and snacks, and, for one meeting of each group, a home-cooked meal from scratch—with plenty of love.

One participant described his A.C.A. experience this way. It allowed him to ventilate his deep anger, hatred, and resentment toward the church. It was an atmosphere of complete acceptance, totally nonjudgmental. No pressure was put on him to get back to the church. The group experience made him realize that others shared many of the same feelings he had. Having a priest in the group said to him, "the official church is listening." Besides all this, he said the meetings were pleasant, socially enriching, and events to look forward to!

Further, the A.C.A. experience restored his integrity and affirmed belief in his basic goodness as a person and a child of God. It opened the door to a life of prayer. His struggles in the journey of faith were validated and accepted, and he was reintroduced, after a fourteen-year lapse, into genuine religious experience. His story is typical.

## PART III: IMPLICATIONS FOR THE RCIA

Whether the experience of Alienated Catholics Anonymous is a restoration of the Order of Penitents or not is an interesting question, and perhaps some would like to pursue it. My purpose here is simply to share what I've learned while attempting to minister to hurting members of our church. And there are millions!

Not all are ready to take another look, but many are. To them we can say, "Come! Share your journey with others. Let us pray with you, search with you, listen to each other's pain, and celebrate each other's joy." The paschal mystery is Good Friday and Easter Sunday intertwined in inseparable fashion.

Should a formal Rite of Reentry be unearthed and/or developed? Or is it enough simply to offer the A.C.A. experience as the hallway, the rite of passage back to the eucharistic dining table? Should A.C.A. participants, and others in similar efforts, be restored to full communion by way of a Lenten, or Holy Thursday, or Holy Saturday public reincorporation into the church? Or is it enough to come back quietly? Is there need for dropouts to formalize and publicly affirm their choice to return, if that is their decision?

The process described in this article is probably needed in every parish in the land. Caution must be observed, however, if new causes of alienation are to be avoided. This ministry, like any other, can fall victim to dishonorable and less-than-selfless motives. Its success seems to require absolute reverence for the movement of grace, a resignation to God's will, and a detached spirit that allows one to serve with unpredictable outcomes, and no hidden agendas. The ministry of healing is, after all, God's work. We are privileged to share in it.

The RCIA is for new members of the church. The process it uses is gentle, caring, nurturing, and reverent. The same is needed for dropouts who want to take another look.

In five years of ministry to these special people, the outcomes have been astounding. Many a night I have retired after an A.C.A. session so excited and moved that I couldn't drop off to sleep. It has been one of the most personally exciting and rewarding ministries I have ever been privileged to share.

The Rev. John Forliti is not only a pastor and educator, but an author as well. He is the director of religious education for the Archdiocese of St. Paul-Minneapolis where he began his outstanding program in reaching out to alienated and inactive Catholics in 1977. As a resource person, Father Forliti is available to groups across the nation and has a series of cassette tapes available, giving instructional materials to parishes wishing to begin a program of outreach in their own communities. His recent publication *Love in the Food* is available by writing to NCR Cassettes, Box 281, Kansas City, MO 64141. Or you can reach Father Forliti himself by writing direct to: Rev. John Forliti, 328 W. 6th Street, St. Paul, MN 55102.

# DR. ROBERT SCHULLER
## THE MAN BEHIND THE MINISTRY

HE is the evangelist of extravagant ebullience, the sultan of religious slogans, the apostle of aggrandizement. And now the Rev. Robert Schuller is preparing to overtake Oral Roberts as the overseer of America's largest television congregation.

Dr. Schuller, a former Chicago pastor who migrated in 1955 to southern California, has found especially hospitable soil for his unconventional ministry and his "possibility thinking" methods. His message has been spread throughout the continent, and Robert Schuller now stands among the most influential religious figures in our nation.

The fifty-six-year-old clergyman, for example, presides over a parish of more than 10,000 members, housed in a multimillion-dollar Crystal Cathedral just down the freeway from Disneyland. His Sunday morning worship service is viewed by more than 2.5 million persons. He is the author of a score of books, the most recent edition being the volume he mailed free of charge to every pastor in the United States, called *Self-Esteem.*

Most American Christians regard him as a chief architect for the modern "church growth" movement. Dr. Schuller prefers to be known, not as a glib and glittery television preacher, but as a "ground-breaking, ecumenical theologian and visionary who is changing the course of Christian history."

It isn't often that a daughter is asked to interview her own father. Surprisingly, the task was not as easy as I thought it would be. First, having family status didn't guarantee a spot on my dad's busy calendar; I had to wait two months for my turn. Second, in spite of being one of his closest confidantes, I still had to work hard to get the real Robert Schuller to open up and share his inner thoughts. I hope I succeeded in revealing the Robert Schuller I know and love.

*Dr. Schuller, the scope of your ministry today is staggering. Your* *Hour of Power television program reaches over two million people* *each week; the Crystal Cathedral is recognized as an architectural* *phenomenon; your newest book,* Self-Esteem: The New Reformation, *was recently mailed to every pastor and church* *leader in America. . . . Did you ever think this would all happen* *to you?*
   No, not really. As a child I did have a sense of destiny. You know when I was four years old, my uncle Henry, then a missionary in China, patted me on the head and said, "Robert, you're going to be a minister when you grow up!" I took that as God's calling for my life. Since then I've known I would be in full-time ministry. As for what you see today, none of it would be possible without the support and faith of countless beautiful people who caught hold of a vision and gave their help.

*What are your personal goals for the coming year?*
   One goal is to get in better condition. I have been traveling and working so much that I haven't been running as much time as I should. I need to get back to running an average of three miles a day.
   Another goal is to cut down on my lecturing so I can have more time to enjoy my grandchildren. I also want to spend more time in my garden. I love to trim the growth and sculpt the plants. I want to take time to smell the flowers. Also I want to

take about four mini-vacations just to rest, reflect, and pray.

My spiritual goal is to become more of what I call an "ecumenical" leader. What I mean is, I want to bring people together and be a catalyst used by God to help create a real sense of unity and community in our world. After thirty-two years of ministry, I am drawing fresh insight from Isaiah 58:12, which has always been a favorite verse of mine. It says, "Thou shalt be called, The repairer of the breach, The restorer of paths to dwell in."

I caught a glimpse of that for one shining hour in Flint, Michigan, during our seminar for the unemployed. The history of that city has been one of diversity: labor against management; blacks against whites; Catholics against Protestants. It was a marvelous feeling to know my influence was helping to bring people together to solve a real problem. I would like to be able to go to any town and find people of all colors, faiths, and persuasions welcoming me to join in unifying the community.

*Do you ever feel depressed if you don't meet your goals? How do you deal with this depression?*

Yes. At first I feel disappointed with myself. That disappointment becomes a gentle nudge. If I don't respond to the nudge, the disappointment turns into discouragement and becomes an added weight. Then, if I don't respond to the discouragement, the pressure builds to a hint of depression. And if that doesn't do it, I start feeling guilty that I've let myself go. If that doesn't do anything for me, then my wife, Arvella, will say, "Hey, get out and run!" Then I usually get to it. Many times Arvella has motivated me, gotten me started again. And, in turn, I have motivated her.

*That's great, but what do you do when someone else can't motivate you?*

I ask my best friend—Jesus Christ—for help. I talk to him almost all the time—in my car, during meetings, anywhere. I really feel he is there. When I've asked him to lay it on the line, he's done it once or twice. But I can't go back all the time and keep asking him for miracles to prove himself. That's an insult. I've got to grow up and stop being a baby. I can just hear him saying to me, "I've shown you in your twenties, thirties, forties, and fifties. I'll show you once every ten years; that's enough. Grow up now and behave yourself!"

*Does he actually speak to you?*

Yes, I feel that he's spoken to me about five times in my life. And then it was with a powerful idea that passed through my brain. That thought had the power to help me, release me, uplift me, or motivate me. From a psychological standpoint, I could take those five instances and explain them away, but I've chosen not to do that because of all the good they've done.

What more can he do for me? I can't expect him to reincarnate himself. If he did, I'd think I was hallucinating. So I don't think there is any other intelligent, responsible, or emotionally healthy way for him to speak to me.

*Do you have any weaknesses?*

Yes, one of them is my tendency to overeat. Recently I prayed about it for more than an hour and a half. During my prayers one sentence came to mind: "I will not let your weakness sink you." Now I know myself well enough to know that I could not create that kind of sentence. It came out of the blue; I think it was his message. "I will not let your weakness sink you." Boy, that says a lot. Everybody has a weakness. Christ let Paul bear a thorn in the flesh. Why? Was it so he'd remain humble? So he'd be dependent on him? Maybe, but I know that Christ did not say that he would remove it. But he did say, "I will not let your weakness sink you." Receiving that message was an extremely beautiful, personal experience. That's all I needed to know.

Another weakness I have is my inclination to become intensely involved when I see an injustice taking place. I have a very strong sense of justice, so when I see a victim of an injustice, I tend to react and project the same emotional intensity that you might see in the pulpit. I can pour the same amount of energy into a negative situation as a positive one. The result is rarely good. In fact, it's almost always counterproductive. So I have to restrain myself so I don't cause greater chasms rather than restoring peace and justice.

Normally your weakness is your strength. And your greatest strength is probably your weakness. Today my greatest strength might be my growing visibility. It might be my greatest weakness because I will be vulnerable to review, misinterpretation, and criticism. Don't let your weakness sink you. That thought has great ramifications that I've not even begun to think through yet. Your weakness might motivate you and goad you, but it won't sink you.

*What do you feel is your greatest accomplishment to date?*

I hope that it is my influence on religious thinking—my theological and professional example to other church leaders. I believe I'm being used to change the personality and emphasis of passive Christianity from negative to positive.

*In your book on self-esteem you talk about a reformation taking place. Do you think that this will happen?*

I believe a reformation can take place. However, it must not take place in the way it happened in the sixteenth century, when it was centered around two men, Martin Luther and John Calvin. But, rather, it must be universal. Someday I hope to hear Roman Catholic, Methodist, Presbyterian, and Lutheran leaders espousing self-esteem. The reformation should be like a wave of consciousness that trickles down from one leader to another until the entire religious world is soaked through.

*What would you do if for some reason everything that you've been a part of—the Cathedral and the Hour of Power ministry— collapsed? Would you start over and do it all the same way?*

First of all, there is no way the Cathedral could collapse. Even if the structures did collapse, we do have earthquake insurance. And if they were all demolished in an earthquake, we'd rebuild them almost exactly the way they are.

The nationwide television ministry won't collapse either, unless the financial support drops off. But I don't anticipate that happening because I believe more and more people see the uniqueness of our message—the substance of what we're saying.

*How did you start believing in possibility thinking?*

I think I've always been attracted to the positive, now that I look back—positive stories, positive books, and positive Bible verses. But I was also strongly attracted to the negative. I was turned on by a lecture on anti-communism. I was concerned about any potential catastrophic problems facing the human race. These problems appealed to my fears, my doubts, and my hunger for a certain degree of sadness. I think my wife, Arvella, helped me see the difference between the negative and the positive. It was a growing awareness—an evolutionary process.

For instance, in my first church, a ruling elder was very negative and critical and presented a strong resistance to my leadership. I told Arvella that I wanted to confront him and stop him from continuing his accusations. Arvella said, "Look, you don't need to defend yourself. There are plenty of good, wise people in the congregation who can do that for you. You just concentrate on what you need to do and ignore the criticisms." So I did. Before long, some of the other elders had enough of the negativism and spoke up on my behalf. The problem was solved when the man finally left on his own.

*What books, besides the Bible, have inspired you and influenced your thinking?*

Early in my ministry, J. Wallace Hamilton's *Ride the Wild Horses* was given to me. This story of a man turning the negative realities and emotions in his life into positive experiences made quite an impression. Dr. Peale's sermons and books have also inspired me, plus Maxwell Maltz's *Psychocybernetics*.

*Who else has influenced you?*

Viktor Frankl deeply inspired me during one of his lectures on man's will to meaning. That was a turning point in my life. Something about the speech indicated to me that there was something deeper than will to meaning. I raised the question: What gives meaning to meaning? Then I hit upon the idea that deeper than all is the will to self-love. And I wrote *Self-Love: The Dynamic Force of Success.*

Billy Graham helped me see how to lead people to a personal relationship with Jesus Christ. Norman Vincent Peale positivized my theology. Fulton Sheen syncretized it, and Frankl then moved me deeper. Frank Laubach really spiritualized my theology by adding mysticism to it, emphasizing prayer. I think more than anybody else, he taught me the concept of prayer as a sense of communication with God: God can communicate with me through my thinking process. Richard Neutra's doctrine of "biorealism" encouraged me to create a beautiful environment out of my habitat.

*The Crystal Cathedral is such a beautiful setting for worshiping God. Could you recount what led up to the building of the structure?*

Well, as you know, our congregation was literally bursting at the seams of our church. I didn't just want to expand our existing building. It seemed that God was calling me to truly dream a big dream. So I asked Philip Johnson, one of the most gifted architects of all time, to design a structure that would be beautiful and worshipful—a true modern-day cathedral.

It took us years to realize the dream. And it took the dedication of thousands of individuals to help pay for the completion of the cathedral. But I think everyone would agree that it was worthwhile.

*How are you different today than when you first began work on the Crystal Cathedral?*

I don't have the drive anymore.

I think there are peaks in life, a mountain that is going to stand out. To say you always have to have a higher mountain is preposterous. I suppose that the Cathedral is the Mt. Everest of my efforts from the standpoint of having to set a goal, with seemingly impossible problems, and not give up. I don't think I could handle any more goals like that one. There are limits to human endurance and perspective.

*Since you are never without a project, would you tell us about some of them?*

First of all, I want to build a retreat. Last year John and Donna Crean gave the church Rancho Capistrano. We want to develop the ranch into a retreat center for marriage encounter groups and other conferences aimed at strengthening the family. Most of the mail I receive concerns marriage problems. It will be a lot cheaper to buy an airplane ticket and come to our renewal conferences than it will be to hire a lawyer and get a divorce. It will be cheaper financially and emotionally. But before we can begin these conferences we need hotel accommodations and a small chapel. To develop the center in the first stage alone requires three million dollars, and raising that money is a number one goal.

We want to develop the property from an emotional and psychological perspective so we'll have the same beautiful feeling that we have at the Crystal Cathedral. I'll also select the staff to conduct the seminars that will feature our possibility thinking principles. And finally, I'll help develop the conference programs, including the renewal conferences for religious leaders.

Another exciting goal is to plan for next year the first "Glory of Easter" musical production in the Cathedral. Staged with choirs and pipe organ, the live drama will depict the last six days of the life of Christ. The play will open with Christ riding a donkey into Jerusalem. He will then appear before Pilate, endure the trial, and suffer the crucifixion. In pitch darkness, Christ's body will be placed in the tomb. Full house lights and glorious music will culminate the production as Christ's body rises during the resurrection. I predict that this play will become to America what the Oberammergau Passion Play is to Europe.

*You mentioned earlier that you felt one of your greatest strengths was increasing your visibility. Do you feel like a celebrity?*

I'm beginning to feel more and more like a celebrity. On airplanes stewardesses come up to me with pieces of paper and ask me if I would mind giving passengers my autograph. Also, I'm kind of shocked when I pass people on the street and hear my name being spoken.

*How do you handle being famous without losing your humility?*

I don't know how to answer that, except that I never boast about what I've done. All of my ideas and commitments were made in prayer. When I made these commitments, I was criticized and misinterpreted; yet I accepted the abuse and sacrificed my ego. When I say that the cross sanctified the ego trip, I know what I'm talking about. When you've finished something you've worked hard at, you end up with a wonderful sense of self-esteem. You can live with yourself and be proud of your efforts. There is no arrogance in me, because God keeps me in line, like an older brother keeping his younger sister in line. Twice a month, I'm humbled when I write letters to the thousands of people on my mailing list. And I'm humbled every

Sunday morning when I stand in the pulpit and deliver a message, because I can't repeat what I said the previous week.

*How do you manage your time?*

I get out my calendar and make sure my priorities are the first thing scheduled. The three most important values in my life, and not necessarily in any order, are my marriage, my personal faith and ministry, and my children. So on Sundays I am in church, on Monday nights I have my date night with my wife, and on the other days, I am always available to my children. Plus, I have a great secretary who knows those priorities and makes me stick to them.

*How about your family?*

When the children were small, we reserved Saturdays and Sundays for the family and for God. Every Saturday night we had our prayer time around the table. We never allowed neighborhood kids to come over on Sundays. I think those days were an emotional oasis for our family. Then my son and I built a small cabin in the mountains where we could escape the pressures of the local community and retreat as a family.

We genuinely love our children very much. We are sensitive to their hurts, aspirations, and sufferings. Fortunately our children haven't all faced difficulties at the same time. Our older daughter faced some lonely times, but she got through them. Then Bob decided he wanted to be a minister, and he also married very young. We had to accept the fact that it was OK for him to marry that young. Then, you, Jeanne, and Carol, and Gretchen have all had individual needs. We have let all the children develop their own characters. I think we've always recognized that each child has to develop as a decision-making individual.

*What difficulties have you experienced as a father of five strong-minded children, and how have you handled them?*

Well, one problem I remember having to handle was a time when our son, Bob, broke our trust and lied to his mother and me. He was still young, dating Linda, his wife-to-be, and was only allowed to see her on certain nights. Well, one night he wanted to see her without permission and told us he was at his friend's house. When we found out the truth, there was a real scene between us. He had violated our trust; it was like a crack in a fine cup that marred its appearance. In the confrontation, I smashed a fine English tea cup on the floor and told Bob that to restore our trust would be like gluing that cup back together again. He said, "I don't know if I can do that." And I said, "Well, that's how hard it is to build confidence and trust again." The outcome was that Bob spent literally weeks carefully gluing the pieces together until he finished. I know he learned a very important lesson. As a father, I then had to forgive him and believe he was sorry. I had to believe the best about him, even if I appeared naive. For I would rather be naive and run the risk on the side of faith than on the side of doubt. If I remained suspicious I would probably drive him to being more unfaithful. "I am what I think you think I am." That's so important with my children.

*Why do you remain nonpolitical in the pulpit? Is it because you don't want to use the church as anything but a place of worship?*

Yes, and there is another reason. I don't want people to perceive me as a political personality because it might intimidate them and prevent them from hearing my spiritual message. My own political views and judgments fall into mainstream thinking. I'm a great believer in the two-party system, shared powers, the Supreme Court, and the free enterprise system. I hold to a position that doesn't swing to extremes—either liberal or conservative.

*How do you feel about the changing roles of women?*

I'm delighted that women have more freedom today to use the creative abilities God has given them, whether at home or at work. I think it's great that women's roles are no longer so specific as they once were. Women now have the freedom to be all they were created to be.

Arvella is a good example of a woman who not only raised five children and is a wonderful wife and homemaker, but is also a creative professional. She serves as program director of the Hour of Power and has a key management role.

*What are your feelings about nuclear disarmaments?*

Well, I sure hope we can successfully negotiate nuclear disarmament, but I don't want to place this country in an inferior position and make us vulnerable to international forces.

*But how do you remain positive when you know there are nuclear missiles pointed directly this way?*

I think of the promise in Isaiah: "The government shall be upon his shoulders." In other words, ultimately, the government is in the hands of the Sovereign God. I have to trust him. I also trust our government and I pray for our leaders. I use my brains to select a leader. Basically, I feel that our collective leadership is basically right on track. If it goes off, it will be corrected in an election. The pendulum may swing to the left or to the right; but it will keep moving until it's meeting the needs of the masses. With free press and free speech, I trust that the collective populace can intelligently vote for a qualified Congress, Senate, and President.

I do not like, approve, or participate in two extreme reactions to political situations. One is a government run by the elite. There are those who say that the masses are not smart enough to elect government officials and that the country should be run by leaders in the intellectual, political, and corporate community. But, don't forget: the average human being with an eighth-grade education still has the gift of common sense.

The other extreme is to let the masses take to the streets, formulate opinions, and protest without knowing all the facts.

There's no way I'd go to the streets and advocate a nuclear freeze, because, frankly, I don't think I have all the facts. I don't think most people do. We should trust the leaders who have been elected by the collective masses, and who have the facts in front of them. Let them debate nuclear disarmament with other world leaders and resolve the issue to ensure peace.

*Dr. Schuller, if you could give every reader one sound piece of advice to change his/her life, what would it be?*

To meet Jesus Christ, the Ideal One. Despite your shortcomings, Christ accepts you as an equal even though he knows who and what you are. After this encounter, you are a different person. You are born again; you are able to trust and love. For the first time you will dare to come out of the bushes and meet your heavenly Father without fearing rejection. You will dare to accept and experience reconciliation.

Can you imagine any psychological or psychiatric therapy that can begin to approach the healing power of this religious experience? Can you imagine the power of an unconditional love between Jesus and a rebellious human who is suffering from insecurity, defensiveness, and feelings of inferiority?

When you have been redeemed into God's family, you are ready to think big—as God thinks. And you are ready to dream that great divine dream of building the Kingdom of God in the world. Cured of feelings of inferiority by your identification with the family of God, you begin to be released from the negative self-image that keeps you from daring or deserving to think big and beautiful as God wants every human to think.

The "I am" will determine the "I can."

Self-esteem will lead to possibility thinking. When we are adopted as children of God, the core of our life changes from shame to self-esteem.

## SIX STEPS TO A POSITIVE SELF-IMAGE THROUGH GOD

1. Pursue God.
   Begin by confessing your sin. Be specific, using words that bluntly describe you as you are. "If with all your heart you truly seek him, you shall surely find him . . ." (Deuteronomy 4:29).
2. Reexamine yourself.
   Ask yourself, "Am I sincerely honest?" Don't play games or pretend. If your problem is doubt, then admit it. For instance, pray, "I thank you, God, that you love me even when my faith is dim, dark, and dreary."
3. Affirm positively what God is able to do with you.
   In your honesty, do remain affirmative. Negative praying only weakens you. Pray, "I know that you love me anyway. I know that you are waiting eagerly to forgive me for. . . ."
4. Yield your self-will to God.
   "Not my will, but yours be done, O God" (Luke 22:42).
5. Expect positive results.
   Anticipate positive emotions, sense the joy, peace, and faith flowing into you. "If you have faith, all things are possible."

6. Rejoice!

   In thanking God, be specific, detail your thanks. For example, "Thank you, God, for eyes to see the faces of those I love, for ears to hear my favorite music, the sound of a friend's voice on the telephone in the middle of a lonely hour of life."

It's not an accident that the initials of these six steps spell out "Prayer." Talk to your heavenly Father often. Remember to entrust your self-image to him.

## A THEOLOGY OF EVANGELISM
## by Robert Schuller

Since we believe that the deepest need of every person is to experience and enjoy a healthy self-respect, a distinctive theology of evangelism evolves from a theology of self-esteem. Then it would follow:

1. The unconverted, the unchurched, the non-Christian is to be viewed as a nontrusting person—fearful and suspicious—instead of as an "evil" or "depraved" or "shameful" soul.
2. We must visualize every person as precious and valuable in God's sight, with vast untapped possibilities of service to God and his fellowman.
3. God longs to release every person's human potential from the imprisoning self-destructive fear and guilt that inhibits positive believing.
4. Our natural inability to trust God's love or to trust Christ's offer of salvation and forgiveness stems from our deep lack of self-worth. We simply do not value ourselves enough to believe that we can truly be loved unconditionally and nonjudgmentally. So we have to "earn love" and "do something" to merit forgiveness. So, lack of trust or a lack of self-worth is the central core of sin.
5. Unsaved souls—insecure, nontrusting persons—will need a great deal of positive affirmation before they will be able to listen or hear and begin to comprehend the truth of saving grace. No wonder Jesus Christ employed a

strategy of evangelism in which he never called a person a "sinner." They were sinners, of course, but he never told them they were. The proclamation of the truth of their sin would only have driven the nail of unworthiness deeper, until promises of forgiveness would lack the power to loosen and extract the spikes of sin, self-condemnation, and guilt.

We have a counseling center on the fourth floor of our Tower of Hope at Garden Grove Community Church. On a certain occasion our staff psychiatrist, a medical doctor, was counseling a patient, and I had been invited to witness the session. I shall use the term "doctor" to refer to the psychiatrist and "anonymous" to refer to the patient.

This patient had a terrible guilt problem. The doctor said: "Is it hard for you to see God as somebody who turns the other cheek?"

> *Anonymous:* "Yes. I see God with his arms folded across his chest saying to me, 'When are you going to get your act together?'"

> *Doctor:* "Are you perhaps confusing your mother with God?" [That was brilliant; I mentally patted him on the back for that.]

> *Anonymous:* "Possibly I have. Maybe I've always gotten God mixed up with both my mother and father. Maybe that's what has kept me from believing."

> *Doctor:* "What is your mental image of Christ?"

> *Anonymous:* "I guess as a baby. Or maybe as somebody dying on a cross. A real loser."

> *Doctor:* "Do you think you could begin to imagine Jesus as somebody who loves you, regardless of what you are or what you've done or where you've been?"

> *Anonymous:* "Oh, if that were possible, what freedom that would be. I would feel then that his arms were open and would come around me."

> *Doctor:* "Can't you imagine Christ doing that?"

*Anonymous:* "I don't know. Why do I resist it? Why do I fight the very thing I want?"

*Doctor:* "You probably feel unworthy."

*Anonymous:* "That's it."

*Doctor:* "You are worthy. God was born in a manger and died on a cross for you. That means you're worth a lot to the Almighty."

With that powerful affirmation of eternal truth, Anonymous began to open up to the healing, inclusive love of God.

The most significant question that an evangelist must ask is: How can we communicate in a way that will lead a person to accept Jesus Christ as Savior and Lord? How do we convert people? By telling them they are what they are—sinners? Or by telling them they are what we wish they would become? This latter technique was the Lord's approach: "You are the salt of the earth." "You are the light of the world." He understood what many of us had to learn through lessons in modern psychology: "I am what I think you think I am."

I shall always remember the night I was asked to make a hospital call on John Wayne, the veteran film actor. He was to be operated on in the morning for what was feared to be cancer. I prayed for divine guidance all the way to the hospital. Should I come right out and ask my friend Duke Wayne if he was prepared to meet God? I was strongly led to reject that approach. Should I ask, "Are you saved and forgiven, and if you die tonight will you go to heaven?" The answer came clearly: "No, that is not what you are to say."

Then I heard the "still small voice" that I identify as the Holy Spirit of the living Christ. It said to me, "Simply bring Jesus Christ into the mind of John Wayne. He will accept or reject Christ. That is what it's all about."

When I arrived at the hospital, I found the famous actor lying in bed. We talked, we related, and then I asked him, "Duke, may I pray for you?"

His response came immediately, "You bet, Bob. I need all the help I can get."

I recall seeing his eyes close tightly, his rugged face taut with tension, as I prayed. Without planning or plotting or contriving to manipulate, I heard the following words come from my mouth: "Lord, John Wayne knows about you. He has heard about you all his life. He admires you. And deep down he knows that you can and want to forgive him of all his sins. Deep down in his mind he accepts you and believes in you and loves you, now." At that point I opened my eyes to see the face of John Wayne as possibly no other person has ever seen it—peaceful as an Easter sunrise, all tension gone. There was absolutely no evidence of embarrassment, spiritual uneasiness, or psychological discomfort. Beyond a doubt, I spoke the right words, and he followed them without resistance and with sincere acceptance.

How then do we convert and change people? We do it by the positive approach Christ himself consistently used. In the stage play, *Man of La Mancha*, the grand idealist, Don Quixote, met a harlot named Aldonza. "You will be my lady," he announced, to the shock of this whore. Then he added, "Yes, you are my lady and I give you a new name—Dulcinea." She laughed scornfully.

But Don Quixote followed the approach Jesus used with Mary Magdalene. Undaunted, he kept affirming her and declaring her to be what he wanted to believe she was. And, of course, the affirmation became a self-fulfilling prophecy.

The play continued and the stage was empty. It was night. Offstage a woman screamed. It was Aldonza. She was being raped in the hay.

She appears onstage, hysterical, blouse torn, hair disheveled, dirt on her face, terror in her eyes, breasts heaving with the fast breathing of a panic-stricken soul. Loud and clear comes the voice of the Man of La Mancha, "My lady!" She can't handle this and screams, "Don't call me your lady; I was born in a ditch by a mother who left me there naked and cold and too hungry to cry. I never blamed her. I'm sure she left hoping that I'd have the good sense to die."

Aldonza is weeping now, her head downcast, humiliated, shame-wracked. Then her shame turns into violence, and as her head rises, she screams, "Oh, don't call me a lady. I'm only a kitchen slut reeking with sweat. A strumpet men use and forget. Don't call me a lady; I'm only Aldonza. I am nothing at all!" She then whirls and runs into the night, but Don Quixote calls after her with a loud voice, "But you are my Lady Dulcinea!"

The curtain drops, but shortly it rises again to the death scene of this glorious dreamer of the impossible dream. He is dying now, like Jesus, of a broken heart—scorned, laughed at, despised, and rejected of men. Suddenly, to his side comes what appears to be a Spanish queen in a mantilla and lace. She kneels and prays.

He opens his eyes and asks, "Who are you?"

"Don't you remember?" The lady rises and stands tall. She is beautiful, perfectly proud and perfectly humble at the same time. She speaks softly, "Don't you remember? You called me your lady. You gave me a new name. My name is Dulcinea!"

The conversion was complete! She was born again!

In summary: a theology of evangelism not based on a theology of self-esteem may be judged unethical, unhealthy, and ultimately unsuccessful if it manipulates, intimidates, or humiliates a person in the process of trying to convert a person.

Bill Bright, founder of Campus Crusade for Christ, told me once: "When I was converted, I was converted not out of a consciousness of sin, but I was attracted to the love of God in Christ. . . . Once I ran to receive him as my Lord I became, in his presence, strongly aware of my sin and imperfections, and I was genuinely repentant." Sinners dare to repent in the presence of Christ, whereas they will fear repentance in the presence of their fellow imperfect human beings.

The gospel must be proclaimed as salvation from shame to glory, from self-doubt and self-condemnation to self-confidence and self-affirmation. Now we are released to become creative, healing, and redeeming persons.

Dr. Robert Schuller completes this entire thesis in his new book, *Self-Esteem*, which can be obtained from Word Books of Waco, Texas. Complete information on the Garden Grove "Tower of Hope" counseling services may be obtained by writing directly to the church, located at 12141 Lewis Street, Garden Grove, CA 92640.

# FATHER ALVING ILLIG, C.S.P.
## WHAT CATHOLICS AND PROTESTANTS CAN LEARN FROM ONE ANOTHER ABOUT EVANGELIZATION

*CHAPTER*

# 9

SINCE Vatican II, when Pope John XXIII announced to the world a new vision for the Catholic Church that had a fourfold objective—Identity, Renewal, Ecumenism, and Evangelization— things have never quite been the same for Catholics. The Pope called us to "put our house in order" so we could once more reach out with renewed vigor to the entire world with the good news of salvation in Jesus Christ.

That was in the late 1950s. It took another ten years before a complete statement on evangelization was given in the papal exhortation entitled, *Evangelii Nuntiandi* ("The gospel must be proclaimed").

It took another ten years and more before the American bishops took up the challenge and began a program of outreach, first to the bishops, then to the clergy, and now to the entire church across the nation.

Probably no other Catholic since the time of St. Paul himself has reached into the church with the cause of evangelization as has Paulist Father Alvin Illig. A priest in the order of the

Congregation of Saint Paul (The Paulist Fathers), Father Illig was appointed to chair the National Conference of Catholic Bishops' newly formed Office for Evangelization, and things really began to happen. Since that date, Father Illig has presented the case for evangelization to over 20,000 of his brother priests and bishops, held conferences in over 50 percent of all the dioceses in the United States, began a Bible study program that now numbers in excess of a half-million readers, opened offices for evangelization in more than a thousand parishes, and brought the field of evangelization into the forefront of Catholic thought and action.

It would be hard to count the results, but the more than one million new members added to the Catholic Church across America in the past two years owe a good portion of their newfound faith to the efforts of this "second St. Paul." Father Illig has a vision for the future that includes some 85 percent of all the parishes having a trained staff person operating an effective office for evangelization, and at least 20 percent of all Catholics having an evangelistic mentality based upon sound training to share their faith with everyone they meet.

Under the impulse of the Holy Spirit, the chemistry of ecumenism is preparing the Christian community for collaboration in evangelization, turning distrust into trust, suspicion into respect, competition into cooperation.

According to *The Search for America's Faith* by George Gallup and David Poling (Abingdon, $8.95), today 73 percent of the American Protestant community looks favorably on the Catholic community, and an amazing 87 percent of Catholics today look favorably on their Protestant brothers and sisters.

Evangelization (i.e., bringing the Good News into every area of life) and ecumenism (i.e., the effort to undo the scandal of disunity among believing Christian peoples) are growing together in America because there is no contradiction between the two. Both compel us to look to one another, to learn from one another, to celebrate what we have in common, to appreciate the special emphasis each one of us brings to evangelization, and to recognize the unique features found in each other's evangelization programs.

Pope Paul VI writes in "Evangelization in the Modern World," which is the modern charter for world Catholic evangelization:

> It is with a strong feeling of Christian hope that we look to the efforts being made in the Christian world for this restoration of the full unity willed by Christ. St. Paul assures us that "hope does not disappoint us." . . . We make our own the desire for a collaboration marked by greater commitment with the Christian brethren with whom we are not yet united in perfect unity, taking as a basis the foundation of Baptism and the patrimony of faith which is common to us. By doing this we can already give a greater common witness to Christ before the world in the very work of evangelization. Christ's command urges us to do this; the duty of preaching and of giving witness to the Gospel requires this (#77).

In this article I will seek to develop evangelization within an ecumenical perspective under these five headings:

1. Images of Catholics and Protestants in America.
2. What Protestants and Catholics have in common.
3. What Catholics can learn from Protestants.
4. What Protestants can learn from Catholics.
5. Three unique features of Catholic evangelization.

This effort does not center on a "hard science" such as mathematics or technology. We are dealing with popular theological speculation and with images, a very "soft science." Since this is the result of study and personal reflection—and personal reflections will be quite subjective—many of the reflections are clearly open to much discussion.

## I. IMAGES OF CATHOLICS AND PROTESTANTS IN AMERICA

Briefly stated, the Catholic Church in America, historically and now, projects an image of a religious community primarily concerned with the nurture and the maintenance of the faith of its own people. Many in the Protestant community see Catholics as a people focusing their time, money, and effort almost exclusively on their 50 million active members, with very little interest in the unchurched American—though with some mild interest in foreign missionary work. Catholics have their own places of worship, their own schools, hospitals, social agencies, publishing houses, rectories, and convents. It is understandable that the Catholic Church is seen this way since only about 2 percent of today's active American Catholics evidence an evangelizing mentality in terms of reaching out to their 15 million inactive brothers and sisters to invite them to come back home, and reaching out to the 80 million unchurched who make up 41 percent of the nation, to invite them in turn to sample the Catholic way of life.

The American Protestant community, on the other hand, presents to the Catholic community an image of an evangelizing church, a religious people certainly concerned with the nurturing and maintenance of the faith of its own members, but a people specially impelled with the impulse to preach the Good News to the American community from the housetops. This image is strengthened by the many powerful Protestant evangelizers on today's radio and television stations.

There are historical reasons for these images. Over two hundred years ago, in the thirteen original colonies, the infant Catholic Church began to face the challenge of meeting the spiritual needs of an expanding immigrant people in a religiously hostile society. In 1776, there were about 30,000 Catholics who made up 1 percent of the nation's population. There were about twenty-five priests, but no bishops, no sisters, no brothers, no dioceses, no visible structures. By 1982, not counting the 15 million inactive Catholics, there were over 50 million active Catholics, or 23 percent of the nation. When George Gallup asks the question in his national polls, "What is your religious preference?" 30 percent of the American people today answer Catholic. At present there are 58,000 priests, 128,000 sisters, 10,500 schools, 174 dioceses, 355 bishops, 1,800 hospitals and major charitable institutions that last year served 37 million Americans, with 19,000 parish families spread across the face of the land.

During this same 200-year period, in which the Catholics were struggling to assimilate the immigrant, many native American Christian and semi-Christian churches were founded in the United

States to become highly visible evangelizing groups such as the Southern Baptists, the Assemblies of God, the Seventh-Day Adventists, the Mormons, the Christian Scientists, and the Jehovah's Witnesses. Today there are some four hundred Protestant denominations in America which have grown to a very large extent through effective evangelization programs. Unlike the Catholic Church, which increased through immigration as well as births, most of these denominations grew through their ability to attract those people already in the United States as well as through birth. Put simply, not too many Southern Baptists originally came from Ireland; not too many Jehovah's Witnesses originally came from Italy.

A leader in Catholic-Baptist dialogue, Glenmary Father Joseph O'Donnell explained it this way recently:

> The whole thrust of the Southern Baptist Convention is so oriented to evangelism that you can hardly escape being an evangelizer if you are a practicing Baptist. Given their theology of salvation and their conviction that God will abundantly bestow graces through evangelizing Christians, Southern Baptists have been remarkably successful throughout American history both in bringing about conversions and in orienting the thrust of their entire convention to worldwide mission and evangelism.

As both great Christian traditions mature in America today, it seems that more and more evangelizing is taking place in the Catholic Church, while more and more nurturing and maintenance programs are active in the Protestant churches. Each has much to teach the other: each has much to learn from the other.

## II. WHAT PROTESTANTS AND CATHOLICS HAVE IN COMMON

a) We are all Christians—not Buddhists, not Muslims, not Maoists—but committed Christians. Christ is our ideal. We model our lives on him and accept his system of values and his world view. We have a Christian view of life and death and resurrection.

b) We evangelize because Jesus first preached the gospel. We all labor under the same Great Commission that is found in Matthew 28:18, "Go therefore and teach all nations." We share in the universality of his mission. As Pope Paul writes in "Evangelization in the Modern World":

> Jesus' last words in St. Mark's Gospel confer on the evangelization which the Lord entrusts to his apostles a limitless universality: "Go out to the whole world; proclaim the Good News to all creation."
>
> The twelve and the first generation of Christians understood well the lesson of this text and other similar ones; they made them into a program of action (#49).

c) We respect each other as people of good will, each following his/her conscience under the light of the Holy Spirit, each searching to do God's will.

d) We reverence the truth because we believe that Christ is the way, the truth, and the life.

e) We believe in the power of prayer, the human response to the God who first loved us, a response that takes the form of adoration, contrition, petition, and thanksgiving.

f) We accept God as our loving Father. He created all of us—all 4¼ billion people on the face of the world today—because he wanted to. His love for his children is unconditional and universal.

g) We accept Christ as our personal Savior and Lord. He so loved us that he made us a "chosen generation, a royal priesthood, an holy nation" (1 Peter 2:9), purchasing us not with the blood of goats and heifers, but with his blood.

h) We have the Holy Spirit as the Vivifier and Sanctifier of all Christians. The Second Vatican Council emphasizes that the Holy Spirit lives in all Christians. As Pope Paul VI writes:

> . . . the Holy Spirit is the principal agent of evangelization. It is he who impels each individual to proclaim the Gospel, and it is he who in the depths of consciences causes the word of salvation to be accepted and understood. But it can equally be said that he is the goal of evangelization: He alone stirs up the new creation, the new humanity of which evangelization is to be the result, with that unity in variety which

evangelization wishes to achieve within the Christian community (#77).


i) Catholics and Protestants have as a common heritage the message preached by Christ, a value system which is a sign of contradiction to much of our society. St. Paul wrote to the Jews of his time that Christ crucified was a stumbling block to them, and foolishness to the Greeks. Today we continue to proclaim a value system that is counter-culture. When we are faithful to Christ, Protestants and Catholics alike preach peace not war; love not hate; forgiveness not revenge; truth not lies; justice not injustice; meekness not power; humility not pride; self-control not self-indulgence; selflessness not selfishness; a spirit of poverty not a spirit of richness; life not death.

j) Together we issue the call to the conversion experience, to the *metanoia,* to the renunciation of the old person with his and her vicious habits of sin, and a putting on of the new person made in the image and likeness of Christ.

k) Protestant or Catholic, we are both caught in the timeless search for balance between fidelity to the eternal message of Christ and the need to interpret the signs of the times to our age. All Christians strive to achieve St. Augustine's dictum: "In essentials, unity: in nonessentials, diversity: in all things, charity."

l) We share in a common evangelistic concern to nurture our own active communities, to reach out to our inactive members, and to invite the unchurched to experience our Christian way of life.


## III. WHAT THEN CAN CATHOLICS LEARN FROM PROTESTANT EVANGELIZERS?

a) We should articulate and emphasize as they do the centrality of the person of Jesus Christ as Lord and Savior. Catholics often show a love for the institution called the church, which is indeed the mystical body of Christ, and this is laudable. But love for Jesus Christ is our first love. The first Commandment is "Thou shalt love the Lord thy God." Structures and organizations are helpful, but God comes first in our loyalties.

b) Protestants have developed an intense love of God's Word in the Scriptures. Their evangelization efforts reflect St. Paul's words:

> . . . and you remember that ever since you were a child you have known the Holy Scriptures, which are able to give you the wisdom that leads to salvation through faith in Christ Jesus. All Scripture is inspired by God and is useful for teaching the truth, rebuking error, correcting faults, and giving instruction for right living, so that the man who served God may be fully qualified and equipped to do every kind of good work (2 Timothy 3:15-17).

c) Protestants are more comfortable with the explicit proclamation of Jesus Christ as Lord and Savior than are Catholics. In this vein, Pope Paul VI challenges all of us by noting:

> There is no true evangelization if the name, the teaching, the life, the promises, the kingdom and the mystery of Jesus of Nazareth, the son of God, are not proclaimed (#27).

d) Our brothers and sisters of the Protestant tradition place a strong emphasis on the priesthood of the faithful. They challenge their laity to teach, to shepherd, to sanctify. They do not empower their laity to do the work of Christ: they stress that the laity already have the power by the fact of baptism in the Lord, and they challenge them to use this power given by the Holy Spirit.

e) They possess a more highly developed notion of volunteerism, throwing out great challenges and calling for great sacrifices, especially to their youth. The Mormons field 30,000 young missionaries who have to support themselves and give two years of their lives to evangelization. The demands of Campus Crusade volunteers, the demands made by the Christian Service Corp., would frighten most Catholic laity.

f) Radio and television as tools of evangelization are much better employed by the Protestant community. The Catholic community to a large extent is still print-bound. It is of note historically, that for sixty years after the invention of the printing press, the Protestant reformers used this mass media tool most effectively before the Catholic community "discovered" it. History seems to be repeating itself.

g) Out of the Protestant tradition emerge powerful national preachers who are promoted and supported by the Protestant community, e.g., Oral Roberts, Robert Schuller, Billy Graham, Jimmy Swaggart, et al. Today there are no comparable national Catholic preachers.

h) The Protestant community has the courage to engage in large stadium events that inspire their active members and are a public witness of faith to the secular community. While the Catholic community actively engaged in large stadium events before Vatican II, this form of religious expression and evangelization has been almost totally abandoned by the Catholic community in the past twenty years.

i) Music as a tool of evangelization is important in the Protestant tradition, while Catholics employ music almost exclusively for the maintenance of the faith of the active community.

j) The Protestant community, for the most part, prefers the small and personal church over the large and often impersonal church community. While there are 19,000 Catholic churches in America with 58,000 priests serving almost exactly 50 million active Catholics, there are almost 300,000 Protestant churches with over a quarter of a million ministers serving about 75 million churchgoing people. The average Catholic parish has over 2,500 women, men, and children, while the average Protestant parish has less than 200 women, men, and children.

k) Personal witness plays a very important part in Protestant evangelization programs, showing a keener understanding of the human condition, the legitimately emotional, in the religious experience. People seek to know what faith in Christ and incorporation into a religious family can do for their personal life.

l) Most of the Protestant evangelizers are more willing to run the risk of being rejected in order to evangelize than are most Catholics. Evangelizers must respect religious freedom and the human conscience, but Catholics certainly could be more aggressive than they are at present.

m) Protestant evangelizers often are more creative and imaginative in designing evangelizing programs, e.g., phone counseling services, Bible hot lines, family camping programs, etc.

# IV. WHAT PROTESTANTS
# CAN LEARN FROM CATHOLICS

a) Evangelization is a blend and balance of both Word and sacrament. Both represent ways of encountering Christ. Although Protestants traditionally have emphasized the Scriptures, and Catholics traditionally have stressed sacraments and liturgy, Christianity from the beginning has always drawn on both elements rather than a choice between the two.

b) If there is to be harmony, unity, and peace among evangelizers, all of whom use their own personal charisms, the need arises for a universal ministry of coordination and oversight able to make responsible and authoritative decisions in major areas of church teachings and practices.

c) In evangelizing, Catholics often display an aversion to a negative world view, an aversion to an imminent Armageddon, an aversion to a preoccupation with apocalyptic speculation. Christ tells all Christians that we simply do not know the time nor the hour of his second coming.

d) Catholics view the conversion experience as a daily experience, a lifelong process of growth and maturation. They see a place for ongoing sanctification after a conversion experience. They note that St. Paul spent three years in the desert after his Damascus Road conversion before he felt that he was ready to preach the Good News of Christ. Grace transforms, but also builds on nature; and nature generally makes haste slowly.

e) Catholic evangelizers present a Christian humanism that reverses the order of creation and the divine plan it contains. It sees that the body is God's creation and therefore good. "God does not make junk," the Marriage Encounter movement states. Pleasure is legitimate. Even in regard to personal sin, Catholic evangelizers present the gentle face of Christ and teach that not all sin is mortal, not all sin is unto death.

f) Catholic evangelizers see a relative value in material signs and in human symbols correctly used to express a spiritual reality. They value time-honored liturgical forms that convey a sense of continuity and stability in this age so filled with change. There is a place for color, design, beauty, drama, and mystery. Vestments, stained glass, candles, incense, holy oils, water, statuary, ashes can be employed in the service of the Lord, just as music and song are used because we human beings have bodies and emotions as well as minds and hearts. St. Thomas Aquinas reminds us that all knowledge comes through the senses, except infused knowledge.

g) Along these same lines, there is a place for communal structures—international, national, diocesan, and parochial—for passing from one generation to the next a religious way of life and a religious value system. Catholics have a felt need for corporate involvement in the church so that the faith of the parents can be transmitted, under God's grace, to their children and to their children's children.

h) The Catholic evangelizer strives to present the church as a humble yet hopeful, lovable yet tragic, non-elitist mass of people of all cultures, colors, educational achievements, economic levels, and ages, all on a great pilgrimage together to eternal glory. The evangelizer works from an ecclesiology that says Christ founded his church for sinners, not for angels. He is the divine Physician who came not for the healthy, but for those who are ill; the Good Shepherd who leaves the ninety-nine to search for the one; the compassionate Christ who will not break the bent reed or quench the smoking flax.

i) Social ministry and spiritual ministry are but two sides of one and the same coin that says that we are to love God with our whole heart and mind and soul, and that we are to love our neighbor as ourself. Christ tells us that we will be welcomed into the Kingdom of heaven because we fed the hungry, clothed the naked, visited the sick, and did not abandon the prisoner.

j) The Catholic evangelizer sees a place for saints in the life of the Christian community, realizing that human beings take encouragement from the study of sinners who became great saints of God, the human example of people who achieved eternal life despite human frailty. The Catholic evangelizer takes hope from Peter who denied Christ, but then became a great saint. He takes hope from Thomas who doubted, but also became a great saint. He takes hope from the ten apostles who all fled from Christ in the Garden of Gethsemane, but then became great saints. The saints give us great hope that someday grace will conquer our sinfulness and draw us close to the Savior, to remain with him forever.

k) There is a tolerance in Catholicism—rather, there is

encouragement—to a broad spectrum of prayer forms and religious life styles, from Pentecostal tongues to rosary beads; from joyful shouting to silent comtemplation; from the Carthusian way of life to street ministry; from Marriage Encounter and Cursillo to the Knights of Columbus, the Legion of Mary, the Catholic Daughters of the Americas.

l) There frequently is a deep sense of joy and peace, a lack of frenzy, in Catholic evangelization. Catholic evangelizers realize it is not they who save people. Pope Paul points out to us in chapter 80 of his document on evangelization that human beings by God's mercy can gain salvation even though we do not preach the gospel to them. Catholic evangelizers work with what they have to work with, do their best, and then confidently leave the rest in God's hands. We are not called to make 5,000 converts in our lifetime. We are only called to be faithful—faithful to our vocation, faithful to the Scriptures, faithful to Christ, faithful to the church. Paul sows seed, Apollo waters the seed, but God gives the increase.

# V. THREE UNIQUE FEATURES OF CATHOLIC EVANGELIZATION

1) Catholic evangelization is ecclesiastically rooted in a 2,000-year-old heritage that springs from the scene at Caesarea-Philippi when Christ asked his disciples, " 'Who do people say the Son of Man is?' And they said, 'Some say he is John the Baptist, some Elijah, and others Jeremiah or one of the prophets.' 'But you,' he said, 'who do you say that I am?' Then Simon Peter spoke up, 'You are the Christ the Son of the living God.' Jesus replied, 'Simon son of Jonah, you are a happy man! Because it was not flesh and blood that revealed this to you but my Father in heaven. So I now say to you: You are Peter and on this rock I will build my Church. And the gates of the underworld can never hold out against it. I will give you the keys of the kingdom of heaven; whatever you bind on earth shall be considered bound in heaven; whatever you loose on earth shall be considered loosed in heaven' " (Matthew 16:13-19, JB).

A Catholic evangelizer is not a "lone ranger." A Catholic evangelizer works in union with the bishops and the Holy Father.

As Pope Paul tells us, "Evangelization is for no one individual and isolated act: it is one that is deeply ecclesial. When the most obscure preacher, catechist or pastor in the most distant land preaches the gospel, gathers his little community together or administers a sacrament, even alone, he is carrying out an ecclesial act, and his action is certainly attached to the evangelizing activity of the whole church by institutional relationships, but also by profound invisible links in the order of grace. This presupposes that he acts not in virtue of a mission which he attributes to himself or by a personal inspiration, but in union with the mission of the church and in her name" (#60).

Writing in paragraph #67, the Holy Father goes on to say, "The Successor of Peter is thus, by the will of Christ, entrusted with the preeminent ministry of teaching the revealed truth. The New Testament often shows Peter 'filled with the Holy Spirit' speaking in the name of all. . . . The Second Vatican Council wished to reaffirm this when it declared that 'Christ's mandate to preach the gospel to every creature primarily and immediately concerns the bishops with Peter and under Peter.'

"The full supreme and universal power which Christ gives to his Vicar for the pastoral government of his church is thus especially exercised by the Pope in the activity of preaching, and causing to be preached, the Good News of salvation."

2) The second unique feature about Catholic evangelization is that it culminates the Eucharist. As Pope Paul writes, "Evangelization is in fact the grace and vocation proper to the church, her deepest identity. She exists in order to evangelize, that is to say, in order to preach and teach, to be the channel of the gift of grace, to reconcile sinners with God, and to perpetuate Christ's sacrifice in the Mass which is the memorial of his death and glorious resurrection" (#14).

Catholic evangelization is an enriching balance of both Word (preaching) and sacrament (Eucharist). It is always both Word and sacrament. It is never either Word or sacrament. Both are ways in which we encounter Christ. We are fed, not only by the body and blood of our Lord Jesus Christ under the form of bread and wine consecrated at the eucharistic table by a duly ordained priest, but also by the Scriptures.

As noted previously, over the past four hundred years the Catholic community to a large extent has emphasized sacraments and other liturgical matters, while not emphasizing preaching. Other Christian churches, on the other hand, have emphasized preaching, while neglecting sacraments and liturgy. Now, as a result of the Vatican Council's new emphasis on Scripture and preaching as well as on sacraments and liturgy, there is emerging a more balanced respect for both Word and sacrament in all aspects of Catholic life, especially in evangelization.

Again, Pope Paul writes: "To live the Sacraments in this way, bringing their celebration to a true fullness, is not, as some would claim, to impede or to accept a distortion of evangelization: it is rather to complete it. For in its totality, evangelization—over and above the preaching of a message—consists in the implantation of the church, which does not exist without the driving force which is the sacramental life culminating in the Eucharist" (#28).

3) The third unique feature about Catholic evangelization is that it has a Marian tone to it. Because Mary, the mother of Jesus Christ who is true God and true man, was the one who bore him into the world, Catholic evangelization will always be marked with a certain Marian spirituality. As we see especially in St. Luke's Gospel, Mary, by the power of the Holy Spirit, was the first person to receive Christ into her life, to allow him to live in her, and then to share him with the world. She is a perfect scriptural model for the evangelizer who, by the power of the Holy Spirit, accepts Christ into his/her life, allows him to live in the person, and then shares Christ wherever the person happens to be.

In the Dogmatic Constitution of the church of the second Vatican Council (*Lumen Gentium,* #65), we read: "In its apostolic task the church rightly looks to the one who bore Christ, Christ who was conceived by the Holy Spirit and born of the Virgin in order that he might also be born and grow in the hearts of the faithful. In her whole life this virgin mother showed herself as an example of that motherly love that must animate all who share in the apostolic mission of the church for the regeneration of mankind."

# PART TWO

# Twelve Outstanding Evangelizing Churches

# CHRIST CHURCH OF OAK BROOK
## OAK BROOK, ILLINOIS
## DR. ARTHUR H. DEKRUYTER, PASTOR
## BRINGING EXECUTIVES
## AND THEIR FAMILIES TO CHRIST

CHAPTER

10

CHRIST CHURCH of Oak Brook has never had an evangelism committee, our people have never knocked on neighborhood doors, and our church does not list evangelism *per se* as a goal. Yet the Lord has blessed us richly in this area. When we started Christ Church eighteen years ago we had five families. Today we have about sixteen hundred families. We have grown at an average rate of a hundred families per year over the last ten years, and we expect that trend to continue for at least another ten years.

Numbers, of course, do not tell the whole story. They are just an outward indication that things are going well in areas far more important to us. The development of this successful outreach into our community has been a by-product of striving for other goals.

In the following pages I will describe some of our methods for reaching people in our area, writing as a pastor-practitioner, not an academician.

One of the first things we did when we committed ourselves to this area was set some goals for our ministry. We envisioned a church that was dynamic. From the days when I first felt called to the ministry, I had always had a goal of pastoring an exciting, active congregation. It also seemed that a church in the Oak Brook area should be fairly large.

A quick look at the people in this area indicated that they were used to specialists. We decided they would react more positively to a church in which a staff could minister to specialized needs. Conversely, they probably would not want a minister who tried to do a little of everything. We also felt that God wanted the church to be a visible part of the community. Hiding away in a small building at the edge of town was never a part of our vision.

The next thing we did after we committed ourselves to the area and set some definite goals was study the people. We wanted to know exactly what they were like and how we could best serve them. We made a genuine effort to throw out preconceived notions and truly understand their situation.

Often ministers make the mistake of going to an area with the idea of changing the life styles of people who live in the area. A better approach would be to find out where the people are in their spiritual development and let them change their own life styles, if necessary. We came to Oak Brook to identify with the people, minister to them, and simply love them.

We learned that we were surrounded by corporate executives and professional people. They constituted a surprisingly homogeneous group in our immediate area, they were well-to-do financially, and they were also aggressive, mobile, and self-sufficient.

"Are these the kind of people to whom Jesus Christ would minister if he were on earth today?" is a question I am occasionally asked. This question often comes from people of modest socioeconomic backgrounds (and many of the clergy come from those backgrounds). Implicit in that question, I am afraid, is a judgment. We might have served God better, it seems to say, by locating Christ Church in a poor neighborhood . . . or perhaps in a blue-collar area . . . or an ethnic neighborhood . . . or an area populated by some other group.

We have nothing against ministries in those kinds of areas—we support many such ministries, in fact—but my answer is this: "Jesus Christ loves executives, and so do I."

Executives and their families are exactly like any other "people group" in having definite needs, problems, strengths, and weaknesses. Personally, I find this ministry tremendously exciting.

The executives in our community have several common traits that have shaped our church. The following list is offered as a product of years of work among executives in Oak Brook, not as social theory.

## CHARACTERISTICS AND METHODS

### 1. EXECUTIVES ARE MOTIVATED FROM WITHIN.

The people in and around Oak Brook do things because they *want* to do them. They have a need, they see an opportunity to fulfill that need, and they move aggressively and decisively to obtain what they want. They are not shy about exploring new ways to do things or about joining new groups—provided they are motivated from within. They haven't risen to their positions in business or professional life by sitting back passively and letting other people tell them what to do.

I find Maslow's hierarchy of needs to be a useful tool in understanding the mindset of our people. Consistently, we learn that the needs they experience are from the "higher" levels on Maslow's chart: self-fulfillment and service to God and man. If our programs meet those needs, we find our people are highly motivated and our programs are successful. Conversely, if we resort to motivational methods that don't take inner motivation into account, such as threats ("If you don't support this program, the future of our youth program is in jeopardy"), we would get absolutely nowhere.

### 2. COMMITMENTS ARE ALWAYS UPHELD.

Commitments are never made lightly. If someone promises to do a job by a particular time, it *will* get done right and on time. In the event that outside contingencies force a delay or a change, the responsible person will immediately call a meeting of all concerned to explain what is happening and how it will affect the results.

This trait comes directly from the business world, of course.

Anyone who has visited a corporate office just before a major deadline or at the end of a fiscal year knows that the pressure to perform is tremendous. Corporate boards are not interested in excuses.

## 3. EXECUTIVES LIVE WITH SPECIALIZATION.
Our people have a high regard for specialization in a profession, in a business, or in talent development. When they consult a doctor, they prefer talking to a specialist. When they need a professional service, they look for a specialist. Their children are taught by educational specialists. They plan their careers along very specific lines. They have a high regard for proven achievement and the way it can be used in a team situation.

## 4. VISION IS IMPORTANT. GOALS MUST BE ATTAINABLE.
They understand long-range goals and are willing to contribute time and money to help achieve those goals—as long as they truly believe that the goals are attainable.

Christ Church was not always large. During its early years it consisted of just a handful of families. But the people in those early days were the same kind we have now; they were able to share a vision for what could happen in the future. We charted a course toward our goals, made the necessary commitments, and over the years the Lord has helped us attain most of our goals.

## 5. COMMITMENT TO EXCELLENCE.
This is a commonly used phrase, but it is difficult to put into practice. It takes time, energy, constant attention to detail, and money.

You don't see second-rate products coming out of the businesses in which our members participate. Staff people in these businesses know that nothing less than their best will be acceptable, and on occasion they will be forced to make sacrifices in order to preserve the quality of the goods or services their company produces.

## 6. A POSITIVE ATTITUDE IS A MUST.
Negative thinking and negative talk are for closed-door sessions only. Negative leadership on any level is considered bad form and it tends to discredit the person who uses it.

## 7. THERE ARE FAMILY PROBLEMS.

Our executives and their families are high achievers and upwardly mobile. There is a constant turnover in the community, with fathers being relocated or taking new positions. This creates job-related pressure and family trauma. The term "generation gap" may not be stylish anymore, but it still describes the distance between too many executives and their children. The executive life style seems to carry with it related problems of broken marriages, alcoholism, child abuse, drug abuse, and wayward children. Money cannot correct these problems, although many people mistakenly expect it to.

## OPERATIONAL PRINCIPLES

When we had a clear picture of the strengths, weaknesses, and general characteristics of the people in our community, we developed operational principles for our church—pathways to use in reaching our goal. As can be expected, there are definite correlations between the characteristics of our people and the way we operate the church. I would expect similar patterns to be evident in other progressive congregations.

(The following list includes some principles that evolved in the years after Christ Church was established.)

- Absolute loyalty to God's Word is required.
- Believers are encouraged to develop their spiritual gifts and talents, and the church seeks ways to integrate them into the body.
- The worship service is dignified, respectful, and liturgically sound.
- Creeds and confessions of the historical Christian church are a base for current faith and life style.
- The ministry must start with a basic understanding of the people to be served.
- Major areas of service are delineated. Programs within those areas are flexible.
- The church makes a sincere effort to serve its community as it ministers to its own members.
- Commitment to excellence.

- No fund-raising campaigns or any other money-making ventures.
- Leaders display a positive, enthusiastic attitude.
- Mission activities and programs are emphasized.
- A prayer base is established for all activities.
- Spiritual need dictates programs, not financial constraints.
- Building(s) and grounds will be secondary to the servant role of the church.

Some of the items on the above list are obvious, and some already have been discussed, as I described character traits of our people. I would like to include a few paragraphs, however, about three of the items on the list: our building, missions, and money.

1. The Christ Church building complex was carefully designed to embody our goals and operational principles. The building points heavenward, constructed of simple, strong, plain materials and quiet colors. Our sanctuary seems to shut out the world while rays of light stream down from windows high above. Worshipers enter the sanctuary by passing under a cross. It is a dedicated, holy place, set aside for one purpose only: worship. People come here expecting things to happen, praying that there will be results. A kind of electric spiritual dynamic often seems to envelop us as we prepare to meet God on a Sunday morning.

2. We do not stage fund-raising events at Christ Church. We might gain a little money as an immediate result, but such activities do not interest the majority of our people. They give liberally—but not because some committee sets a goal and then pleads for money. They enjoy becoming financially involved when they see for themselves how a project will meet a real need. (Financial support from enthusiastic, committed people is far greater than support from people who need to be cajoled or threatened, anyway.)

3. Christ Church helps support mission programs in Chicago, other parts of North America, Singapore, India, Kenya, France, Mexico, Israel, Hong Kong, Korea, the Philippines, Indonesia, and many other countries. Our congregation's mission committee also provides at least partial support to members of the church who feel the call to serve on a mission field themselves.

Worship services are broadcast on commercial radio and television stations in the Chicago area. This media ministry is only an extension of the pulpit of Christ Church, not a tool for bringing new members into the congregation or raising money. The media ministry is regarded by the church to be one among many mission activities—in our mission booklet, in fact, it is listed on page 22 as "The Pulpit of Christ Church," between mission programs in Upper Volta and the Niger Republic.

## THEOLOGICAL TENSION

Although Christ Church has never formed an evangelism committee, the concept of evangelism always has been very important to us. It is so important, in fact, that it has led to some theological tension. We have consciously worked through these questions, and I believe the process of resolving them has made us a stronger, more unified congregation.

The first question was this: "Should our church be an evangelistic instrument or should it be a body of believers?" That question could be restated this way: "Should our church be a soul-winning entity, or should it be a community of growing, developing, and maturing believers?"

Some people, I realize, would advise us that we are setting up an unnecessary polarization between the two choices. The answer, they would say, lies on a continuum between the two extremes or in some other formulation of the relationship between the two. At Christ Church, however, we used that model to come to some specific conclusions about the nature of our church and its responsibility to our community. The conclusion affected the nature of our worship services, the content and purpose of our preaching and teaching, the attitude toward youth programs, and our emphasis on programs in which new members are involved.

We decided that our church would be primarily *a body of believers.*

In any given place and time God raises up people and institutions which are used by him for very specific purposes. We felt that the church has always been defined in Scripture as a body of believers who must grow and be nurtured. The primary task of the church, therefore, would be to create and develop the process by which these members will grow and be nurtured.

We recognized that the church also has as one of its mandates to go into all the world and evangelize. To achieve this task, the

Holy Spirit equips certain persons with special gifts. Not all organizations, as far as we could see, had this gift—only a select number. There are organizations that arise from the Christian community with evangelism as a specific mandate. Churches benefit from cooperating and interlacing their programs with them. New members join the body of believers as a result of their efforts.

But once the new believer is drawn into the church, he must grow. The process of growth is the responsibility of the local church. In our judgment, the worship service and the study groups must be the gathering of believers who assemble primarily to honor God and study his Word. These assemblies are not places of explicit evangelism.

The church, we felt, was a place for nurture and instruction of those who are committed to Christ. To try to do the two functions simultaneously would not be wise. We were founding a church in Oak Brook—we were certainly not organizing an evangelistic institution.

While hoping to extend the boundaries of the church and invite the community to become part of it, we had to recognize that our primary responsibility was to the believing community, not to the unbelieving community.

We could not, therefore, give equal priority to both. "But," we were asked, "what about finding a happy medium—developing a church and also putting at least some emphasis on becoming an agency of evangelism?" Or, put another way, "Could we in fact be an arm of evangelism while existing in the community as a church and not as an evangelistic association?"

Our conclusion was this: Since the Holy Spirit reserves the right to bless certain people with specific gifts (including those relating to evangelism), and he promises to bless *all* believers with the fruits of the Spirit, our emphasis would be on the latter. We trusted that the Lord would use this stance to create a strong, healthy fellowship that would appeal to unbelievers. We would encourage those with various gifts, and if we developed into a truly Christlike community we trusted that we would see a fulfillment of the truth stated by Christ: "And I, if I be lifted up, will draw all men unto myself."

Our program, therefore, has not included any direct door-to-door canvassing or heavy-handed campaigns to convert unbelievers. Our church, on the other hand, has placed a strong emphasis on personal and collective understanding of biblical truth, the practice of Christian living, and the enthusiastic communication of the Christian life style.

On a typical Sunday morning at Christ Church, you can see members showing visitors various parts of our church, sanctuary, chapel, library, bookstore, missionary displays, and children's areas. Printed in each Sunday morning bulletin is a complete list of the week's activities: youth group meetings, adult groups, prayer groups, choir rehearsal, language class, recreational activities, fellowship suppers, Bible studies, businessmen's breakfasts, discussions of current topics, and new member classes. From the pulpit we announce that all events—even those held in private homes—are open to visitors and everyone is cordially welcome to attend.

There are many offerings within any one of our departments. No one volunteers to participate in any program out of a sense of duty to the institution. We do not put tacit pressure on people to participate in anything—if no one joins a particular course or special activity it means that the church staff failed to gauge correctly the need for that activity. We feel that people should learn to respect our faith and to become more Christlike through their own commitments, rather than by what we are seeking to do as an institution. Christianity should never become an institutional demand.

A businessman's friend may feel a need for group prayer and meditation—he feels free to join our prayer breakfast at 6:45 every Thursday morning. A family interested in providing a church home for a restless teenager might find that one of our youth programs appeals to their son or daughter. A recently widowed or divorced woman might find companionship and strength in one of the women's Bible study groups. We strive to provide programs that meet real needs among the families in our community and we make it easy for visitors to become involved. A more thorough understanding of the gospel message, repentance, conversion, and eventual church membership are *natural* results of the coming into our body of believers—not emotional, highly orchestrated decisions extracted from a person at a prearranged time.

Instead of an evangelism committee, Christ Church has a staff, a board of trustees, a board of elders, and many program chairpersons who are always asking the question: "How can we better meet the needs of the people in our congregation?" Or, "How can we make this congregation healthier and more nurturing?" Or, "How can we be more Christlike?"

If people in the community sense that we are aware of genuine human needs and that we are sincere about ministering to those needs, they will respect us and come to us for help. We will then be able to minister to them.

We will be aggressive, positive, and creative as we develop our programs. We may become aware of a particular need, and even though we have never heard of a program that offers a solution, we will propose one, plan it carefully, and if it seems workable, we will implement it. The people in our constituency appreciate our efforts. In fact, they expect as much of us.

This brings us to a second area of theological tension that we faced and resolved as a church. We are basically a *spiritual* entity in the community. There are a hundred thousand needs to be met among the executive and professional families in this area, but we must remember that we have a spiritual calling, not a social calling. It is fine to be socially concerned, but in our community there are country clubs, YMCAs, garden clubs, Rotary, Lions, Kiwanis, and many other socially concerned clubs. If we had intended simply to compete with them, we had to admit that they could do many jobs better than we could. As we worked to build a church that met needs, we always had to address ourselves to the spiritual dimension of life.

We are part of Christ's church, and if we abandon that central spiritual responsibility, no other organizations will pick it up. Some other group could take care of social awareness, neighborhood problems, or educational issues, but not the spiritual side.

The need to reemphasize spiritual action became very real to me recently. I spent some time studying in Spain, and I became acquainted with the mystical movement that occurred there in the sixteenth century. Christians have all but forgotten the movement, whose leaders were St. Teresa of Avila and St. John of the Cross. These two individuals brought about changes that deeply affected their compatriots in the church of Spain and even won the favor of the Pope. St. Teresa challenged the church to understand its spiritual dimension. She focused on the experiential. She constantly looked for Jesus Christ in the hearts of those who had been redeemed by his Word, as well as in her own heart.

The movement surrounding St. Teresa was private and personal. It affected the hearts of people who sincerely wanted to talk with Jesus Christ. They practiced the disciplines of prayer, solitude, and meditation, and thereby drew close to God. History tells us that the movement won the hearts of many people.

We renewed our emphasis on the spiritual dimension of our programs at Christ Church shortly after that trip.

I preached a series of sermons on the "marks of spirituality" that included such topics as healing, fasting, meditation, and simplifying our busy lives. Someone who was not acquainted with the people in our congregation might have wondered, "Would hard-nosed executives and professional people *really* sit still for a sermon on fasting or meditation?"

They did. Exploring the spiritual dimension of life is important for any church, and in a church filled with people who are searching for fulfillment and meaning in life it becomes especially important. We had ninety people sign up for a church-sponsored course in spirituality, and later many individuals told me that they had begun practicing meditation (in the biblical sense) and fasting.

In the drive to be dynamic and meet all kinds of needs, a church should remember its spiritual dimension. That makes it distinctive in the community. When our members speak of Christ Church among their friends and associates, other people begin to think: "Those people really have something to say that no one else seems to be saying. We should go and see for ourselves."

The power of the Spirit moving in a community of believers is far different from anything in the secular community. It has nothing to do with how wealthy our people are, what kind of homes they live in, or whether they are busy, creative, self-motivated, educated, or anything else. It is related to a quality of life that can apply to anyone anywhere. I think that *this* is what Christ meant when he said that it is for the poor as well as the rich, the ignorant as well as the brilliant.

A third major tension we faced was related to our methodology and style of leadership. From the beginning, we saw that it would be necessary to decide on a style of leadership. *How* would we approach the people of Oak Brook and surrounding communities? *How* could we best represent the attractiveness and irresistible magnetism of Christ? If we felt a spiritual emphasis would benefit the believers in our area, *how* would we bring it to them?

The extremes of the tension in the third problem seemed to be these: demands and dogma vs. freedom and faith.

Our choice: freedom and faith.

We felt we should emphasize the liberty of the true Christian conscience and the development of faith in a pluralistic, creative way. Leadership by demanding, ordering, shaming, or threatening was out of the question. Our method would be to offer a reasonable explanation for our faith, provide biblical principles, and give wide latitude for unique, creative, and individual application of the Word of God.

Some people in our society react to emotionalism. Some are thinkers, and their wills are moved through the intellect. Some follow personalities and involve themselves in a cause because of loyalty to a charismatic person. Some react to threats. Others to fear. History tells us that men have been frightened into Christianity by graphic pictures of hell. Some personalities need domination, some thrive on legalism, and some crave freedom from decision making. We recognize that many of these people are true Christians and are part of the body of Christ.

But the people in our particular area demand a certain kind of leadership style. They are comfortable with decision-making, they are well educated, and they expect to use their ability to reason their way through complex problems in their daily lives. Our approach was influenced by all those characteristics.

We decided that faith would really come alive at Oak Brook if we took seriously the mandate of Scripture which counsels us to give a reason for the faith we possess. Therefore, we adopted methods which accept the demand for obedience, but go beyond mere blind obedience to an understanding of the Mind which requires obedience.

Our style, therefore, is reasonable, historically defensible, and spiritually rooted. Our people respond enthusiastically as I preach "the reasonably superior way of life in Christ."

Before leaving the subject of leadership in our congregation, I should note that a long pastorate is essential for the kind of leadership we have in Oak Brook. A true commitment to a community and its people is necessary before trust and understanding can develop.

The reason I have been able to provide strong leadership for this congregation is because I have been here for almost twenty years and the people know I intend to stay until death or retirement. I think of my pastorate in terms of a marriage in which I am investing all I am and all I have. I am part of this community and I have a stake in it. The people in this congregation can depend on the fact that I am going to live with them through all their problems. I am not here on temporary assignment for a couple of years—descending on them with a lot of temporary idealism.

A DYNAMIC CHURCH CANNOT BE IGNORED.
"We trust that you will find God here" is a sentence I use often in the pulpit of Christ Church. I mean every word of it.

I have a great respect for churches that are able to organize successful evangelistic campaigns and I also respect evangelists and the great para-church evangelistic organizations that cooperate with churches. But to churches who do not seem to reap blessings from specific evangelistic programs I would offer the words of Christ: "And I, if I be lifted up, will draw all men unto myself." In our church, attention to a collective understanding of biblical truth, the practice of Christian living, and an enthusiastic communication of the Christian life style is a way of lifting up Christ. Community people are naturally drawn to him through the people of the church.

A dynamic church cannot be ignored by the community it is in. People are going to know it is there, and it is going to be attractive. It will be attractive because it is meeting the needs of people, including areas in which the community people are hurting. It is going to be stating things to the community through its people—not necessarily great statements from the pulpit that get quoted in the media—but a very natural witness by a laity that speaks its mind in the marketplace. Enthusiastic, committed church members are naturally going to have an impact on the areas in which they live. The church develops creative citizens of God's Kingdom who can go out from the church into a vocation or into the community and redeem the things they touch. The church is a kind of nursery for siblings. It is a place where we launch ideas.

God's truth, we find, does indeed set all men free, including those who make their homes in this western suburb of Chicago and come into contact with Christ Church.

# ELMBROOK CHURCH
## WAUKESHA, WISCONSIN
## DR. STUART BRISCOE, PASTOR
## FROM 500 TO 5,000 IN FIVE YEARS

CHAPTER

11

## THE PHILOSOPHY OF
## ELMBROOK CHURCH'S MINISTRY

Our Lord wasted no time in demonstrating that he proposed to use human beings to achieve his divine ends. His public ministry started with the calling of disciples and he very quickly mobilized them into a force to be reckoned with. We, his contemporary disciples, follow in their train.

St. Luke succinctly explained the initial mission of Christ's disciples as follows:

> "Then he called his twelve disciples together, and gave them power and authority over all devils, and to cure diseases. And he sent them to preach the kingdom of God, and to heal the sick" (Luke 9:1, 2).

We can summarize this under three headings.

1. They were to announce the Kingdom of God.
2. They were to attack the strongholds of Satan.
3. They were to address the needs of mankind.

While we can divide these three aspects of mission into convenient and neat compartments for the sake of clarification, it should be noted that all three are interrelated and cannot be separated in practice. We must concentrate our efforts in the contemporary church in the fulfilling of this mandate. This, I believe, requires a strong emphasis on proclamation or preaching. Undoubtedly, there is place for dialogue and debate, but that place is not to be found at the expense of solid, systematic preaching and teaching of the Word of God.

Elmbrook Church clearly reflects this emphasis, not only in programming, but also in architecture. The sanctuary is circular, the pulpit and the communion table stand in the geometric center, and the people literally gather around the pulpit and table for the ministry of both Word and sacrament.

Any honest, forthright proclamation of the Word of God cannot avoid the harsh realities of sin and Satan and the evidences of their nefarious operations in individual lives and in corporate society. Our preaching and teaching, therefore, seek to apply the truth to the secular scene with the objective of bringing people to repentance and faith, leading to forgiveness and reconciliation. Of course, human need is overwhelming and the problem facing the church is knowing to what extent we must involve ourselves in addressing such a monumental problem. We have not come up with any easy answers, but we are trying!

## THE PRINCIPLES OF ELMBROOK CHURCH'S MINISTRY

1. THE PRINCIPLE OF PRAYER.
Elmbrook has increasingly embraced Tennyson's thought:

"More things are wrought by prayer, than this world dreams of. . . ."

In our organized and systemetized world it is all too easy to overlook the necessity of prayer in the work of the ministry.

Programs, presentations, promotions, and projects have too often usurped the prime place that prayer must have in the work of the Lord. This conviction has led to numerous efforts to call the congregation to a ministry of intercession. Personal prayer is, of course, encouraged, and public prayer in the congregation meeting is regarded not only as a corporate calling on the Lord, but also as an opportunity to present models and encouragements to prayer. Prayer chains of believers committed to this ministry can be reached and mobilized day or night when necessary. Prayer groups meet regularly to deal with specific requests for prayer, and occasional "half night" or "twenty-four hour" prayer services are arranged, to which a growing response has been in evidence.

## 2. THE PRINCIPLE OF DISCIPLESHIP.

Elmbrook Church takes seriously the fact that Christ's earthly ministry commenced with the calling of disciples and concluded with the mandate to disciple all nations. Discipleship, therefore, cannot be overlooked. Contemporary Christianity has sometimes displayed a tendency to downplay the demands and delights of a personal commitment to our Lord demonstrated in a uniquely Christian ethic and a distinctively attractive servant spirit. The blurring of ethical norms and the intrusion of secular attitudes has so infiltrated the church that an undemanding "easy believism" has become almost endemic. To remind professing believers that our Lord called us to a life characterized by the denying of self and the daily taking up of a cross is of the utmost importance— as is the proclamation to unbelievers that life in the Kingdom of God is considerably more than life as usual with occasional visits to church.

The emphasis on serving rather than being served touches many sensitive nerves in today's self-absorbed society, but the call of Christ is such that the church which fails to preach and require this approach will quickly lose its spiritual distinctive and eventually its *raison d'etre*.

New members of Elmbrook are reminded of these things in a required premembership class lasting three months, and unless they renew their commitment to this type of discipleship on an annual basis, they are automatically assumed to have withdrawn from church membership.

### 3. THE PRINCIPLE OF EVERY-MEMBER MINISTRY.

For too long churches have operated on the basis of a small professional clergy doing the work of ministry for a congregation which has become accustomed to treating "church" as a spectator sport. Elmbrook Church is solidly committed to the biblical principle that every member of Christ is not only indwelt by the Spirit of Christ, but is also gifted for ministry by that same Spirit. This emphasis in no way detracts from the necessity to have pastors and teachers who can devote themselves totally to ministry, but it does mean that the responsibilities of these pastor-teachers are to equip church members to discover and exercise their spiritual gifts, to mobilize them in ministry, and to ensure that adequate opportunities and resources are available to them.

Clearly this approach can lead to problems if not properly handled, but this is no excuse for failing to operate in a manner that reflects the concept of the body of Christ rather than one or two body members trying to act like a body. The balance of ministry which comes from a multitude of gifted people properly functioning, the multiplicity of ministries which can be developed and perpetuated, and the sense of participation which formerly bored observers can now experience all point to the advantages of church leadership encouraging every member to engage in a ministry in the context of the body of Christ.

## THE PRACTICALITIES OF ELMBROOK CHURCH'S MINISTRIES

The pastoral staff of Elmbrook Church, at present comprised of twelve people, along with interns and residents, is responsible to the Board of Deacons for the oversight and administration of ministries. Responsibilities are broadly defined as follows:

1. Children
2. Junior High
3. Senior High
4. Singles (including college age)
5. Neighborhood Group Coordinator
6. Church Administrator
7. Pastoral Concerns
8. Worship and Foreign Missions Coordinator

9. Couples (including premarital)
10. Social Concerns
11. Study Center Director
12. Senior Pastor

The objective in all these areas of ministry, it must be stressed, is to lead people from the point of their "felt need" to a commitment to Christ as Savior and Lord (which will lead not only to help in the area of "felt need" but also to salvation in the area of "real need," whether felt or not).

## CHILDREN
In excess of 1,500 children from crib to sixth grade are ministered to through innovative Christian education, club activities, and camps. Parents are also instructed and assisted in order that the spiritual well-being of the children might be a priority in home life. Many hundreds of lay people are involved in this ministry.

## JUNIOR AND SENIOR HIGH
Programs for the youth of the church are designed to explain, offer, and nurture spiritual life to those not yet committed to the Lord. Extensive group and individual activities are available to those who know Christ; and, in addition, the young people are encouraged to take the lead in their school activities with a view to witnessing the power of Christ in their lives. Special opportunities for social service and overseas missionary experience are also provided for our young people.

## SINGLES
This group covers all manner of people, from those who are in college, to widows and those who have never married, to those who have suffered the tragic trauma of divorce. It is a sad commentary on our society that we have found the latter group one of the fastest growing in our sphere of influence and one of the greatest areas of need. Considerable effort has been put into arranging all manner of activities for these people, ranging from extremely popular small group Bible studies, to retreats, social occasions, special seminars dealing with problems related to divorce, single parenthood and related problems. College age young people are encouraged to take the lead in campus

organizations such as Navigators, Campus Crusade, and Inter-Varsity, as well as denominational groups that are attempting to stand for Christ in the learning centers of the city.

NEIGHBORHOOD GROUPS
Elmbrook Church, with approximately 5,000 adults attending weekly, has long recognized the necessity for midweek, small group experiences to supplement the large group Sunday-based activities. Accordingly, three types of small groups have been organized: peer groups (which tend to spring up spontaneously); interest groups which deal with specific matters of concern or interest; and neighborhood groups, where people meet regularly with other believers who live in the same geographical location. Neighborhood groups have proved invaluable as a means for mutually enriching spiritual experiences. Many people have become aware of gifts which they would possibly not have discovered in the larger situation. The immediate needs of individuals and families have been met on an intimate, caring basis, and all manner of ministries have sprung up because people developed a vision for their neighborhoods. These neighborhood groups have also become the core groups for two new churches which have been planted in the metropolitan area.

PASTORAL CONCERNS
In keeping with our philosophy of every-member ministry, we have found that many hundreds of members are anxious to minister to sick people, shut-ins, those experiencing marital problems, family and child disturbances, and all manner of other problems which can hinder the healthy spiritual and social growth of those committed to our care. Accordingly, extensive training opportunities are offered to those who wish to be involved at a caring level in the lives of those who are hurting. These many ministries come under pastoral oversight.

WORSHIP
As mentioned above, the exposition of Scripture is given high priority in the worship services, and this has proved to meet a need in the lives of many who sense that their grasp of Scripture is considerably less than desirable. The musical aspect of worship takes many forms, with strong emphasis on congregational

praise; but a wide variety of choirs, ensembles, instrumentalists, and soloists lead the congregation in worship. In addition lay people regularly lead the congregation in prayer, and opportunities for personal testimony to the gracious intervention of the Lord are readily provided.

## MISSIONS

Strong emphasis is placed on the necessity for the church to be aware, not only of the rich harvest close at hand, but also of that which is flourishing overseas. The church actively supports over 150 missionaries by prayer and material gifts; the pastoral staff has a number of members with international missions experience; missionaries on furlough are encouraged to become Missionaries in Residence, seconded to the pastoral staff; and lay people are encouraged to visit mission fields either in the context of their secular occupations or on special work or study tours arranged at regular intervals. In addition, Elmbrook has recently identified a region in Northern Kenya where a ministry to a nomadic desert people will be initiated and for which major responsibility will be accepted by the church. Each year the members are invited to share in a Faith Promise commitment to missions which is quite independent of the church's budget, and the interest and involvement of many hundreds of members in missions has been one of the most obvious aspects of maturity and growth.

## COUPLES MINISTRIES

In addition to many remedial ministries designed to help in the area of marital breakdown, the church has established numerous preventive ministries in family life. Not least of these is the premarital class which is mandatory for all who wish to be married in the church's facilities. In addition, marital enrichment classes and special couples events have proved not only popular but most beneficial.

## SOCIAL CONCERNS

It is not surprising that many social concerns have emerged in a church where so many people are encouraged to be concerned. Perhaps the most visible of these ministries are the refugee and prison ministries. Many people are involved in both, and steps have been taken to reach these types of persons, whatever their condition and need. Three churches have been established among refugee communities, and many visits to prisons, both statewide and nationwide, are made by staff and lay people. Other areas of concern such as overseas famine relief and immediate needs for food and shelter among the disadvantaged of the neighborhoods are constantly addressed.

STUDY CENTER

In keeping with the solid commitment to teaching, the church has established a study center where courses of Bible school and seminary equivalence are offered to those who are not in a position to leave their homes and jobs for full-time training. This new venture has proved most effective, and approximately 200 people are enrolled in courses in which the highest caliber of theological training is theirs for the taking. The objective in this, as in all other aspects of the church's ministry, is to encourage, to mobilize, and to support those who, knowing Christ in their own lives, recognize the privilege and responsibility to make him known to others.

This brief summary of ministries—which has not mentioned all manner of media outreaches, special events in shopping malls, orchestral and dramatic presentations, and organized surveys of people's opinions and needs—does nothing more than touch on all that is going on, but may serve to portray a church where people are excited about the Lord and are eager to serve him.

# FIRST ASSEMBLY OF GOD
## ROCKFORD, ILLINOIS
## ERNEST J. MOEN, PASTOR
## "WE SEE 4,000 PEOPLE EVERY SUNDAY"

CHAPTER

12

THE CHURCH is never a place, but always a people; never a fold, but always a flock; never a sacred building, but always a believing assembly. The church is *you* who pray, not where you pray. A structure of brick and marble can no more be a church than your clothes of satin or cotton can be *you*. God does not live in buildings. He lives in bodies of born again believers. The church is not where we meet, but the church is who we are. The church is a mighty, militant army designed to overthrow Satan's kingdom and to establish the Kingdom of God in the lives of people and in our communities.

*—Pastor Ernest J. Moen*

### THE CHURCH WITH 20/20 VISION

I called an optometrist to find out the definition of 20/20 vision. He told me it means that at twenty feet a person is able to read the chart set before him. Then, according to how close one moves toward the chart, the ratio becomes 20/40, 20/60, etc. If you have normal vision, you can read the sign at 20 feet.

Now, let me speak to spiritual 20/20 vision. This is another matter. As a pastor, it is primary that I carefully teach my church to have vision. I must lay out before them the way of salvation and the way to live out that salvation received by faith, and then teach them to have a passion for the unsaved. Like Paul, I need to be able to say to my flock, "I kept back nothing that was profitable unto you, but have showed you, and have taught you publicly, and from house to house." My job is to win the lost, educate them, and give them vision! Following are guidelines I deem important to accomplish this task.

## THE PASTOR IS THE KEY TO CHURCH GROWTH

"I kept back nothing that was profitable unto you, but have showed you . . . and have taught you." The first thing that goes into building a wonderful church is a God-called, God-blessed, God-ordained, God-anointed pastor. You cannot build a church without him. I often hear men who say that they felt the "call" of pastoring in their lives but fled from the ministry. They testify that it was only God's coercive judgments that finally brought them to a place of surrender to be a preacher. But let me tell you that my story is different.

When I was a little boy, I believed that the most marvelous thing in the world was the thought of God letting me be a pastor. I've not had every job offer in the Assemblies of God denomination, but I've had several. My instinct is that there's nothing to compare to pastoring a church! If I were to be elected to the Presidency of the United States and had to resign my pastorate to do so, I would feel I was stepping down! I love being the undershepherd of God's flock. Scripture says, "It pleased God by the foolishness of preaching to save them that believed." I love to preach! The gospel message burns within my soul and must find release. I love to pray over the message, to prepare the exposition of a sermon, and to stand in the pulpit and deliver the message. It is the highest honor God can give to man.

It would seem obvious that the pastor must want the church to grow. However, Larry Richards interviewed 5,000 evangelical pastors and found that less than 38 percent really wanted their church to grow. One reason is because they were lazy. It takes work! Another reason is that some are committed to a negative philosophy; that is, they bad-mouth a big church. They've decided that God can't do anything in their church anyway, or they're insecure in their own personality. Yet the opposite is true. If Shamgar used an oxgoad, if Moses used a rod, if Jesus used a donkey, then it is also true God would use one of us . . . flesh and blood, bone of his bone, joint heir with Christ . . . and anoint the one whom he calls to preach his Word. He *will* use us for his glory!

Now, in building the local body, do it right. Do it scripturally. Reevaluate the Great Commission. It is the mandate, the obligation, the sworn duty for every one of us preachers to win the world for Christ. Reexamine the New Testament church. Three thousand souls won in one day. Don't bad-mouth a big church! A few days later, 5,000 were added to the church. "And the word of God increased; and the number of the disciples multiplied in Jerusalem greatly." Re-echo Paul's statement in Colossians 1:28, "Whom we preach, *warning every man,* and *teaching every man* in all wisdom; that we may present *every man perfect* in Christ Jesus." Be willing to watch the ushers sweat. Experience the choir filling up and the Sunday school classes filled with excitement. Read and pray and work like you've never worked before. Preach and pray and plug away, and Sunday morning you'll see a new family in your congregaton.

THE PASTOR MUST HAVE PEOPLE
The above may not sound like a profound statement, yet I have been around churches were the people did not want the church to grow! Their attitude is one of discouragement. Paul was a great church planter and pioneer. Study his travels. They took him to the major metropolises of Asia, Philippi, Thessalonica, Macedonia, Athens, Corinth, and finally the imperial city of Rome. Wherever he went, people were there. Get a burden for people. Feel for people.

> Let me have my church by the side of the road,
> Where the race of men go by.
> The men who are good—the men who are bad,
> As good and as bad as I.
> I would not sit in the scorner's seat,

Or hurl the cynic's bend.
Let me have my church on a downtown street,
And be a friend to man.

I repeat again, the people have got to want the church to grow. They've got to see this. Just recently, we made the decision to put in parking for ninety-eight cars in the front of our church. We dug up the grass, put in curb and pavement, and made room for more people. It was a step of faith. The day we opened it up, it was full! In some churches it's easier to get the sinners coming than it is to get the saints going. Just know this: If you make much of Jesus, he'll make much of you. If you work for God, God will work for you.

Now, once your church has caught the vision for growth, keep in mind that the best kind of growth is steady growth. Don't expect to jump from 500 to 5,000 in eighteen months. I have studied the growth patterns of Richard Jackson's church in Phoenix, of Baily Smith's in Del City, Oklahoma, and of Charles Stanley's First Baptist in Atlanta. Theirs are massive churches with growth of 200-300 every year. Why does this happen? They plan for growth. They organize for growth. Everything has to have a system. We need to break out of tradition, i.e., three songs, a prayer, the offering, then the sermon. There's no life! There's no creativity! There's nothing fresh! When you give an altar call, be specific. Afterward, go after those who come forward and get them into a new Christians' class. Have water baptism often. We have it every Sunday night! Put greeters in the narthex who have a friendly smile and a warm welcome. Think how you can handle traffic flow. Discover ways you can make your people feel a part of the plan. Develop a growth consciousness in them. Break out of old patterns and don't let the method be more important than the task.

THE PASTOR MUST HAVE A PROGRAM—20/20 VISION
We have quoted the Scripture verse, "It's not by might nor by power but by my spirit" so much that we've virtually destroyed creativity. And who gives creativity and inspiration? They come from the Almighty. I pray constantly, "Lord, give me means, give me ideas—something fresh, something that will glorify you." I

don't want the bizarre or the weird. I want something from God that is fresh and new, interesting and appealing.

TO GROW—
THE PASTOR LEADS THE CHURCH IN A GREAT PROGRAM
Let me share some appalling facts with you. DeWitt Talmage was one of the greatest preachers in America. He was articulate, oratorical, and he packed his building throughout the whole of his ministry. The building would burn down, they'd build it up, and he'd fill it up again. Yet, in spite of the power of this man's ministry, historians cannot find the exact location of his church! Now, I'm not just talking about a building. I'm talking about a body of believers. Where are they? The memory of the man is not sufficient to be able to locate the church! Charles Spurgeon, the prince of preachers, is another example. The body he built no longer exists. Now these are great men of God! But I'm talking about building a church . . . a lasting church. And there is no such thing as building a great church without a great program. It is not done! You cannot build a lasting church in four walls.

Charles Spurgeon died at age fifty-eight. It is told that he said to a friend, "My friend, I am afraid that London has lost its listening ear." I had never heard this before, but history tells that scattered throughout the great metropolitan tabernacle where he preached were empty seats and a dwindling congregation.

God is not pleased when we build the church just on the preacher or his sermon. He doesn't like to be contained. He likes expanse. He likes diversity and creativity. He likes genius, the contribution of the mind.

I have established this priority in leadership: My staff plans ahead and formulates a program. If I didn't do this and our philosophy and spirituality only amounted to "it's just going to be me and you," the church would suffer. I believe in a monthly emphasis to inspire and lead the people. Following is an overview of our church programming for one year:

January—"Prayer"
February—"Family Month"
March—"Youth Emphasis"
April—"Easter—Living Cross"

May—"School Functions"
June—"Weddings"
July—"July 4—Old-fashioned Sunday"
August—"Charismatic Conference"
September—"School & Sunday School Emphasis"
October—"Fall Evangelism Emphasis"
November—"Missions"
December—"Singing Christmas Tree"

You might want to ask the question, "Why plan for a program?" I see the reason being as simple as: it's just good stewardship of time and of God's property. Utilize it well! Seek the heart of God for how to use his money, his time, and his people. Plan for special days: anniversaries, old-fashioned Sunday, Labor Day, laymen in the pulpit. Keep summer alive! Schedule conventions or conferences for missions, family life, and Holy Spirit renewal. Make your Sunday school classes interesting. Plan field trips and emphasize the gospel with points of interest. Our Teen Challenge pastor holds a class for junior high boys and has taken them to visit the city jail. These things have great impact. Plan for banquets and fellowship dinners for stewardship, Valentine's Day, graduation, senior citizens, singles. Hold retreats for staff, couples, singles, college, and career. We even give our secretaries a day of retreat.

I know it's not by might or by power, but if you fail to plan, you plan to fail. The church cannot afford to wait when God says move. Nor can it afford to move when God says wait. We cannot afford to walk by sight, to plan small, to be moderate, to accommodate the world, or to have the word "impossible" in our vocabulary. I believe church and Sunday school can bulge at the seams. Run those buses, fill those classrooms, print bulletins, sing songs. Give altar calls, inspire the people—preach as a dying man to dying men. The church cannot afford prayerlessness, carelessness, faithlessness, lateness, or powerlessness. Here's more! The church cannot afford insipid leadership, shoddy discipleship, cheap stewardship, or watered-down Lordship. The church cannot afford popularity at the cost of principle. We cannot afford not to go, give, reach, teach, or disciple.

At First Assembly of God Church, Rockford, Illinois, the primary focus and function of our congregation and pastoral staff is evangelism. This single-mindedness of purpose has contributed greatly to the steady growth of the church. With membership at 1,358 people, our average Sunday morning attendance is about 4,000. Last year the annual budget of the church approached $3,500,000.

The philosophy of the church can be stated as, "We reach and teach." Evangelism with education builds a strong, healthy body of believers.

The church has a pastoral staff of twelve pastors working in specialized ministries. I believe that each ministry must have evangelism built into it as its reason for being. Each ministry's primary goal is an individual's decision for Christ. Developing discipleship, a vital extension of successful evangelism, is also a top priority in the work of First Assembly.

In all areas of ministering, we are interested in quality along with quantity. So, with people coming to Christ in record numbers, the job of producing disciples from decisions grows in each pastor's ministry. Every pastor is building a church within a church.

Pastor Ken Smith is our Evangelism Pastor. It is Pastor Ken's conviction that every Christian is called to be a witness for Jesus Christ, and he is committed to equipping people for that responsibility.

Evangelism Explosion III International, otherwise known as E.E., is the program through which the laity of First Assembly is being trained to witness at home, on the job, with friends, or wherever the Holy Spirit leads them. E.E. is a seventeen-week session involving about 100 hours of study, trainer-trainee discipleship, and on-the-job training.

Five years ago, we began with twelve people. We now have 100 people making weekly calls on homes to present the gospel. Since 1978, E.E. has harvested 650 decisions for Christ and trained 300 laymen.

Pastor Ken explains that once a person is trained, he's then qualified to teach two trainees. This team of three goes out on visitation together, using visitors' cards as a resource for potential calls. During the call, a member of the team will share the gospel. This training ministry takes foundational, biblical facts and puts them in an order easily understood by an unchurched person. When a person accepts Christ through E.E., he is followed up with another personal visit and encouraged to attend church services and Sunday school.

The thirteen-week New Christians' Class was developed to meet the needs of the new convert. The program teaches basic, fundamental biblical principles, and promotes individual study of God's Word. After thirteen weeks, the routine of attending Sunday school and church is established, the new Christian is invited to join one of the church's many ministries—and he has become a vital, active part of the body of Christ. Pastor Ken is gratified that many people who came to Jesus on an E.E. call have gone through the program and are now leading others to God.

Pastor Ken uses evangelism workers as altar counselors. They pray and counsel with people after they've made a decision for Christ by responding to an altar call in our church service. Following up and discipling are done in the same manner as with converts in E.E.

A young wife invited an E.E. team to visit her home to share the gospel with her husband. Pastor Ken led the young man to the Lord that evening. The next week the couple asked Pastor Ken and the E.E. team to come again and talk with his brother and sister-in-law. This couple accepted Christ also, and the following week the E.E. team led the sister-in-law's ex-husband and his wife to Jesus. They and their families are all active members of the body at First Assembly.

Ten years ago, the people of First Assembly built Christian Life Center Elementary School. The high school was added in 1978. Enrollment has gone from 43 to 700 students in ten years, with Pastor Mike Elias as Administrator and Principal of the elementary and high schools. The community's exposure to the gospel through Christian Life Center is immeasurable. All school programs and athletic events are begun with prayer. Pastor Mike feels that the school is a strong Christian witness, and through the attitudes and behavior of faculty, parents, and children, many people can be won to the Lord.

In the school program itself, children are guided toward a personal experience with Jesus Christ. Teachers are sensitive to which students are lacking in their spiritual lives and minister to the children as well as teach them. Christian children are urged to share the Lord with their fellow students. Probably the most amazing thing about Christian Life High School is that the "in" group is the students with the most vibrant, exciting spiritual lives, who are living for God and planning a life of service for him.

Two Hindu students from India who had initially balked at the mandatory Bible class, just recently accepted Christ as their Savior.

Another part of the ministry of First Assembly is Christian Life School of the Bible. Dean of the Bible school is Pastor Dave Ytterock. According to Pastor Dave, the Bible college trains Christians for the work of evangelism and to become disciples of Christ. A course on personal evangelism, based on Evangelism Explosion III International, is offered at the college.

Pastor Curt Johnson ministers to the singles of the congregation and also administers our Needy Family Outreach. His singles group meets for Sunday school and on Thursday evenings for a social activity. Many Thursday evening visitors are not Christians when they begin attending "Positive Christian Singles." A new member who doesn't know the Lord may attend several activities, receive some counseling from Pastor Curt, hear the message of salvation, and accept Jesus Christ as his personal Savior.

Pastor Curt is planning a witnessing program for his group to go into the singles bars to bring the gospel to lonely, hurting people.

First Assembly sponsors a Teen Challenge home that ministers to boys with "life-controlling" problems such as drugs, alcohol, or rebellion. Pastor Mike Lindquist manages the Teen Challenge home and is the spiritual leader of the young men in the program.

"Teen Challenge is centered on evangelism," explains Pastor Mike. "We try to show them that sin is the problem, not drugs. Through salvation, they can get the problem taken care of. Then we concentrate on discipleship, teaching them how to live a Christian life." Teen Challenge students are in Bible study for an hour every day, they attend three church services a week, and they go through the Sunday school's thirteen-week New Christians' Class.

Pastor Mike visits Juvenile Detention twice a week, where he shares a message of hope and gives an altar call for boys who want to come to Christ.

Teen Challenge reaches into the community with literature,

television, and radio commercials, and street ministry on weekends.

Our street ministry is led by Don Bienemann. Recently, Don received a letter from a bartender after he had been witnessing in a local bar.

"God is always there. Just like the first time I saw you. You came into the tavern on that Friday night for church. I desperately needed someone to talk to. I went to the tables and picked up the leaflets that everyone left. I read them over and over again."

The street ministry has shared the good news of Jesus at bars, rock concerts, malls, or just street corners all over the city of Rockford.

Pastor John Davis is our Pastor for young marrieds, home fellowships, and counseling. Pastor John believes that counseling is "an arm of evangelism." In counseling sessions, unsaved people often see their need for Christ and come to him, or new Christians are equipped to become disciples.

This spring, Pastor John is launching a lay-counseling clinic which he believes will reach many hurting, troubled families. "People are very receptive to counseling now, and the gospel will be the basis of our counseling methods," Pastor John shares.

Bill and Mary Ellen were ready to get a divorce. Bill was out of work and all seemed lost. Friends from First Assembly encouraged them to speak with a pastor. They met with Pastor John jut before their appointment with their attorney. During that first counseling session, they both accepted Christ. They went through the thirteen-week New Christians' Class, are active in Pastor John's Sunday school class, and are both growing in the Lord.

In home fellowship groups, I've challenged the leaders to reach out to unsaved friends and neighbors. Many times people will visit a Christian friend's home for a Bible study before they will come to a new church.

The New Wine fellowship group, for people with drug or alcohol dependencies, now has a motorcycle gang visiting every Monday night at their meeting.

Pastor John exhorts his Sunday school class of young marrieds to be soul-winners. He believes that very often a Christ-centered family is the greatest witness to neighbors and relatives.

Leading our music department is Pastor Nathan Bouren. With

175 choir members, an 80-member teen choir, 40-piece orchestra, and a handbell choir, Pastor Nathan produces three musical spectaculars a year which draw thousands of people into the church.

Pastor Nathan recognizes that through the Singing Christmas Tree, the Living Cross, and the Living Flag presentations, he reaches out to the community in a unique way. People who may not visit for a service will come to see a musical production. The choir also ministers in song in the shopping malls and nursing homes around the area.

Within the music department, members are involved in small group Bible studies, to strengthen and encourage one another in their walk with the Lord.

First Assembly acquired radio station WQFL in the spring of 1980. Pastor Curt Reinke, the station's manager, stating the purpose of the radio ministry, explains, "WQFL is a channel of God's purpose to build up the body of saints, being perfected in the image of his Son, and an agency of God for building up Christians to encourage them to evangelize Rockford and beyond."

Pastor Curt believes that the most effective evangelism is on a one-to-one basis. He feels it is the radio station's job to motivate the Christian to do his job, with inspirational music and programming. Pastor Curt's first goal in his radio ministry is to lift up the name of Jesus.

The church's ministry for young, single adults, College and Career, is a dynamic evangelistic force in our community. Leading this group of 200 young people is Pastor Dale Crall. It is his philosophy that it is God's will for every person to be saved, and that God's heart is broken when some go into eternity without ever knowing him.

Pastor Dale has had many opportunities to preach on college campuses in the city. These meetings are especially important since he can speak to young people about Christ who may not have any knowledge of God or his Word.

The College and Career group is very active in discipleship programs, where people work together in developing a more intimate relationship with the Lord. Pastor Dale says, "The witness of our lives must be equal to the witness of our words. The quality in our lives should make the gospel attractive to the unbeliever."

Along with living their faith, these young people are busy touching lives and bringing others to Christ individually and through services at the church. In a six-month period, College and Career had 600 visitors. The members are active in the street ministry and E.E. They minister to youngsters in Juvenile Hall, pass out tracts at rock concerts and bars, and conduct Bible studies in nursing homes. One exciting result of Pastor Dale's ministry is the high percentage of his people who enter the mission field. Wherever their lives take them, the young people of College and Career continue to be witnesses and disciples of Christ.

Pastor Oda Jones is in charge of our hospital visitation. Pastor Jones visits our members who are hospitalized and often ministers to people outside of our church body as well. During times of illness, people who have never been interested in God will often turn their thoughts to him and the emptiness in their spiritual lives. Pastor Jones has had the opportunity to lead many people to the Lord during his hospital visits.

Glen was sixty-eight years old and suffering with cancer. Glen's wife, Mary, attended First Assembly and asked Pastor Jones to visit him in the hospital. Pastor Jones saw Glen a number of times while he was in the hospital. One evening, Pastor Jones went to Glen and Mary's home to have communion with them. Before they took communion, Pastor Jones asked Glen if he would like to ask Jesus to come into his life. Glen answered that, yes, he would.

Pastor Jerry, our Youth Pastor, feels that the essence of his ministry is evangelism. A new ministry this year for the youth group is Youth Evangelism Explosion. There are twenty-two teens in the E.E. session and another forty-four waiting to get involved in the spring session. Pastor Jerry says that the program is "revolutionizing" these young people. When a team of teens leads another teen to the Lord on an E.E. call, there is a six-week followup. They're invited to social activities, youth meetings, and church services, and made to feel a part of the youth group.

Pastor Jerry is also working in a jail ministry for young people. Besides counseling our teens, he gets referrals from public high school counselors. While counseling, Pastor Jerry can often share with a youngster his need for salvation and lead him to Christ.

The youth group is also involved in street witnessing, and on several occasions they have stood outside at rock concerts, handing out tracts and witnessing to other young people.

Pastor Jerry estimates that 50 percent of his group is from public schools. With his teaching and exhorting his teens to witness and share Jesus with their friends, the gospel reaches far beyond the halls of Christian Life High School.

Pastor Jerry is heading up Sonlight Ministries. This new children's ministry is spreading to churches across the country. The weekly meetings lead children, from kindergarten to eighth grade, to a personal knowledge of Jesus Christ and an understanding of God's Word.

Pastor Marc Solmes is the Administrator of Christian Life Retirement Center. Built in 1981, the center has 145 residents. Evangelism in the retirement center is accomplished as a friend shares with another friend what Jesus has done in his life. Christian residents have organized small, daily Bible studies in their apartments. People also invite their friends to church services and programs. The children of Christian Life Center and Sonlight Ministry visit the center to minister in song during the holidays. Pastor Marc and other pastors are always available for counseling and meeting the special needs of our elderly friends at Christian Life Retirement Center.

Pastor Marc also is the director of our daycare facility, Kiddie Kollege. While the principle function of Kiddie Kollege is quality care and education for its 177 children, age six weeks to kindergarten, the gospel often reaches the unsaved parent indirectly. Through counseling with parents, Kiddie Kollege programs, or their little children coming to Jesus, parents are often drawn into the church.

The direct evangelizing of children from nursery to eighth grade is the responsibility of Pastor Marc, director of Christian Education. Children are taught the good news of salvation through lessons, films, songs, object lessons, and an exciting puppet ministry. Once a year, we host a Kids' Krusade with a guest child evangelist. Hundreds of children come to Christ during these fun and exciting meetings.

One family in our church has an especially moving testimony evidencing the power and love of God in restoring broken lives and bringing a family together to serve him.

Gloria and Roscoe have three children. Both of them were alcoholics, and Roscoe also had a drug problem. They were on public aid for all of their married lives. Divorced from Roscoe twice, Gloria was living alone with the children when someone invited her to a home Bible study at the Gary Phipps home. Gary and Mary Phipps began New Wine ministry to bring alcoholics into the church, believing that God holds the only hope for deliverance from alcohol addiction. Gloria accepted Christ that evening.

Roscoe, during one of the darkest moments of his life, recalls, "I was morally, mentally, and spiritually sick. The fact that there was a warrant out for my arrest meant little to me, for I was on suicide watch, lodged in 'time out' in a mental ward." Gloria led Roscoe to the Lord during a phone conversation. Both were delivered from drugs and alcohol. Their children have all accepted Jesus as Savior. Gloria and Roscoe were remarried this summer and given a beautiful wedding by their friends in New Wine. Roscoe's business is thriving, and they even returned money to the public aid office, explaining that Jesus had turned their lives around. All three children now attend Christian Life Center. The family is involved in New Wine, E.E., and other church ministries.

Perhaps Roscoe expresses it best when he says, "Jesus came into my life, forgave me, unshackled me, and set me free! Oh, amazing grace! As for me and my family, we will serve the Lord!"

Here is the cornerstone of First Assembly—to see the love and grace of God be made a reality in people's lives through Jesus Christ.

# THE CORAL RIDGE PRESBYTERIAN CHURCH
## FORT LAUDERDALE, FLORIDA
## DR. D. JAMES KENNEDY, PASTOR
## 12,000 PEOPLE FOR EASTER SUNDAY

*CHAPTER*

**13**

CORAL RIDGE Presbyterian Church began twenty-four years ago in the heavily churched area of Fort Lauderdale, Florida. With forty-five prospects for membership, it fell in size to less than twenty in the first year. Then the pastor, Dr. D. James Kennedy, asked himself, "What is evangelism?" "How do you do it?" And things began to happen.

Today Coral Ridge is one of the largest churches in the nation, with a television ministry reaching millions of people and an impact upon the life of America that calls people to a renewed commitment to Jesus Christ.

Here is living proof that evangelism is the key to growth: Jesus Christ is the Way, the Truth, and the Life of any church that hopes to grow.

Listen to what a visitor to that great church had to say as she personally investigated "what goes on there" at Coral Ridge. As you read her article, you'll discover the plan for church growth—it simply unfolds as you look at this modern-day miracle of church growth for the 1980s.

It's Easter Sunday morning, and as the sun comes up over the Atlantic, you'll find thousands of enthusiastic worshipers flocking toward the Coral Ridge Presbyterian Church. All told, you'll be able to count some twelve thousand of them—that's roughly as many people as live in St. Augustine. They come to sing their hosannas at the four services being held in what is measurably the fastest-growing Presbyterian Church in the nation. It is a temple of superlatives, a huge 3,200-seat spiritual supermarket built by the hand of one man and the grace of God.

This is Coral Ridge Presbyterian Church located in Fort Lauderdale, Florida. Coral Ridge is about as far from the "Little Brown Church in the Vale" as one can get. It is a megachurch—vigorously, fervently evangelical—and it is on the march!

The pastor, Dr. D. James Kennedy, is fifty-two years of age and is the founder and senior pastor. He reminds you that Easter isn't the only time his church is packed—this happens every Sunday of the year. It takes a dozen ministers, two organists, a 200-voice choir, fifty-three ushers, and ten public washrooms to accommodate his congregation each and every Lord's Day.

When Kennedy, a one-time Arthur Murray dance teacher, came to Florida to start this place twenty-four years ago, his congregation consisted of forty-five prospects. There were no members; there was no building. The little group met at 8:30 Sunday mornings at McNab Elementary School. Then everyone had to clear out and leave the room free for an equally fragile fledgling congregation of Baptists. Virtually everything about the situation was lousy, and God seemed to be preoccupied with the troubles of other folks. Within a year, the Baptists had plain given up, and Kennedy's flock had dwindled pitifully, to seventeen.

"I thought the whole thing might be a mistake. When you're preaching to seventeen people, you get a very distinct impression that big would be better," says James Kennedy.

Today, he has better than big. He has enormous.

Consider these facts:

The largest Presbyterian congregation in the country, Highland Park Church of Dallas, has 7,700 members. Coral Ridge has about 6,200. This year, it will add 600 new names to its rolls. There are so many people running around on Sunday mornings—as many as 1,600 in Sunday school alone—the church issues plastic nametags so its members can keep each other straight. Not too long ago James Kennedy wandered up to a man who looked unfamiliar and introduced himself.

"Then I asked him if he was a member of the church. He said he was. I said, 'How long?' He said, 'Twelve years.' "

Anne Kennedy, the minister's wife, says she probably knows only a third of her husband's flock by name. This is the price you pay.

"Big," says James Kennedy, "can sometimes be a tremendous heartache."

The church has an annual income of $10 million. Tithes and offerings given directly to the church bring in about a third of that. The rest comes from the church's various communications ministries and Westminster Academy next door. Last year the church gave $4 million to missions. In two decades, it has produced two offspring congregations in Coral Springs and Tamarac, and sent 120 people out to be ministers, missionaries, or youth workers.

The fifteen-acre church complex on North Federal Highway has itself become a neighborhood landmark. The present building, dedicated in 1974 by James Kennedy's friend Billy Graham, cost $4.25 million. At that time, it was the largest and most expensive church facility ever built in South Florida. Its tower soars 303 feet into the air—so high it must carry two flashing aircraft warning lights, and strong winds moan their way painfully around it.

When the sanctuary was under construction, James Kennedy could summon only one reaction to the place: "I was scared to death. It looked as big as the Roman Colosseum."

It still does. There are eight balconies, three communion tables, 18,000 pieces of colored, faceted glass in its windows, an eight-story-high vestibule, and two fountains that tinkle merrily before services begin. The twin spiral staircases are pure whimsy, there solely because Kennedy, who never lived in a two-story house as a boy, wanted them. Outside, above the central front door is an inscription: Come Unto Me.

The church's immense Ruffatti organ with its seventeen ranks and five manuals is the biggest in the South and the second-largest European-built instrument in the country. It cost $200,000 to build and could not be replaced for much under $1 million today. The largest of its 6,600 pipes is forty feet long and weighs 800 pounds; the smallest is not so big as a pencil. Together they give the instrument a magnificent fiery, French voice, rather like that of the great organ of Notre Dame Cathedral in Paris.

Senior organist Diane Bish, who began playing piano at five and switched to organ once she had grown tall enough to reach the pedals, has been at Coral Ridge twelve years. There are those who say that, with the deaths in recent years of both Virgil Fox and E. Power Biggs, Diane Bish hands-down coaxes glory from a church organ better than almost anybody in the world. The night of Palm Sunday, 1,800 people showed up to hear her perform one of her own compositions, a majestic work she calls Passion Symphony. She also has recorded twenty long-playing records (Bish, "Bach and Baroque"; "Christmas with Diane Bish"; "The Artistry of Diane Bish"; etc.) and has a weekly television concert series, "The Joys of Music," that plays on cable as well as UHF stations in seven major cities.

As a Fulbright Scholar, Wichita-born Diane Bish had studied with Gustav Leonhardt at the Amsterdam Conservatory. She was the first American woman to record on the famous "Mozart" organ of Haarlem. Still, she says, "Music is not an end in itself. None of this would be worth it if it weren't to glorify God and help change people's lives."

The Ruffatti is but the centerpiece of Coral Ridge's $200,000-a-year music ministry that involves 500 people from pre-kindergarten children (Cherub Choir) to adults. There are five handbell choirs. A hired orchestra plays at the church fifty times a year, including one morning worship service a month. This year the church's $200,000 self-supporting concert series presented a ten-performance schedule that featured the U.S. Army Field Band and Soldiers' Chorus, George Beverly Shea, the Vienna Boys Choir, and pianist Roger Williams. And Carol Lawrence, Della Reese, and Sir Simon Preston, the organist at Westminster Abbey, are already firm for next year.

"Some people who see worship as a quiet, introspective kind of thing might think what we do here is a little too showy," says Roger G. McMurrin, Coral Ridge's music director. A week ago, McMurrin conducted an unconventional dramatic version of Bach's "St. Matthew Passion" with 300 singers, dancers, musicians, and actors. Sometimes it jarred. Coral Ridge's St. Peter was a short and portly apostle, and St. Matthew was a distractingly handsome blond.

"If you close your eyes, the music's still there," McMurrin says. "We see worship as a celebration of the resurrection. We believe people get fed when they come here. If all we had was music, they wouldn't come."

You want to know why they come? Just ask.

"This church has given me the best circle of friends I could have," says John Hixon, a twenty-six-year-old manufacturer's representative who moved to South Florida two years ago.

"These people didn't desert me," said Cathy Jackson, a divorced mother who supports her two children working for a trio of psychologists. "For a time, things were rough, and (thanks to the church) we've had food, we've had clothes. We haven't fallen through the cracks."

"I was looking for answers to a lot of questions, and God led me here," says Ralph Wittenkeller, a church elder who owns a real estate company.

"We heard about this church, and we lived not too far away," says Priscilla Kovach who, like her husband, Ron, was raised Catholic. "At first we felt guilty walking in the door, but some people came to our house and shared the gospel. We felt their concern. We had a marriage that was falling apart. The church has put a lot of love back into our marriage and into our lives."

"I have eyes that go blink, blink, blink. . . . God has made my eyes," sing the three-year-olds in Anna Kornrumpf's Sunday school class. Their parents cluster with other adults in groups of three or four to large gatherings of 150 and study everything from biblical archaeology, to the book of Esther, to building a Christian conscience. In the class on the epistles of Peter, Ken Wackes, Westminster Academy's headmaster, tells his Sunday morning adult students, "Even psychologists tell us that children who have no fences built around them are very insecure. They want us to have enough love to build fences."

Meanwhile, Joy Thornhill and Kathy Garner have just established The Channel, a helping-hand, by-members-for-members ministry. Sick and need supper brought in? Call The Channel. Lost your job and can't buy your children new shoes? Call The Channel. "With all the government programs being cut, I see a big vision for this," says Joy Thornhill. "I think we're going to need this more and more."

There are prayer groups, Bible study groups, special programs for singles, married couples, men, women, mature people, children, new members. On alternate Sundays, Gil De Leeuw teaches a special class for the handful of Coral Ridge members who were born in Taiwan.

John Cochrane, a former policeman who joined the church staff in January as director of community services, has begun a rehabilitation and outreach program for prostitutes. One woman already has been established in a new job, but on the whole it is sure to be slow going. "Very few prostitutes come to church," he says.

At Coral Ridge, there are ministers for pastoral care, youth visitation, education, community outreach, discipleship, and even singles. There are Wednesday night study courses in Christian financial planning, the Gospel of John, effective prayer, and an intriguing aerobic dance class called Firm Believers. It is quite possible that you could show up here on Monday night and find so much to do you would not make it home again for a week.

Audrey and Harry Theobold are among 120 people welcomed as new Coral Ridge members on Palm Sunday. They drive down from Boca Raton to attend services. "We tried every church in the area," says Audrey Theobold. "We think the minister gives a wonderful sermon, and we love the music. The only thing we worried about was that it's such a big place."

Says Cathy Jackson, "It's up to you. We have all these things available. You're invited. All you have to do is show up. You can get lost, but if you do, it's your own fault."

"There is only one reason people come here," says James Kennedy. "They come here because we're giving something away free. We're giving away eternal life."

Inside the vestibule, over the church's main front door, are the words, "Go ye into all the world." You are virtually forced to look at them as you leave. And they do not let you alone. You lug them home with you as if they were made of stone. They are there for one purpose, to remind you of the mission of this place. The quote is a verse from the Gospel of Mark: "Go ye into all the world and preach the gospel to every creature." James Kennedy regards it as no less than marching orders straight from Jesus.

"John Wesley said, 'The World is my pulpit,'" he says. "I'm going to take as big a whack at that as I can."

It was not always so. In 1953, this Georgia-born glass jobber's son was twenty-three and working in Tampa as an instructor at Arthur Murray. He had studied clarinet and saxophone at the University of Tampa and thought he would go through life literally tripping the light fantastic.

He was wrong. "I came into the ministry kicking and screaming. The Lord dragged me in by the ankle."

Here is why. One morning, James Kennedy was awakened by the crackling radio voice of Dr. Donald Grey Barnhouse, pastor of Philadelphia's Tenth Presbyterian Church. "Suppose you were to die tonight," said Barnhouse, "and God were to say to you: 'Why should I let you into heaven?' What would you say?"

Simple, thought Kennedy. He had obeyed the Ten Commandments. He was a good guy. That would get him in.

"I was certainly sure, as most Americans are sure, that one earns his way into heaven by having been a good boy," he says.

No way, said Barnhouse. You only get in for one reason: God lets you in. You cannot earn your ticket, buy it, steal it, trade or bribe for it. It is a gift.

"The idea of grace was totally out of my mind," said Kennedy. "I went straight out and bought a book, if you can imagine a tango dancer doing a theological investigation." The newsstand sold him Fulton Oursler's, *The Greatest Story Ever Told*, a fairly classic docu-drama of the life of Christ.

It took God, Donald Barnhouse, Fulton Oursler, and a young believer named Anne Craig Lewis from Lakeland to redeem James Kennedy. "I did not know a Christian at that time. To my knowledge I did not know a single Christian. I had not been to church for ten years." Anne Lewis was one of James Kennedy's dancing pupils. They fell in love, and he fell into grace.

James Kennedy quit Arthur Murray and by 1959 had graduated from Columbia Seminary in Atlanta, Peter Marshall's alma mater. He thought he would like to become a missionary to the Congo. "It was so long ago, I don't even remember why," he says. His application for mission service was not accepted, and he came to Fort Lauderdale, charged with starting a new church from nothing.

Today, Kennedy, who says he was once so shy his boss had to

shove him bodily out onto the dance floor, is an awesome preacher. He holds an earned doctorate from New York University, is fluent in Hebrew and Greek, and is a clear contradiction to those who think evangelical ministers always talk aw-shucks like good old boys and have hay behind their ears.

In twenty years, he has presented more than 2,000 sermons on topics that range from proof of life after death to Felix Mendelssohn to nuclear warfare to humanism. He spends as much as twelve to fifteen hours on each message and then speaks without a text in a rumbling, resonant baritone, hopping smoothly back and forth from biblical text to classical reference: "Even the great wheel of Ixion, where the giant is strapped, pauses in its circles, and the great vulture even stops his attack on the giant."

On Palm Sunday, he leads off a sermon on the penitent thief of Calvary with a description of dawn on that first Good Friday. "The sun had only just now begun to climb reluctantly over the hills of Moab. . . . It had begun to purple the peaks of the mountains. . . . Then the white city, the holy city seemed by some magical levitation to rise out of the black sea of night. . . ."

He is no mere jack-in-the-pulpit. His magnetism is riveting, but his message almost always meanders back to one theme: The Gift. "If eternal life were a wage that we had to earn, we'd have to wait a long, long time to collect," he tells his Palm Sunday congregation. "Heaven is free. Paradise is free. Wonderful to tell."

Today, Coral Ridge's Sunday worship services are taped by the church's own million-dollar television studio and shown in 3,300 U.S. cities and twenty-one foreign countries. Each week, James Kennedy preaches electronically to a congregation of one million souls spread from South Florida to Orting, Washington, to Australia.

In addition, Evangelism Explosion, a phenomenally successful evangelism training program for laymen which Kennedy started twenty years ago, has been used by 10,000 churches representing 200 denominations in fifty countries. Coral Ridge's FM radio station, WAFG, is on the air from Miami Beach to Stuart, broadcasting Christian music and messages twenty-four hours a day, seven days a week. And Coral Ridge's print shop reproduces Kennedy's sermons in pamphlet form. Put a quarter in the slot at the back of the church and select, "What Is a Christian?" or

"Possibilities Unlimited," from the rack and take it home to keep forever.

"Big in itself is not better," says James Kennedy, who has sixty teams of members practicing the same basic shoe-leather witnessing that started this church's growth two decades ago. They call on 180 new prospects every week.

"But on the other hand, if in a community of unsaved people, you can only afford to reach 100, and the 101st turns out to be someone you love, that makes it all worth it.

"People have asked, 'Isn't the church too big?' and I've said, 'Too big for what?'"

The experts at Evangelism Explosion have told James Kennedy that by 1990, his pervasive ministry will have reached 100 million people. They also say that by the year 2000, he literally will have done it. He will have reached every single creature in God's whole wide world.

# GARDEN GROVE COMMUNITY CHURCH
## GARDEN GROVE, CALIFORNIA
## DR. ROBERT H. SCHULLER, PASTOR
## MUCH MORE THAN GLASS

CHAPTER

**14**

## THE CRYSTAL CATHEDRAL

Throughout the centuries, churches and cathedrals have been recognized as some of the world's most beautiful structures. Already the Crystal Cathedral in Garden Grove, California, has taken a foremost place in historic religious architecture.

Designed by AIA gold-medal winner Philip Johnson with his partner John Burgee, the Crystal Cathedral is a dream fulfilled. Johnson has called it his *capo lavoro*—the crowning achievement of his career.

The Crystal Cathedral is more than just an architectural phenomenon—it is the home base for the Robert H. Schuller International Ministries, including the internationally televised "Hour of Power" and a congregation of 10,000-plus members.

The Crystal Cathedral is also the fulfillment of a dream of Dr. Robert H. Schuller. On September 14, 1980, he dedicated the Cathedral "To the Glory of Man for the Greater Glory of God." Since its opening, the Cathedral has been seen by millions around the world via the "Hour of Power" program and by thousands of daily visitors.

The structure spans a full 415 feet in length and is 207 feet wide and 128 feet high. The size of the Cathedral is enhanced by the all-glass covering that encloses the entire building.

More than 10,000 windows of tempered silver-colored glass are held in place by a lacelike frame of white steel trusses. These 16,000 steel trusses were specifically fabricated for this engineering feat.

The sanctuary seats 3,010 persons including 1,778 seats on the main floor, 403 seats in the east and west balconies, and 306 in the south balcony. Over 1,000 singers and musicians can perform in the 185-foot-long chancel area.

In addition, two ninety-foot-tall doors open electronically behind the pulpit area to allow worshipers in the drive-in sanctuary to participate in the services.

The Cathedral organ, made possible by a gift from Mrs. Hazel Wright of Chicago, will be one of the world's largest pipe organs upon completion. Designed by the late organist virtuoso, Virgil Fox, the concept calls for the uniting of an Aeolian-Skinner organ from the Avery Fisher Hall, Lincoln Center in New York, a Ruffatti Organ built for the former sanctuary in 1977, and a new Ruffatti addition that will bring the total ranks of pipes to 223. White oak organ cases will hold the 10,000 pipes in the chancel area, including forty-four thirty-two-foot pedal rank pipes from Bovard Auditorium at the University of Southern California—a gift of the Mt. Olive Lutheran Church of La Crescenta. Another nearly 3,000 pipes, of which there are 549 trumpets, will be in the four corners of the Cathedral.

The chancel area is constructed of Rosso Alicante marble, quarried in Spain and cut and polished in Italy. The communion table and pulpit area are made of granite, and the seventeen-foot-tall cross is antiqued with eighteen-carat gold leaf.

Huge white concrete columns, the largest ever poured, hold the balconies in place. About 10,000 yards of concrete, equal to 20,000 tons, were poured for the foundation of the structure. All visible concrete has a white marbleized appearance. The columns are hinged at the balcony and/or foundation to permit movement and to withstand an earthquake of the magnitude of 8.0 on the

Richter Scale, as well as wind tunnel tests of 100 miles per hour.

Special facilities offer simultaneous translation of the worship services into four different languages. At present, German, French, Spanish, and Korean are offered with special translation for groups upon request.

The Cathedral's concourse level accommodates the music ministry, performing arts offices, and related rooms, including three rehearsal halls, practice rooms, choir robing areas, and rooms for Christian education classes, as well as bride and groom rooms and ushers' rooms.

The Cathedral's concourse also houses a technically advanced audio studio and television production studio where all video and audio recording of the television services takes place.

Only the lower level is air-conditioned, as the sanctuary itself is cooled by fresh air which flows from the ground level through clerestory windows which open and close automatically. Heat flows from underground pipes to regulate temperatures in the cooler months.

In addition to the Sunday morning worship services, the Crystal Cathedral is open daily to visitors from 8:30 A.M. to 4:30 P.M. A Visitors' Center is located south of the main entrance of the Cathedral, and guided tours operate regularly. All groups tours are scheduled in advance through the Visitors' Center.

Weddings, seminars, and cultural events, including the Crystal Cathedral Concert Series and high school baccalaureates, enhance the Cathedral's role as an active, living facility which draws people from all races and beliefs to experience a common bond.

Already the Crystal Cathedral has become the setting for holiday traditions. Each Memorial Day weekend, a nine-story high American flag is unfurled within the Cathedral during a special service. Every Christmas Eve, five identical services see the Cathedral packed with standing-room-only crowds. In December 1981 a new tradition was born with the dramatic production of "The Glory of Christmas—A Living Nativity"—a pageant that includes a cast of 250 musicians, performers, and live animals in over forty public performances.

The Crystal Cathedral is located on the corner of Chapman Avenue and Lewis Street in Garden Grove, California—just off the junction of the Santa Ana, Orange, and Garden Grove freeways.

# MUCH MORE THAN GLASS

When one considers that Dr. Schuller began his ministry with $500 in his pocket, and his wife as his helper, and now enjoys a worldwide outreach and a Sunday congregation of over ten-thousand people, you know that there is much more to his ministry than a glass cathedral.

His "Community Church" is just that, a community. With over two thousand trained lay ministers, his church offers programs and instruction that surpass the best seminaries. Little known to the rest of the "churched world" is the fact that the Garden Grove Community Church offers some of the finest Christian education to be found in the nation today. The nationally acclaimed Bethel Bible Series is the standard program. For example, the series begins this year with the following listing of Wednesday evening courses to choose from:

BIBLICAL STUDIES
Psalms and the Twentieth-Century Christian
Beginning Bible 1
The Bible and the Future
Beginning Bible IV
Book of Acts II

CHRISTIAN LIVING
Christian Life II
Stress Management
Feelings, Emotions, and Aliveness, Part II
Inner Healing and Peace of Mind
Growing Towards Wholeness
Appreciating the Child
Life After Divorce
Vitality and Health
Vocational Guidance

THEOLOGY AND CHURCH HISTORY
Christian Beliefs
Christian Doctrine II
Church History II
Lay Ministry Is for You
Paraprofessional Counseling

New Hope Telephone Counseling
Laubach Tutor Training
Christian Toastmasters
Film Workshop

LAY MINISTRY SKILLS
Hospitality Training
Teacher Training
Communication Training
Women—Discover Your Gifts
Small Group Leadership
Training for Home Bible Study

This is for Wednesday evening. They offer over thirty courses and charge a tuition to all who attend, as well as charging for the materials they use.

The courses are offered by trained people, many with professional degrees in the subject. Dr. Schuller himself offers the Sunday Evening Bible Studies in the main sanctuary of the church throughout the year. Thus thousands in his congregation receive a continual biblical training for life and ministry.

Throughout the rest of the week, hundreds of courses are offered, some which carry graduate degree credit. Fuller Seminary offers a Certificate of Graduate Studies or a Master of Arts Degree in Theology for the members of the parish who attend and fulfill this parish program.

One can only imagine the evangelistic outreach the Crystal Cathedral music programs have upon the entire community. Heralded as "The Largest and Most Spectacular Christmas Pageant in the Nation," the Cathedral's "Living Nativity" is witnessed by 100,000 individuals who attend on nineteen performance nights.

The Crystal Cathedral is not only a place to worship Jesus Christ, and is not only a place to learn about Jesus Christ, but most of all, it is a place to serve Jesus Christ. This is true evangelization, says Dr. Schuller: "We bring them to Jesus, then we fellowship them in Jesus, then we help them to learn about Jesus. This fulfills his divine commission: 'Go make disciples, baptize them . . . and teach them.' We add one more dimension— train them to then go on and make disciples—a continuing life cycle."

# THE HOUR OF POWER

No account of Garden Grove Community Church would be complete without mentioning the Hour of Power, the television ministry of this great church. It is now an international telecast which emanates from the weekly services at the Crystal Cathedral.

The Hour of Power reaches the "greatest number of households and the greatest number of adults of all the televised ministries in the nation today."

It began in Los Angeles in 1970, and today is seen on 175 stations in America, Canada, Australia, and the Armed Forces Network. This telecast outreach has an evangelistic effect. Each week, tens of thousands of letters are received from all parts of the world. They ask for guidance, for prayer, for help, and for spiritual answers to life's major problems. As a direct result of this outreach ministry, countless thousands are brought into church membership all across the nation.

Pastors and people who believe such televised worship services lead people away from church are mistaken—they simply do not know the facts. Many a parish has reaped where it has not sown. Through effective programming, souls are motivated to seek Jesus Christ, and at the Garden Grove 24-Hour Counseling Tower, they are directed to find Christian fellowship in a neighborhood church where they live.

Finally, schools and conferences for professionals are conducted to share the success story with other pastors. There is the National Conference on the Training of the Laity held each year, and the National Institute for Church Leadership at which thousands of pastors of all denominations have found training. There is also the annual Creative Management Symposium for business and professional people.

Persons interested in learning more about the exciting programs of Garden Grove Community Church can write for information to:

THE GARDEN GROVE COMMUNITY CHURCH
12141 Lewis Street
Garden Grove, CA 92640

# FIRST PRESBYTERIAN CHURCH
## CHATTANOOGA, TENNESSEE
## DR. BEN HADEN, PASTOR
## "WHY WE ENJOY OUR LARGEST CONGREGATION EVER"

CHAPTER

15

WHILE most inner-city parishes slowly die and lose their membership to suburban churches, this is not the case with First Presbyterian Church of Chattanooga, Tennessee.

Under the visionary leadership of their senior pastor, Dr. Ben Haden, this church enjoys its largest membership in its long one-hundred-year history.

The concept that the "Old First Church" slowly dies while the exciting growth is headed toward the suburbs is simply not true.

Not only does Dr. Haden meet the needs of his congregation of some 1,500 people, but he has a nationwide radio congregation in the millions. His sermons are favorites all across the nation on weekly Christian radio stations.

"You may have gone to church all your life, given a lot of money, a lot of time, a lot of attention—and yet you don't personally know Jesus Christ.

"Your life may be just a little better than hell. And you frankly wonder if that's the way life is meant to be. Jesus says, 'I have come that you might have life, and that you might have it more abundantly.' That's either a lie or the truth.

"If you have the slightest doubt that you know Jesus, would you give me or any other officer of this church the privilege of talking with you at your convenience—today or by appointment—about the claims Jesus makes on my life and yours.

"Then understanding the claims of Jesus—that his death was for the forgiveness of your sin and that he demands personal obedience—you may reject him as a liar and not live under either the burden or pretense of loving him.

"Or by the grace of God, you may receive Jesus as the Truth—and with just an inkling of how much he loves you—then live for him without apology.

"Any discussion will be without reference to denomination and without reference to membership in any church."

This brief announcement is made *before* the message, not afterward. There is no altar call. The public invitation is for a private discussion of Jesus.

Inner city . . . thirty feet from the worst of the ghetto area. Older than any organization in the city. Just three pastors in the preceding 100 years. That's the First Presbyterian Church of Chattanooga to which Ben Haden was called in 1967.

"We understood the membership was 2,000," he recalls. "After two special committees purged the rolls, they had purged 750."

Today the membership is 2,300. The Sunday morning attendance is 1,500 with 300 visitors. From a predominantly older congregation, First Church now attracts 45 percent under thirty at all services.

First Church has broadcast its Sunday morning service live on local radio for fifty years. It has telecast its special music and sermon in a thirty-minute format on local TV since 1971. There is also an indirect national outreach through an independent and nondenominational ministry of the pastor. Worldwide the church has invested $4.5 million in missions alone since 1955 and is projected to invest an additional $5 million in the next ten years. The church supports missionaries under different boards and members of other denominations. The Lord has given this church more outreach each week than any church in Tennessee history.

Heading the unique church is a team of very young pastors working with the older Haden. "We are all pastors in this church," they explain. "There is none of the usual emphasis on senior pastors, assistants, titles. We all counsel, we all teach, we all preach, we all evangelize, we all visit hospitals. We are a team—minoring in different minors but majoring in the same majors. Evangelism is a major!"

David Bryan—converted by Fellowship of Christian Athletes—is a former college basketball star. A native of Chattanooga, he graduated from Gordon Conwell Seminary north of Boston and joined the staff out of the Presbyterian Church US. He has been trained in evangelism in England.

Peter Van Deison is a native of Texas. He headed up the college ministry of Campus Crusade for Christ in Tennessee. At one time he served with five other young men in overseeing the U.S. college ministry. After graduating from Dallas Theological Seminary, he joined the staff out of an independent Bible church in Dallas.

Randy Stringer is director of Christian education. He is a native of Pennsylvania and graduated from Trinity Evangelical Divinity School in Deerfield, Illinois. He joined the staff out of the Christian Missionary Alliance Church. He heads the 127-acre camp of First Presbyterian, where evangelism is a major thrust. Today 45 percent of the attendance at the camp is by nonmembers.

Glenn Draper is director of music and quickly completed the transition from the tradition of a paid quartet to a seventy-voice volunteer choir. Music plays a major role in the strategy of First Church. Draper is nationally known as leader of the Lake Junaluska Singers of the United Methodist Church.

Haden is a native Virginian, with a political science degree from the University of Texas, a law degree from Washington and Lee University, and a divinity degree from Columbia Theological Seminary. He was formerly executive vice president and general manager of a morning, evening, Sunday newspaper operation. He is also a former businessman and attorney. During the Korean War he served with the Central Intelligence Agency. He has served as an associate evangelist with Billy Graham.

He is speaker on Changed Lives TV-radio, a national weekly nondenominational thirty-minute program. It has a potential radio audience of 200 million each week and a potential TV audience of 75 million each week. Starting first on national radio in Philadelphia, Haden is in his seventeenth year as a national weekly broadcaster.

The church strategy is simple and specific: reach as many people as possible with the gospel in whatever time remains before Jesus returns. Denomination is not it—it is Jesus crucified, risen, ascended, and returning. Evangelism is not a suggestion but an absolute order to demand repentance and to offer the forgiveness of sin in Jesus with love and compassion.

The strategy is to create an atmosphere in which the unbeliever is sincerely welcomed and appreciated for any honest doubts and reservations he has toward Jesus as the Messiah God promised. The same atmosphere is also to encourage and challenge believers to live for Christ.

"My burden is for the unbeliever," Haden says. "I have been an unbeliever most of my life and understand him best. I can more readily understand his doubts than I can understand my faith."

Were there to be an emphasis on denomination, the staff feels additional barriers would be created to the conversion of the unbeliever. For instance, where great issue is made of baptism, experience indicates that the unbeliever may culturally react from the religious background of his family. He may instantly become preoccupied with the "right" mode of baptism rather than confronting squarely the claims of Jesus.

The staff believes that Satan often uses denominational differences to divert attention from the Cross and the Christ. Here unbelievers from different denominational backgrounds are not made to feel out of place or unusual. From time to time the choir may include as many as nine denominations.

The church is affiliated with a national denomination. The strategy, however, is to present the gospel on a nondenominational basis. Haden feels comfortable with a Methodist choir director, a Seventh-Day Adventist organist, a Southern Baptist personal secretary, and three other pastors from different states, different seminaries, different denominational backgrounds. His own background includes Episcopal (high), Methodist, Baptist, Presbyterian, and Catholic—"and a pagan in all of them."

New members of the church and inquirers are strongly urged—but not required—to complete a seventeen-week course in evangelism and a nine-week course in discipleship. Once a member or visitor completes these two courses, the staff feels he will understand the "guts of the gospel" and the basic Christian faith and will have a usable technique for sharing Christ in a loving and compassionate manner. Most Christians feel they can't talk Christ, share Christ, or cope with a hardened unbeliever. Evangelistic teams go out twice a week under instruction not to "push" anything but Jesus the Person.

In this strategy, there is a strong aversion to confessing Christians who love the idea of evangelism and converts—but have no love for the individuals themselves.

"Scalp collectors have run off so many individuals who might have come to Christ," the staff feels. "Evangelism requires patient savvy and compassionate directness."

First Church feels there is a contradiction in so many theologians today who claim to believe in evangelism but have contempt for the top men doing evangelism—such as Billy Graham, Bill Bright, Jay Kesler, Jerry Falwell, and Pat Robertson.

"If the Lord obviously blesses the evangelism of an individual," Haden says, "then that servant deserves my prayers, my good will, and my appreciation."

The philosophy of First Presbyterian Church is simple though often unorthodox. There is the conviction that the Lord did not establish the church to have the world come to the church, but to have the church come to man. At least 90 percent of everything First Church accomplishes is done by its officers and its members—not by the pastors.

There is a strong liturgical emphasis on the eucharist (Lord's Supper) with an evangelistic thrust. It is freely served to all confessing Christians who first examine themselves. The staff feels it offers an evangelistic opportunity.

"Many doubts and many arguments are simply crushed by the simple serving of the Lord's Supper—showing forth the death of Jesus for our sins until he comes again," Haden says. "Even the individual most prone to ridicule everything Christian becomes strangely silent when the Lord's Supper is served. In our evangelistic zeal, we so often overlook the life or death issue, the guilt and forgiveness issue, the hell and heaven issue clearly presented at the Lord's table."

Love and the forgiveness of sins is the major philosophy of First Church. Equal emphasis is given to repentance. The conviction is that repentance is ignored in evangelism despite the fact that it is one half of the Great Commission.

"Repentance is the death gurgle in the church's throat," Haden observes. "For generations we have dropped our voice on repentance and emphasized forgiveness of sin to the exclusion of Christ's demand for a new life of obedience under his leadership. We have also falsely taught that repentance is crying over the past rather than living the future under Christ. The Great Commission is not just to evangelize but to make *disciples* of all nations. A disciple is a learner and a follower of Jesus—nothing less."

Haden retains warm friendships among evangelical Christians of different persuasions. He dislikes the tendency to attack other groups differing in minor respects but agreeing on the basics of Christ. He cannot imagine a pastor, with a pastor's heart for souls, carefully insisting on *his* theology to a dying man.

Though Gentile by background, Haden considers himself Jewish by faith, since he believes the promises of the Old Testament have been fulfilled in Jesus.

The church staff hits the issue of election head on. They feel an overemphasis on election undercuts any real zeal for evangelism and misrepresents the urgency of the ministry of Jesus.

"As between the free will of God and the free will of man, obviously God's free will (his sovereignty) will always win out," Haden explains. "But I don't feel that is the issue. Election, God teaches—it is therefore true. Personal responsibility for accepting or rejecting Jesus, God teaches—it is therefore true. Many of us are slaves to human logic and 'logically conclude' that election is all that is ultimately involved in salvation. But being trained in logic all my life—and a third-generation attorney—I know the limitations of logic. Logic contradicts love; but the reality of love is nonetheless acknowledged by every logical person.

"God would not order us to go to every square foot of this earth and evangelize if it were not essential to the salvation of the lost."

Most evangelistic churches have little or no history in social action. First Church has a history of over 100 years of extensive social action—not for the sake of society but as part of evangelism. An 1898 church yearbook reveals that in December—then, as now, the best giving month—all gifts were earmarked for foreign missions and blacks. In 1934 the church hired a full-time pastor to work among alcoholics, prostitutes, and the poor. The object was to evangelize and to help financially.

More than $300,000 was spent on blacks from 1952-1972. The staff has included a black for more than twenty years.

Before there was a United Fund in Chattanooga, First Presbyterian Church served as the welfare center for the city. When the United Fund was finally formed, Dr. James L. Fowle, pastor 1928-1967, was elected president for ten consecutive years.

In an independent study by a local university class, it was confirmed that First Church has traditionally had the greatest social emphasis in the city's history.

"I have more fellowship with many Catholics than I do with many Protestants," Haden says. "The reason is that a high percentage of Catholics know the basics of the Christian faith and traditionally accept them. They don't spend their lives questioning whether Jesus is God, whether he was born of a virgin, whether there is a hell or a heaven, whether there is a judgment."

When Haden seeks to lead an unbelieving Catholic to Jesus Christ, he makes crystal clear that by conversion, he means conversion to the person Jesus and not to Protestantism. He uses a Catholic Bible with the imprimatur of the late Cardinal Cushing. He makes it clear that his interest is in the person coming to Jesus—not in changing churches, and not in accepting a different version of the Bible.

Ben Haden, newspaperman, attorney, author, and now pastor of one of America's largest churches, is known across the nation for his outstanding radio and television programs. He is a Bible communicator to young and old; he has preached at the White House and is regularly seen on television in some 3,000 U.S. markets on what he calls, "Changed Lives."

# ST. JOAN OF ARC CATHOLIC CHURCH
BOCA RATON, FLORIDA
MSGR. RONALD J. PUSAK, PASTOR
EVANGELIZATION AT
ST. JOAN OF ARC

CHAPTER

16

## INTRODUCTION

Several major concerns precipitated the formation of a viable
Evangelization Program in our parish. These areas of concern
included both our active and inactive members, as well as our
"unchurched" friends and neighbors among us.

Because the Catholic Church's central mission has always been
evangelization, a distinction had to be made between our renewed
efforts of Evangelization (with a capital "E") and all of the other
evangelization efforts which historically and traditionally have
been integral and necessary functions of the church, such as the
religious education of our children in grammar schools and
catechetical classes.

## ACTIVE CATHOLICS

There was a feeling that, despite the fact that ours is a eucharistic
church, many of our active, practicing parishioners did not seem
to have a living faith in the resurrected Lord Jesus. Parishioners

seemed to take a passive stance in the church and in their own faith lives: they were catechized, sacramentalized, and theologized, but, perhaps, not evangelized.

In other words, while they attended Mass regularly and fulfilled their obligations for membership, they did not appear to be living the full, rich, joyful life which Jesus offered to all of his followers. So, in one sense, we hoped to evangelize our active members by inviting them into a deeper personal relationship with God, thus building up their faith and enriching their lives. In order to be an evangelizing church, it was necessary for our own members to be evangelized first—"You cannot give away something which you do not possess."

## INACTIVE CATHOLICS

Second, recent trends had shown that since Vatican II, a large number of Catholics were leaving the church for a variety of reasons. Some of these reasons included "too many changes in the church" or "not enough change in the church"; disagreement on issues such as divorce, remarriage, birth control and abortion; and a high degree of mobility.

We also were experiencing a genuine proselytizing effort by other local denominations whereby some of our flock were joining other churches after having been evangelized by lay members of other faiths. For years, we were aware that some of our membership were attending nondenominational neighborhood Bible studies and, while finding a certain degree of nourishment there, they were also coming away with some confusion regarding Catholic doctrine. This confusion also seemed to indicate a lack of secure knowledge of the doctrinal teachings of the church, as well as a basic unfamiliarity with Scripture.

## "UNCHURCHED" AMERICANS

Third, we realized that a large segment of the population within our parish boundaries had no church affiliation whatsoever. Nationally, it is estimated that there are 80 million "unchurched" Americans, or approximately 40 percent of the general population. As evangelizers, we felt the responsibility to spread the gospel message of Jesus Christ to these friends and neighbors and to invite them to experience the fullness of faith in a Catholic faith community.

## HISTORY AND RATIONALE

In 1975, the Apostolic and Exhortation, *Evangelii Nuntiandi* ("The gospel must be proclaimed") was issued by our Holy Father, Pope Paul VI. This teaching subsequently set in motion evangelization concerns not only at the international level but also at the national, diocesan, and personal level, as an awareness grew of the importance of encouraging and nurturing a deeper personal faith in Jesus Christ among all people.

Reflection on the need for a renewed interest in active evangelization in the church by all of its members revealed that, until just prior to Vatican II, there *had* been an active lay involvement in evangelizing. There had been a great call to the laity to be witnesses to the faith in the teachings of Pope Pius XII (1939-1958) through his redefinition and affirmation of Catholic Action as a lay apostolate. Earlier, the efforts of the Catholic Truth Society and the work of street preachers had been quite effective in various parts of the country.

"Why, then," we asked ourselves, "are our people of the seventies not as committed to evangelizing as the Mormons or Jehovah's Witnesses?" It seems that many Catholics believed that only the professional religious were supposed to be carrying out the evangelizing mission of the church. In reality, though, through their baptism, the laity have both the right and the responsibility for extending the Kingdom.

Among the Catholics who truly desired to share their faith with others, most simply did not know how to evangelize effectively. They had not been trained or empowered in evangelization methods and techniques. Also, they did not feel supported in their ministry. "Evangelization," the very term itself, carried a strong Protestant connotation, and, as a result, these few zealous Catholics were misunderstood by both clergy and laity alike.

Impetus was added to our growing awareness for the need for evangelization in our parish when, in 1979, the Archdiocese of Miami formed an Office of Evangelization and was recommending to parishes that an evangelization committee be set up in each parish to evaluate its existing evangelization efforts.

A group of clergy, religious, and laity who had been dialoguing informally on the need for evangelization was activated in January 1980 by the formation of the St. Joan of Arc "Parish Evangelization Resource Committee." Through a process of prayer, discernment, and discussion, our goals began to emerge clearly.

## GENERAL GOALS

1. To raise the consciousness of *all* Catholics to their vocation as evangelizers.
2. To invite, nourish, and nurture our active members into discipleship through a deep, personal, and intimate relationship with Jesus as Lord and Savior.
3. To train and equip these disciples to share their faith with others accurately, effectively, and confidently, empowered by the Holy Spirit.
4. To reach out to our inactive members in a spirit of reconciliation, inviting them to return to a loving, understanding, compassionate, accepting faith community.
5. To invite our friends and neighbors who had no church affiliation to experience the fullness of a personal relationship with God in the context of the Catholic Church.

With these defined goals in mind, specific objectives and methods of implementation developed, some of which we will present in detail here. It should be noted, however, that there are other programs and support groups which exist in our parish, which we believe should be considered as evangelizing efforts.

Before we discuss specific evangelization programs, mention must be made, however, of the movements that have blossomed since the Vatican Council. Cursillo, Marriage Encounter, and various prayer groups have not only been participated in by numerous people of the parish, but, most significantly, these movements have been widely encouraged and supported by the parish staff and priests and have produced a core of committed lay leadership.

We are presenting here our new Evangelization (with a capital "E") efforts, or, in other words, programs and activities which have been designed since 1980 to emphasize explicitly Jesus Christ in such a way that he clearly stands out as the Good News, the central focus in our lives and in our church. In short, these Evangelization programs endeavor to put Jesus "up front" in all that we do.

## MONTHLY COMMUNION BREAKFASTS

"I tell you, whoever acknowledges me before men, the Son of Man will acknowledge him before the angels of God" (Luke 12:8, NIV).

The first effort of the Evangelization Resource Committee of "shouting the Good News from the rooftops" came in the initiation of a unique series of monthly communion breakfasts held the last Saturday of each month. The series offered a radical departure from the traditional communion breakfast, which was usually geared to a specific organization within the parish. At these events the Women's Guild or the Men's Club would attend Mass together and then gather for a breakfast meeting which would include a speaker on a timely issue or a project within the parish.

We felt that all too often programs offered by the church, while based implicitly on the gospel message, were usually intellectual, informational, or social in nature and rarely presented Jesus Christ explicitly. Therefore, at the new communion breakfast series, there would be bold, straight-forward, explicit personal testimony presented—no "beating around the bush" or "watered-down versions." The emphasis would be on personal salvation offered by Jesus and the resultant changed and empowered lives. Also, the breakfasts would be open to the entire community and would be held in a local country club instead of the church hall.

The first communion breakfast was held in May 1980, and Bill Glass, a local businessman who had returned to the Catholic Church after an absence of eighteen years, gave his personal testimony:

I have found joy, peace, love, and understanding otherwise not attainable except through Jesus Christ. He has taken away the gluttony, profanity, and selfishness, and he is planting seeds of patience, kindness, self-control, gentleness, and goodness.

1979 was a very good year! I came back to the church, my son was baptized and received his first Holy Communion, and my sixteen-year-old daughter and my wife came into the church. Since then, the Lord has really been working in our lives. We are a closer family. . . . God has used many people to awaken my awareness of his love, and I thank him and praise him for that. I can now see the fullness of his presence in my Catholic faith!

Concluding his twenty-five-minute address to the group, Bill, who also serves as a member of the Evangelization Committee, invited the 199 guests attending the breakfast to pray with him, accepting the forgiveness of the Lord and openly inviting and receiving Jesus into their lives as Savior and Lord. It was probably as close to an "altar call" as ever had been seen in the Catholic Church! This format has remained the same for all subsequent breakfasts.

Cards are filled out by all in attendance. For those persons indicating a desire for spiritual followup, vital to the effectiveness of the series, an invitation is subsequently issued to join one of the many growth programs offered by the parish. These include Bible classes and discussion groups, spiritual renewal programs such as Genesis II by the Rev. Vincent Dwyer, Free to Be Me by John Powell, and Romans 8 by Franciscan Communications.

Usually nine breakfasts are held in the course of the year from September to May. An average of eighty to ninety persons attend each breakfast, with overflowing crowds for such speakers as Dion, formerly of Dion and the Belmonts.

Many of the speakers are members of the parish and have varied from Bill, a formerly inactive Catholic, to men and women who have shared their personal relationship with Jesus as parents, as career men and women, as divorced and singles. One father and daughter teamed up for a breakfast and shared their testimony to Jesus' love and forgiveness in their family. Another speaker was a young tennis pro who shared his liberation from drug experimentation and usage to the direct result of meeting Jesus. One of our associate pastors shared the story of his conversion to the Catholic faith and his subsequent call to the priesthood.

Monthly parish communion breakfasts are now in their third year. It is often difficult to continue to find speakers who are willing to share their faith journey and the impact of Jesus on their lives. However, the Resource Committee considers them to be a viable means of encouraging the spiritual growth of the practicing Catholic, as well as a nonthreatening, pleasant way of exposing both the passive and inactive Catholic to the abundant life that Jesus came to bring us.

## GOOD NEWS OUTREACH MINISTRY

There was no doubt as to the need for a direct method to evangelize, and there was no doubt that the laity, and not just the professional religious, were called to evangelize. But what about the "how-to" of the problem? *Evangelii Nuntiandi* says, "There is no true evangelization unless the name, the teaching, the life, the promises of the Kingdom, and the mystery of Jesus of Nazareth, the Son of God, are proclaimed." The laity needed to be equipped with the practical and necessary skills for evangelization.

In an attempt to solve this problem, a staff member participated in a clinic on one-to-one evangelism sponsored by Evangelism Explosion International, and then experimented with the approach in the parish. Two diocesan staff members subsequently attended a similar clinic and then, inspired by the experience and encouraged and supported by the Archbishop, the three of them set out to prepare and write a manual for training the laity in one-to-one evangelization. This fifteen-week training program is entitled the Good News Outreach Ministry.

What is unique about the Good News Outreach Ministry?

1. Participants are trained and equipped to make an intelligible, interesting presentation of the basic gospel message to another person.

2. Participants are not only trained to present the gospel but are equipped to be trainers, so that in time, they train other evangelizers and the multiplication process begins.

3. Participants are trained on the job. In other words, they spend a certain number of hours (eight classes of two hours each) in class, and then they go out, accompanied by an experienced

evangelizer, and thus have first-hand experience of how to bring another person to Christ. Little by little, during the fifteen weeks of training, trainees take a more and more active role in the presentation, until finally they are secure with doing the whole visit themselves. This kind of on-the-job training gives one the confidence that no amount of classroom training could give.

Also, each participant recruits two prayer partners who pray for the evangelizer and the people he or she visits. The involvement of prayer partners not only makes the work of the evangelizer more fruitful, but gives the wider sense of participation that is necessary for a concerted effort in evangelizing the community. The whole ministry is based on the principle that God makes "divine appointments," and that people come to the Lord in his time, so that each time the evangelizers go out, they go trusting in the power of the Word of God and the action of the Holy Spirit.

Currently at St. Joan of Arc, there are twenty-four trained evangelizers who go out each Tuesday evening in twos, visit homes, and share the Good News with others. Currently, visitation is being aimed at registered Catholics, many of whom are passive or inactive. For the inactive, the acceptance of the Good News is often the way back to the Lord and his church; for the practicing Catholic, it is the door to that "abundant life" and personal relationship with the Lord that Jesus came to bring us. These visits are, of course, also an opportunity to personally invite others to attend Bible study or communion breakfasts, or to get involved in the many church activities that are available.

## "WELCOME HOME PROGRAM" FOR INACTIVE CATHOLICS

Our evangelization program to welcome inactive Catholics "home" to the church of their childhood eventually evolved into a broader program which encompassed both the active and inactive Catholics in our parish.

Initially, however, the program was designed as an open forum for the estimated 25 percent of our Catholic population who, for various reasons, had left the church and were no longer practicing their faith.

There were a number of reasons for leaving, and it appeared

that many of these problems could easily be resolved through teaching, instruction, and dialogue.

In many cases, there was simply misunderstanding which could be cleared up; for others, there was bitterness that needed to be healed; and still others simply had "drifted away."

Some people labored under a grammar school understanding of religion and never had learned about their faith on an adult level. These people were virtually ignorant of their faith and were easily overwhelmed by the knowledge of other Christians of different denominations who kept up with their religion at various age levels. These Catholics, who had never cracked the binding of a Bible, an adult catechism, or any religious instruction book since they left elementary or secondary school, seemed to have an inferiority complex about their religion.

For them, religion seemed "childish"; it seemed "filled with fairy tales." Often, when non-Catholics told them that Catholicism was filled with "superstition" or "inordinate rules," they could not explain the foundations of their religious practices or see the reasoning behind the rules. This often was a final blow in a faith that was never nourished.

Other inactive Catholics seemingly had strong faith and knowledge about their faith but somehow had been hurt personally in the past by a priest, sister, or parish worker. When one person had hurt them, they generalized that every "official" member of the church would act the same way.

In any case, it was felt that if these misunderstandings and past wounds could be addressed openly, the necessary healing and reconciliation would occur. However, it was stressed from the very inception of this program that mutual responsibility would be accepted for the many reasons these Catholics had left the church. It was very important that the atmosphere of these meetings would be one of reconciliation, compassion, and acceptance. We, the people of God, the church needed to be able to say, "We're sorry if we hurt you. We are sorry if we failed you in some way in the past."

Notices of the first "Welcome Home Program for Inactive Catholics" were placed in the parish bulletin, and the active Catholics were urged to invite their inactive or alienated friends and relatives. Advertisements also were placed in local daily papers, inviting inactive Catholics to come and air their views.

Some columnists wrote articles on this novel idea, thus giving more publicity to the meetings which were scheduled biweekly for four weeks.

The forum was chaired by three people: a priest, a sister, and a layperson. Critical to the "peer ministry" aspect of the program was that the lay facilitator be a person who also had experienced differences or disillusionment with the church, had left for a period of time, and had finally returned to the church with a renewal of faith. With the open sharing of the lay facilitator and with refreshments available, a fairly relaxed atmosphere prevailed, even though many people who came felt rather tense initially.

In the first session, after the layperson had told her "story," we asked the participants to share their reasons for leaving the church. When many points and questions were brought up, answers were attempted by the facilitators, but their primary role was mostly one of listening, understanding, and caring. Sometimes it happened that some of the alienated Catholics actually defended the church on various issues which arose!

At least one third of the people present at the sessions had been divorced and wanted to find out how to be reconciled with the church. Many misunderstandings were cleared up, the process of annulment was explained, and the possible reconciliation of remarried Catholics was discussed. It was surprising how many people resolved their difficulties and made an appointment with the priest for a private conversation and/or confession. Some had their questions answered but still had doubts of faith which could not be resolved then and there. We saw that faith is truly a gift from God, and that talking and instructions do not always help to stir up faith.

We soon discovered that terminology is very important. Many of the participants felt uncomfortable and resented the sessions being labeled for "inactive" or "alienated" Catholics. They did not want to appear as Catholic "lepers," especially when so many active Catholics were going to other classrooms in the same school for Bible study or prayer groups.

As a result, we soon changed the label from "inactive/alienated" to "inquiring/questioning" Catholics. The positive tone of this label brought in many more people to our session, which we found more profitable. The Questioning Catholic Sessions (usually two or three meetings) brought in the active Catholic wanting some questions answered; the confused Catholic who had been disillusioned by the liturgical changes in the church over the past twenty years or the stand the church took on birth control, divorce and remarriage, war and peace, etc.; and the inactive Catholic who was seeking reconciliation and understanding. During these sessions, very little hostility was shown, and many active Catholics gave testimony to their faith in reacting to questions.

Of the two types of sessions, the "Inquiring/Questioning" forum was more profitable in that it gave the Catholic who attended Mass regularly and participated in parish life a place to ask questions never alluded to in Sunday homilies. They would not go to meetings entitled "Alienated/Inactive," as they did not feel this label applied to them. However, the inactive Catholic felt no problem coming to the inquiry sessions, which now are held two or three times a year, along with those for the active but questioning Catholic.

## RITE OF CHRISTIAN INITIATION OF ADULTS

We are now in our fifth year of using the RCIA (Rite of Christian Initiation of Adults). We advertise in our Sunday bulletin for possible converts to the faith and those who want to come into full communion. Many future converts may be attending church with a spouse or friend and respond. Other Catholics may know someone who desires to enter the church and invite her or him to this "inquiry class with no strings attached."

The RCIA is designed for nonbaptized persons coming into the church in a gradual, liturgical way. The faith is introduced to them, the symbols of the faith are handed on to them, and the community of believers who witness this process have their own faith rekindled. However, the RCIA document is a rather adaptable ritual. Very few Roman Catholic rituals are as flexible as the RCIA. Since many people in the U.S. entering the Roman Catholic Church are baptized Protestants, one must adapt this ritual to them as well as to the nonbaptized coming into the church who are the only ones strictly to be entitled "converts." However, the term seems to be a generic one in popular usage, and knowing the theological difficulty, we still call all those entering the church "converts," for lack of a term equally short.

Our whole convert class revolves around the academic year. Before any ritualization is begun in the RCIA, we invite prospective converts to a Bible study class. Surprisingly enough, very few have extensive biblical backgrounds, even though many come from the Protestant denominations. In the instructional part of introducing the faith to converts (the precatechumenate period) we have biblical instruction (study of one of the Gospels) from mid-September through mid-December. From mid-January through Easter and beyond, we have the formal catechetical teaching with various instructions (extensively based on *Christ Among Us* by Anthony Wilhelm, Paulist Press).

Southern Florida has many part-time residents, popularly called "snow birds," who come to Florida when the weather starts getting cold up north. For this reason we continue to advertise our inquiry class at various times during the academic year. We intensify this around Christmastime and the beginning weeks of the New Year, and usually get some newcomers to the inquiry class in January. While they have not attended the Bible study class, we may waive this requirement and urge them to pursue some Bible study after entering the church.

The first step in the process of entering the Catholic Church comes through the formal entrance into the Order of Catechumens, the first stage of the RCIA. A catechumen is a theological term for a learner. They formalize their entrance into the Catholic community in a liturgical entrance rite enacted in February of each year. One can be a catechumen for many years, but we feel this is generally not necessary. Perhaps we should reexamine this, but this has been our parish's practice in recent years. We try to be faithful to the remaining rites of the RCIA and have the converts installed in the other orders at the precise traditional days in Lent. We hand over three symbols: a Bible and two scrolls of the Creed and the Our Father. The converts enter the church at the Easter Vigil, to the delight and applause of the believing congregation. We have baptism, confirmation, and Eucharist for the converts; and profession of faith, confirmation, and Eucharist for those coming into full communion. As the RCIA highly recommends further catechesis, we save the post-baptismal or mystogogical catechesis until Pentecost Sunday. This is a practical necessity, as the instruction has not been completed (since the converts meet only once a week for one to one-and-a-half hours of instruction). The church desires this post-baptismal instruction to indicate to the new church member that his faith should be continually nourished by instruction and attendance at Mass and other liturgical services.

The parishioners enjoy praying for those entering the church and are encouraged in their own faith by seeing new members enter their church. They feel proud that people share their same desire to be part of the Catholic Church. It makes everyone feel they are on the winning team, especially when so many people have left the church. We ask the parishioners to witness to the catechumens, to encourage them in the process, to welcome them and introduce them to the parish societies, and to pray that the Spirit will continue to give his gifts to the catechumens in their faith journey.

The parish catechumen team has not fully developed a good sponsorship program, but this is our goal this particular year. The Bible study group is composed of converts and interested Catholics who will be the sponsors for the converts in the RCIA.

## BIBLE STUDY

As people returned to or joined the church and sought to deepen their faith and grow in their relationship with the Lord, the importance of Bible study loomed larger and larger.

> For just as from the heavens the rain and the snow come down and do not return there till they have watered the earth, giving seed to him who sows and bread to him who eats, so shall my word be that goes forth from my mouth; it shall not return to me void but shall do my will, achieving the end for which I sent it (Isaiah 55:10, 11).

The Word of God is powerful in transforming the lives of those who seek it as their daily source of spiritual nourishment. Yet the average Catholic rarely, if ever, opens the Bible. In an attempt to familiarize people with the Scriptures, various methods have been tried over the past three years: neighborhood Bible groups, lecture series, etc. While the lecture method is still being used for beginners in introductory courses for the Old and New

Testaments, the method that has proved to be most successful is the program prepared by the Diocese of Little Rock, Arkansas.

The Little Rock Bible Program is a discussion series; each participant has a study book with discussion questions, a commentary on the particular book being discussed, and a Bible. Participants are divided into small groups and discussions are led by trained lay leaders. Guided by the leaders, members of the group share the answers to the questions they have prepared and studied. The purpose of small group discussion is to establish an atmosphere of openness and love in which God's living Word and its application to daily life can be discussed. These groups provide an opportunity not only to discuss God's Word, but also to discover and speak about one's experiences in faith, of life with God. And, of course, an encounter with God's Word always challenges the reader to follow it more closely.

After the group discussion, all groups convene in a central area to hear a lecture intended to develop and clarify the themes covered by the lesson. In the absence of a speaker, the group may listen to a taped lecture either on cassette or video, which is also available from Little Rock.

Participants are encouraged to make a definite appointment with God, setting aside a certain time each day to answer three questions. This is to encourage daily, regular study. Each day one needs spiritual food for the soul, just as one needs food for the body. As people begin to experience God speaking to them through the Scriptures, they are encouraged to share with family and friends, thus fulfilling the gospel command to spread the Good News.

Our groups have studied the Acts of the Apostles, using the Little Rock materials. As they studied the life style of the early church community, strong bonds of friendship and community were formed: On the last night, the entire class gathered at the home of one of the participants to celebrate the presence of the Lord Jesus, just as the early Christians gathered in their homes to break bread. Since then we have studied the Gospel of Mark, the captivity letters, and the Gospel of John.

Classes are held in the evenings in the parish facilities, in the morning in homes, and Sunday morning during CCD time, for parents whose children are in religious class. Gradually more and more people are coming to an awareness of the importance of the Word of God to guide their daily lives, and as an aid in developing a strong personal relationship with the Lord.

> Your word is a lamp to my feet and a light for my path (Psalm 119:105, NIV).

## PARISH WEEKEND RENEWAL PROGRAM

More recently, the Parish Renewal Program was introduced in our parish after the pastor and one of the associate pastors attended a week of intensive training by Father Chuck Gallagher, S.J., who created and piloted this program.

The Parish Renewal Weekend is a conversion experience designed to be given by a parish priest for the people of his parish, and it is based on the concept expressed by Pope John Paul VI: "The Church is an evangelizer, but she begins by being evangelized herself by constant conversion and renewal, in order to evangelize the world with credibility" (Evangelii Nuntiandi).

The pastor or associate and pastoral staff lead the weekend and, together with the participants, form and experience community. It is a strong recall into belonging to the people of God, the church. The reestablishment of belonging occurs through an emphasis on and an experience of reconciliation.

The weekend focuses on relationships and sharing with one another the values received from the faith. There are four objectives: (1) intellectual—a sharing of information about the faith, what we understand it to be; (2) compunction—the need we have for forgiveness, to be forgiven and to forgive; (3) conversion—to kindle and renew the faith, and to share that faith with the faithful and with the world; and (4) to evangelize others by living the faith.

Since the program's introduction in the parish in the fall of 1982, six Parish Renewal Weekends have been held, with approximately two hundred parishioners participating in this unique renewal experience.

## THE BORN-AGAIN CATHOLIC SEMINARS

Another problem that had to be dealt with was the number of people who had had a "born-again" experience in a non-Catholic church, or who had heard their friends talk about being "born again." For many Catholics, the very term "born again" had negative connotations. Somehow, they could not equate either the experience or the terminology with traditional Catholicism.

A real treasure was found in a book entitled *The Born-Again Catholic*, by Albert Boudreau, published by Living Flame Press, which holds a Catholic imprimatur. This book says that not only can we have a born-again experience and still remain a good Catholic, but proves that the born-again experience is Catholic Christianity at its best. It answers questions, dispels doubts, and leads the reader into a rich and exciting relationship with his or her heavenly Father. It provides a chance to recapture the faith that so many find slipping away.

A study guide is available with this book, and so we have had several seven-week discussion groups in homes, using this book as the basis for discussions. These discussion groups not only dispelled many doubts, but led many spiritually hungry Catholics to discover the exciting core of the Christian message.

## CATHOLIC EVANGELISM PRESS, INC. AND THE CATHOLIC EVANGELIST

An unforeseen result of the many efforts of so many dedicated people was the creation of the Catholic Evangelism Press. Through actual "hands-on" experience as members of the Parish Evangelization Committee, it soon became evident that there was a tremendous need for simple, "down-to-earth" Catholic evangelistic literature to be distributed during the Communion Outreach Breakfast, the Good News Outreach Ministry visits, and various other parish events. The committee members found that there was an abundance of non-Catholic literature, but that very little quality evangelistic material was coming out of the Catholic press.

As a result, Catholic Evangelism Press was organized informally in 1980, became operative in 1981, and was incorporated in 1982 as a nonprofit corporation founded with the sole purpose of spreading the gospel message of Jesus Christ through the printed word. Initially several members of the committee began writing, editing, and printing small tracts and pamphlets which called individuals to a personal, living, intimate relationship with Jesus. Several of these tracts have since been reprinted in Spanish, and, to date, over 200,000 tracts and pamphlets have been reprinted and distributed.

The obvious need for this type of Catholic evangelistic literature was a significant factor in the decision to launch a new, full-length (forty-eight-page) national Catholic evangelistic magazine, *The Catholic Evangelist*. Six months of prepublication work resulted with ecclesiastical approval to publish by Archbishop McCarthy; a strong endorsement from the Rev. Alvin A. Illig, C.S.P. (the Director of the U.S. Bishops' Ad Hoc Committee on Evangelization); an impressive list of contributing editors; a staff of volunteer writers, artists, and photographers . . . and the premier issue of *The Catholic Evangelist* was printed in January 1983.

Since then, with little or no promotion or advertising funds available, we continue to be amazed at the acceptance of the magazine as thousands of subscriptions have come in from throughout the United States and Canada. Also, we are now receiving subscription orders from South and Central America, various parts of Europe and Africa, and from Guam, the Philippines, Vietnam, Sri Lanka, and New Zealand.

The magazine is available bimonthly for twelve dollars per year, and can be ordered from Catholic Evangelism Press, Inc., P.O. Box 1282, Boca Raton, FL 33432.

## CONCLUSION

Besides the results enumerated above relative to our various approaches to evangelization, it can be said that attitudes have changed. Evangelization is now better understood by many more persons in our community. People are beginning to have a greater awareness of the basic preaching of the earliest Christian community. Numerous persons, though we do not have an exact count, have joined or returned to attendance at church. There is a greater preoccupation on the part of many of cultivating a personal relationship with Jesus Christ. And, all in all, more and more people are coming to understand that "Jesus Christ must be put up front."

Working together, we continue to spread the Good News and build the Kingdom in this small portion of the Lord's vineyard known as Boca Raton, Florida.

# SOUTH MAIN BAPTIST CHURCH
## HOUSTON, TEXAS
## DR. KENNETH L. CHAFIN, PASTOR
## THE WORK OF EVANGELISM AT SOUTH MAIN BAPTIST

*CHAPTER*

**17**

## INTRODUCTION

During the ten years between 1972 and 1982, although South
Main Baptist Church was located in a transitional community and
had lost ground for seventeen consecutive years, the church
experienced unprecedented growth. More than four thousand new
members joined the church, the attendance at Bible study doubled,
the number of converts being baptized quadrupled, and the
church was forced to buy new property to adequately take care
of the growth. This growth took place as a result of several
factors which will be discussed here. The best place to begin
would be to take a look at the church, her history, and her
makeup. Then we will look at the church's assumptions about
evangelism. Finally, we will look at some of the ways this one
church was able to reach out to new people with the gospel.

## UNDERSTANDING THE CONTEXT OF WITNESS

While the church has only one gospel, the way in which each
congregation does the work of evangelism will vary greatly,

depending upon its age, maturity, location, membership, and leadership. All of these factors contribute to what it can and should do to reach individuals for Christ. It would be impossible to understand the ministry and outreach of our church without knowing something of its makeup and setting.

The church was organized in November 1903 and celebrated its eightieth anniversary in the fall of 1983. When it was begun there were not more than a half-dozen Baptist congregations in the city, and all the churches combined would not have numbered forty. Today there are 240 Baptist churches in the greater Houston area and approximately 600 other congregations.

The church was located in its present spot when it was the edge of the city. It was the point where the streetcar tracks ended and the rice fields began. Now the city spreads for twenty miles in every direction and, without having moved, the church finds itself located in the central city less than twenty blocks from downtown. The Baptists who founded the church had their roots deep in rural America, but today's members are urbanites.

The church peaked in 1954, and then went into a slow seventeen-year decline. The atrophy was slow enough that very few even noticed and no one stopped to analyze it. There were many factors involved: the growth of suburbs and the building of churches in them drew many of the young families who found it easier to involve themselves and their children in a church closer to home. Second and third generation persons felt the need to create a little distance. The major factor was the changes taking place in the community. During these years, what was once a neighborhood became a community of people in transition. From a predominantly Anglo neighborhood of nuclear families, it became a racially mixed community of the poor and rich, the young and old, and of couples and singles.

## ATTITUDES THAT UNDERGIRD REACHING PEOPLE

When I came to the church as its pastor in August 1972, I found five things which became resources in leading the church in the work of evangelism. First, I found a membership full of gifted persons. To me the laity represents the great untapped resource of the church, and South Main was loaded with talented, mature

Christians. Second, I found a church where there existed a very genuine love for people and a willingness to minister. The question of "What's going to happen to us?" had not been asked. Instead, I was constantly facing the question, "What can we do to help people?" There are churches which grow, not because they love people, but because they are in love with growth; but that is never a healthy kind of growth. Third, the church had never considered "flight" from its present location. The fact that the question wasn't even on the agenda gave more stability to the church. Fourth, there was a feeling in the church which was articulated by key lay leaders that "God has us here for some purpose." There is no better atmosphere in which to lead a church than one in which there is an interest in what God is trying to do in and through the church. Finally, there was an eagerness and openness to be led. Some churches don't want anyone to lead, but South Main did. I've been in a lot of inner-city churches, but I've never observed that combination of spirit, attitude, and maturity that I found when I came to this church. They were foundational to the church's success in evangelism.

## ASSUMPTIONS ON WHICH EVANGELISTIC CHURCHES BUILD

Three assumptions served as foundational for the church's evangelism during the period of great growth. First, the church became increasingly aware that it was in the midst of people with profound spiritual needs in their lives. There were internationals, many of whom knew no English and who were walled out of a full life because of great cultural differences. There were single adults, many of whom had been married and were now divorced. They were desperately in need of help in processing the failure of their marriages. There were students training for leadership in our society, but needing leadership in their lives. There were the elderly whose mobility and income were decreased but whose needs were growing. There were young professionals who had naively bought society's definition of success and were reaching it, only to be let down. We were an island of hope in a sea of need.

Second, we assumed that the gospel of Jesus Christ still speaks to the deepest and most profound needs of modern man. We truly believed that it is only in a living relationship with God through Jesus Christ that individuals experience the love and acceptance that give them a sense of worth, and the purpose that rescues life from meaninglessness, and the hope which makes us unafraid to face even death. While we engaged in many helping ministries at a very elemental level, our church felt that the best ministry it had was to spread the "good tidings" of Jesus Christ to all who would believe.

Third, we assumed that the work of evangelism is the work of the whole church and not just its staff. Church programs may go faster if they are run by the staff, but the evangelism of the church will be broader and more effective if it involves the laity. Most of the ministries and programs which our church has used to reach people were created by the laity and staffed by the laity. The idea of a church doing evangelism by hiring professional staff to do the work in our place is not a biblical idea.

## A SCRIPTURAL MODEL FOR EVANGELISM

One of the most radical models for evangelism in the Scriptures comes in that section of 1 Corinthians where Paul is defending his ministry. In 1 Corinthians 9:19-21 we found a scriptural model for our congregation in the work of evangelism. In this passage Paul lists some of the characteristics of the people who win others to Christ.

(1) People who win others must be free. "I am a free man and own no master" (1 Corinthians 9:19, NEB). The freedom Paul spoke of was spiritual freedom, for the gospel is a liberating word and the church is a liberating community. God had freed the apostle from the smothering effects of his legalistic background, from the expectations of his peers, from personal ambition, and from compromising sins. The work of evangelism must be done by those who have experienced Christ's freedom.

(2) Those who reach people for Christ must be a servant people. "I have made myself every man's servant" (1 Corinthians 9:19, NEB). What one does with his freedom determines his character, and Paul had decided to become a servant. His model for this was Jesus Christ, who was the fulfillment of the suffering servant prophecies in Isaiah. Christ's coming, his teaching, and his life were the acts of an obedient servant. The church needs to be

very careful not to draw its models for evangelism from the corporate models, or its definitions of success from the business community.

(3) People who reach people must be adaptable. "I have become everything in turn to men of every sort, so that in one way or another I may save some" (1 Corinthians 9:22, NEB). This is not a word of compromise but of adaptability. It is a word of incarnation. It speaks of Paul's ability to identify, with love, with all sorts of people. To be with people who were different without being censorious or judgmental for the sake of the gospel. A church which cannot identify with all sorts of people will never do effective evangelism in an urban setting.

(4) People who reach people need goals which stretch them. "To win over as many as possible" (1 Corinthians 9:19, NEB). Most churches don't have goals which are ambitious, but set goals which reflect what they are already doing with a small increase to accommodate growing families. A church has to begin to measure itself not by those who have been reached but by those yet to be reached. That is the tone of the parables which Jesus told of the lost sheep, the lost coin, and the estranged son in Luke 15.

(5) People who reach others must be disciplined. "Every athlete goes into strict training" (1 Corinthians 9:25, NEB). This is the price tag for reaching people. To love people, pray for them, spend time with them, and minister to their needs is a costly matter. There are really no inexpensive, get-rich-quick ways to do the work of evangelism. The price must be paid in prayer, planning, and hard work.

## ONE GOSPEL AND MANY METHODS

To do the work of evangelism is to share the gospel of Jesus Christ in the power of the Holy Spirit so that individuals may respond to God's love with repentance and faith and may enter into a vital relationship with him. But while the gospel and the goal never change, the different methods by which the church and individuals in the church come to contribute creates an endless variety. I will share just a few which are ongoing and very basic.

(1) Our church's most important place for doing evangelism is in the worship service. This is where Christian fellowship is experienced, where what God has done in Christ is celebrated,

and where the gospel is preached in the sermon. In every worship service there are persons with spiritual needs who are listening for a word of hope, a word of love, a word of forgiveness, and a word of salvation. Worship also creates an excellent climate for decision for those who have been exposed to the gospel in a Bible study group or some other way. In our tradition we have a hymn of commitment at the end of each worship service when people with whom God is dealing may come to make public their interest in becoming followers of Christ.

(2) Of equal importance in reaching people for Christ is our Bible study organization. Unlike many denominations for whom Sunday school is a children's organization, we have multiple classes for all age groups. These are not limited to believers; an aggressive effort is made to enlist people who are not yet Christians in these groups. They all meet at the same time on Sunday mornings at the church building so that members of large families can go to their own classes. It is easier to get individuals to join a Bible study class than to join a church. In the class much more happens than the study of the Bible. There is the exposure to Christian fellowship and love and to the ministry of a loving fellowship. Community is built and experienced. This creates a marvelous nurturing place for potential converts.

Neither of my parents attended church, and my introduction to the gospel was in a Bible study class for nine-year-old boys. I am a believer today probably because of the love and interest I saw in the teacher of that class. Our church presently has several hundred persons who are not members enrolled in one of our many classes. During the coming year many of those individuals will personally receive Christ into their lives. The decision will have been prepared for by their involvement in a Bible study class.

(3) The most productive evangelism we have done has come as a by-product of ministries which the church has performed to persons with special needs. During the past decade our church has done major ministries with the formerly married, the internationals living in our community, cancer patients in a local hospital, undocumented aliens who need counseling, the poor who cannot afford medicine, and a host of other individuals and groups who have needs. All of these ministries are led by the laity of the church and grew out of a love they have for people

and a desire to help them. There are among evangelicals some who feel there is a built-in conflict between those who believe in evangelism and those who believe in ministry. This has not been our experience. Rather we have discovered that the church's evangelism effectiveness has been increased by our loving ministries. There are several reasons.

First, ministry to persons often creates a legitimate point of contact for the gospel. An excellent illustration is our seminar for the formerly married which was designed to help people who have experienced failure in a marriage to apply God's redeeming love to their situation. For over a decade, four times each year, we have conducted this four-day seminar. We advertise in the papers. We have from 80 to 150 in each of the seminars and over the years have an accumulative enrollment of over 5,500. We discovered from the beginning that 85 percent of those who have enrolled had never been to our church before. One of the most difficult aspects about evangelism is finding a legitimate point of contact with persons. Our ministries put us in touch with people with spiritual needs.

Second, the ministries to persons authenticate the gospel the church preaches. It is easy to believe that God is a loving and forgiving father after you have met one of God's people who is able to accept and love. The secular world pictures the church as being interested only in itself and as being judgmental of those who have made messes of their lives. As the church reaches out to persons with needs and meets those needs, this caricature is destroyed. Many of the people we win to Christ have been sent to us by people who have learned that no matter what kind of problems a person has, our members are able to love them and help them. Christians enjoy sharing the word of the gospel more if they have "enfleshed" that word by some loving deed.

While the ministries may vary with the needs of persons, the gifts and interests of the church members, and the resources of the church, every church can enhance its evangelism by its ministry to persons.

## CONCLUSION

I do not know what the future of South Main Baptist Church will be. In the twelve years I have been the pastor I have seen many changes in the church and in the community. Everything which affects the people, whether it's the price of gasoline or the interest rate on a new home, affects our church. As time and circumstances change, we must change, and this is never easy. We have a very basic commitment: to stay in this place and to make whatever changes are necessary to both act out the gospel in our lives and share the word of the gospel with those who are lost. We think that this is the will of God for us and we will try to be faithful servants of God and leave the results to him.

Dr. Kenneth Chafin is not only one of the nation's finest pastors, but a scholar and author as well. His list of accomplishments in the field of evangelization qualifies him to speak with the utmost authority. His success as a pastor proves without question that he is a man who puts theory into action. His 7,000-member Southern Baptist Church, located in Houston, Texas, is one of the nation's finest.

Dr. Chafin has been professor at the Southwestern Baptist Theological Seminary in Ft. Worth, Professor at Southern Baptist Theological Seminary in Louisville, Kentucky, Director of Evangelism for the Home Mission Board of the entire Southern Baptist Convention, a board member of Houston Baptist University, and a member of the Executive Board and Administrative Committee of the Baptist General Convention of Texas.

Probably his most effective ministry has been as Dean of the Billy Graham Schools of Evangelism, where, since 1967, he has conducted intensive seminars in evangelization in over fifty cities and has taught some 50,000 pastors the art of evangelism.

Dr. Chafin's books likewise reflect his scholarly and pastoral skills. He has published *Help! I'm a Layman, The Reluctant Witness, Is There a Family in the House?*, and *How Do You Know When You've Got It Made?*

He can be reached by writing to South Main Street Baptist Church, 4100 South Main Street, Houston, TX 77002.

# EASTWOOD BAPTIST CHURCH
## TULSA, OKLAHOMA
## DR. C. B. HOGUE, PASTOR
## EXCITING EASTWOOD—
## A CHURCH ON THE GROW

CHAPTER

18

EXCITING Eastwood . . . the church people all over
Tulsa talk about. The fame of this church touches large segments
of population even outside the residential boundaries of the city.
Some people travel forty miles from towns and villages in various
directions to visit Eastwood to see what makes this church so
exciting.

The story is not new, but reminiscent of New Testament action.
Less than thirty years ago a strong mother church in Tulsa
named Immanuel Baptist Church determined the need to establish
a mission on the growing east side of the city. Beginning with a
few families, the church developed into a full-grown fellowship of
believers who thought their responsibility was to reach the
community for worship and Bible study.

In keeping with the geographical location, they named their
new fellowship Eastwood. Building their first unit on approximately two acres of land, the pastor and people set out to become
a center of ministry for those who needed the gospel and strength
for daily living.

At the end of approximately sixteen years, attendance reached an average of 650. Stunned silence greeted the pastor when he announced his resignation one Sunday morning. His ministry had been fruitful and loving, yet he was leaving the church without a spiritual leader. What would they do?

The church's strong lay leadership finally came to the conclusion that God really had something special planned for this church. A pastoral search committee was elected by the congregation and an interim pastor was selected. The interim period proved to be the turning point in the dreams of these stalwart lay persons.

One Sunday morning the interim pastor preached a sermon on the possible future of the church. Vision and possibilities captivated the imagination of the congregation. They really *could* become a dynamic organism to touch a city and the world! When that vision crystalized, the search committee knew clearly that the next pastor must fit that concept. While visiting noted pastors across the country, the committee became convinced that a young man who shared their vision, and had the energy to match, was the one they must find. They found him in Texas.

Thomas D. Elliff, who had an outstanding record of growth in a small town, just suited this congregation. Growth was the touchstone of his ministry, and he was full of youthful zest. Eastwood was destined to be the fulfillment of a vision captured by a young congregation which would never be satisfied with anything less than the ultimate of their capabilities.

"We will not be locked into tradition," said the young pastor. Consequently, they became open and sensitive to the Holy Spirit, using new methods of reaching people. "We can't do it; we've never done it this way before" were anathema statements to them.

In the interim period the church had been challenged to begin a bus ministry. Elliff brought in an assistant to direct this ministry and lead the church in evangelism. The bus ministry became the vehicle to prove that people could be reached. It also built an awareness of the needs of all races and economic levels of society regarding the Good News of Christ.

Immediately, attendance began to climb until now the church averages 2,400 in Bible study and worship.

Soon the church determined to make a larger contribution to its members and others in the area through Christian education. The Eastwood School System was organized and began with thirty-three pupils. Today the kindergarten through twelfth grades have nearly 700 enrolled in a strong academic program which equips youth as Christians to face a pagan and hostile world.

Television has played a vital part in public awareness of the church. "To Tulsa with Love" specials have brought Eastwood into the homes of thousands at varied seasons of the year. During the programs counselors are inundated with calls from the community regarding special spiritual problems. Positive answers and caring responses greet the callers, always with the purpose of assisting the caller to know God and discover personal fellowship at Eastwood.

"Our main factor in growth," said one of the lay leaders, "is our people. They really believe in Eastwood, so they energetically witness. They really love their church." Their efforts are given strength by prayer. "It's the connecting link with God," this leader continued.

And that is the way it has been! Two worship services and two Bible study hours run concurrently each Sunday morning. Sunday evening the church comes together for massive worship and celebration preceded by a vital training period for Bible teachers and workers. Wednesday evening the church is together again for worship and prayer. People at the altar praying for friends to come to know Christ in a personal way, or for the healing of a sick family member, friend, or neighbor, is quite common. Reports are given regularly testifying to answered prayer.

These visible programs are but the highlights of many weekly activities. Volunteers meet each week to visit class members, unbelievers, and prospects. Youth have special programs designed to fit their particular age groups. Men gather for prayer at a local restaurant on Tuesday morning; women meet regularly on Monday morning to pray. Tuesday morning many women are involved in Bible study groups, with nursery and preschool activities to match. A Continuing Witness Training program equips lay persons to share their faith in assigned witnessing or in the normal course of their lives. Thursday evenings feature a medical group dispensing medicine and examining patients in economically depressed areas of the city. Food baskets are delivered regularly to the poor and hungry. Counseling by the staff is a continuous responsibility—for distressed families, those contemplating divorce, and those with various emotional needs. And much more. . . .

How does one assess the extreme success of this exciting and growing fellowship? Two words stand out: *caring* and *sharing*. And the tried and proven methods of church growth have been put into practice. It could be summed up by Fuller Seminary Professor Peter Wagner, who said, "Church growth means all that is involved in bringing men and women who do not have a personal relationship to Jesus Christ into fellowship with him and into responsible church membership."

Eastwood practices the broad-based criteria for church growth by:

1. Building a warm evangelistic atmosphere. Evangelistic results are generally impossible where there is a cold, indifferent, and apathetic attitude toward reaching out to others and bringing them to Christ.
2. Developing a deep and compassionate concern for those outside of Christ. The passion and concern for these people should be the same as that which was in the heart of our Lord, and must be the heartbeat of the congregation.
3. Practicing prayer, believing that prayer really does change things. Through prayer Christians become channels of power, are usable instruments of God, and discover that ordinary persons do ordinary tasks in extraordinary ways.

While some people feel physically unable to be a part of this vibrant church, others come to where the action is. They have discovered that the church is strongly pastor-led. The pastor graciously takes charge of his expected leadership role with the church's support. The pastor is visible and available. He is a good administrative decision-maker. He believes in the objectives the church has put forth and has a willingness to lead the church to accomplish those objectives.

Proclamation of biblical truths is done by expository preaching. Using verse by verse teaching/preaching of the Scriptures for inspiration, personal application, and logical persuasion is an indispensable element which brings people back to worship again and again.

Every worship experience is a warm-hearted, bright, and exciting celebration of the gathering of God's people; an atmosphere charged with the expression and freedom of the spirit of praise. The music is preparatory to the proclamation. That loving, warm, and rejoicing praise-time enthusiastically welcomes the presence of God and believers wait expectantly for him to do mighty works.

Eastwood has an obvious sense of conquest, an urgency to cross the next mountain to victory. These people feel they must keep on—go for broke—until they reach their vision . . . their place in Christ.

It is really very simple. Eastwood works on the premise that the urgency with which the first believers viewed their task should not be diminished by time, but seriously practiced today. This congregation accepts that legacy of action, passed from one generation of believers to another, and believes it remains as relevant to Tulsa as to the first-century church members. Methods by which this church plans its actions in witnessing and ministering are influenced by the nature of their cultural circumstances and the ability of people to respond. The mission of Eastwood remains unchanged from the day it captured a vision to touch Tulsa and the world.

Frankly, there really is no reason for Eastwood to continue to be on the grow. It is still located on its original two acres. Additional annexes were purchased across the street and an adjoining public elementary school is used each Sunday morning for two children's Bible study periods. Shuttle buses must transport people from parking blocks away, and others park on the sides of busy streets down a half-mile stretch. Yet . . . Eastwood remains an exciting fellowship.

Here at Eastwood God's people consider themselves a viable and visible institution for accomplishing world evangelization; the body of Christ ministering to one another and to persons out of Christ and out of the church. Upwards of 455 adult baptisms have been registered in a single year, with groups of youth and lay persons going to Uganda, Washington-Oregon, Canada, and other parts of the globe to bear witness.

What of their future? Admittedly, only God knows. The people have declared, "Where there is no vision, the people perish." They continue to believe that the vision has not yet been fulfilled, nor ever really will be until the Lord Jesus comes again. Until then, the vision keeps demanding far-reaching objectives and reachable goals, creating constant expectancy.

Shifting priorities into action, Eastwood continues to mobilize to reach people in Bible study and celebrative worship through a ministry which extends Christ's influence to secular society, and for the conversion of sinners.

Sum it up this way: Eastwood is accepting priorities, developing vision, identifying needs and resources, and working through goals which will bring results and show the world, as well as ourselves, the church is growing. Eastwood . . . exciting Eastwood!

Dr. C. B. Hogue, Pastor of Eastwood Baptist Church, was formerly Director of the Southern Baptist Convention's Home Mission Board. As Director, he was responsible for building up what has been the fastest-growing denomination in America's history. Through church-planting programs, the mission has been able to grow at the rate of some one-half million members per year, and plans to continue this to the year 2000.

Dr. Hogue has authored several books and manuals and is a much-sought-after speaker on church growth. Persons wishing to contact him may do so by writing: Eastwood Baptist Church, 948 So. 91st East Avenue, Tulsa, OK 74112.

# THE ASSEMBLIES OF GOD
## DR. THOMAS F. ZIMMERMAN,
## GENERAL SUPERINTENDENT
## A DENOMINATION ON THE GROW

CHAPTER

*19*

THE Assemblies of God is a denomination conceived in the cauldron of the Holy Spirit outpouring seventy years ago. Honest, sincere, and holy men and women of old went everywhere under the anointing of the Holy Spirit, laying the foundations for what our church has become today.

On their foundation we have been privileged to continue to build, until today the Pentecostal movement encompasses some 75-100 million Christians worldwide.

I believe the coming of the Holy Spirit upon so many and in such a broad sweep of the church world is God's way of counteracting the liberalism, secularism, humanism, and occultism that plague our society.

The Assemblies of God has experienced phenomenal growth during the past decades—a 70 percent increase in membership from 1970 to 1980. Three areas in particular, I believe, have contributed to this growth: biblical preaching, evangelism and new church planting, and programs which meet human needs.

# I. CHURCH GROWTH THROUGH BIBLICAL PREACHING

The Assemblies of God has ever maintained a high view of Scripture. A review of the founding of our church and the resultant doctrinal statements shows the early leaders insisted that the Bible, not experience, must be the rule of faith and conduct. The authority of Scripture has been and continues to be at the core of our doctrine.

Our churches and pastors are committed to the belief that the Bible contains answers to the questions people ask. It contains balm for those who hurt, direction for those who are lost, light for those in darkness, and joy for those who sorrow. Most of all, God's Word directs us to Jesus Christ who, through faith, may become our Savior.

The Bible is central to our preaching and teaching. I personally know of no period in history more in need of authoritative preaching based on "thus saith the Lord" than now. Our ministers do not believe it is enough to stand in the pulpit and quote great thinkers or give pat answers based on human experience or knowledge. Rather, as they minister the powerful, *living* Word of God, it alone probes, convicts, heals, gives hope, creates faith, and leads men and women to repentance and abundant life.

Moreover, we staunchly teach and preach that the Bible is our all-sufficient rule of faith and practice. While we Pentecostals believe Christianity is a living, viable experience, we also affirm that the Holy Spirit will never take us beyond the boundaries of Scripture. The Spirit and the Word always agree.

There will always be a need for ministers who have totally immersed themselves in God's Word and its teachings. Only then can the servant of God come to the pulpit with the Word of God burning in his heart and on his lips to preach with power and authority under the anointing of the Holy Spirit.

The end of the nineteenth and beginning of the twentieth century were marked by a decadent liberal theology which robbed individuals of a belief in a God who intervened in human affairs. There was a resultant drift away from a New Testament vitality within the church and a very obvious lack on the part of the church world as far as any hunger and heart cry to know God in a living, vital way.

Into this climate, God sent a movement of the Holy Spirit, and small groups of people from various church backgrounds began to express a real hunger for God. This resulted in extensive prayer and searching of the Scriptures.

This widespread outpouring of the Holy Spirit has now taken root in every part of the globe. God never manifests himself in a vacuum. Rather, he manifests himself for a purpose, and one purpose that has been evidenced in this twentieth-century Holy Spirit revival has been an increased world evangelization.

## II. CHURCH GROWTH THROUGH EVANGELISM AND CHURCH PLANTING

*Evangelism* as a priority has formed the basis for our church since its inception. We believe that the Great Commission that Jesus gave his disciples almost 2,000 years ago to "go . . . and preach the gospel to every creature" (Mark 16:15) is still the mandate to all believers until he comes again.

In the 1960s when our denomination was fifty years old, we undertook an extensive self-study of our church. A sampling of our constituency revealed some creeping ambiguity about our reason for being. We needed to take a look at ourselves in light of the biblical mandate to see how well we were fulfilling our mission.

This self-study was an attempt to consider our strengths and weaknesses and to identify and protect those forces that had served us well; but also to bring to light those needs for fine-tuning adjustments that would help us to meet today's challenges.

The analysis of our statement of purpose revealed a degree of ambiguity. While our statement of purpose identified evangelism as "the entire work of the entire church" and "the whole work of the whole church," the statement did not delineate or define what it meant by evangelism.

The committee directing our self-study saw the necessity of removing this ambiguity concerning the meaning of the term *evangelism* by defining the mission of our church in a way which would bring unanimous agreement.

The committee presented to the church body the following priority reason for being of the Assemblies of God:

1. To be an agency of God for evangelizing the world.
2. To be a corporate body in which man may worship God.
3. To be a channel of God's purpose to build a body of saints being perfected in the image of his Son.

Thus ministry to the world, to God, and to believers became the threefold purpose of our church and has guided all our activities and programs to this day.

Prayerful consideration of Scripture and the history of the Pentecostal movement made us increasingly aware of the importance of spiritual renewal as a necessary preparation for evangelistic outreach. The unprecedented growth we have experienced in the last decade, I believe, is the result of a healthy spiritual condition of our church. The reexamination of our priorities led to an all-out emphasis on the importance of maintaining a deep emphasis on individual spiritual life. This continued emphasis on spiritual dynamics is more rewarding than advocating mechanical techniques or programs that result only in temporary growth.

The real basis of our church growth is that our fellowship has gone through a time of spiritual renewal which has drawn the people as a whole closer to God.

It is impossible for us to draw closer to God without sensing his love for lost mankind. God's love and grace extend to every person, and he would that all accept his mercy and love through salvation in his Son. In brief, God's heart beats for evangelism.

The Great Commission Christ gave his disciples almost 2,000 years ago is still the imperative under which the church marches. This commission has two sides, however—reaching the lost and discipling them through the church. We dare not stop with the first part, because once people have accepted the Lord as Savior they must be taught and discipled. After they are discipled, they in turn become yet another outreach to people.

It is not God's plan to just superficially reach people. Any outreach that does not build or establish the local church has missed the direction of God as to what evangelization should be. We have an unfinished job if all we have done is reach people and let them fend for themselves. The end result of discipleship is to integrate them into the local church. This was the basic emphasis of our intensive self-study.

So, coupled with individual and corporate spiritual renewal and a clearly defined sense of mission, we also enacted an intensive plan to effect church growth.

This action evolved from a decision of our 1971 General Council to muster all the resources of the church into a concerted effort for new church evangelism. A New Church Evangelism Department was established under the auspices of our Division of Home Missions in 1975. Since this was made a priority, the Assemblies of God has started 2,428* new congregations and today is opening new churches at the rate of about one a day. Church planting in our fellowship is not a matter of master planning from the top down, but rather of individual burden and district encouragement.

Usually, potential pioneer pastors approach their districts to share a burden they have for starting a congregation in a particular area. If district officials concur, they endorse the new work and often help find a meeting place and provide some financial assistance for it.

I believe this "grass roots" method is responsible for the continued number of new assemblies. The method parallels our belief that evangelism is everyone's duty and not just the job of leadership. Not only does this method recognize God's leading for an individual's ministry, but it also emphasizes a total dependency on God's sovereignty as Lord of the harvest.

This dual emphasis of evangelism and church planting has led naturally to the third area affecting church growth: programs and methodology.

## III. CHURCH GROWTH THROUGH PROGRAMS AND METHODOLOGY

Programs and methodology of evangelism are the natural outgrowth of any fellowship born in the fire of the Holy Spirit, united in adherence to the entire Word of God, and cohesively bound by one great purpose—the mission of evangelism.

There are some who, regretfully, establish programs without first establishing a well-balanced superstructure. Such organizations end up stilted and unbalanced. The first real storm

*Period reported from May 1, 1974, to December 31, 1982

passing by washes away the fruit of unfounded methodology.

The Assemblies of God has always been committed to a strong and comprehensive Sunday school program. We are committed to the fact that Sunday school is for everyone—all ages. In fact, many of our congregations had their beginnings as Sunday schools which later evolved into full churches. Our churches offer Bible classes to every age group. God's Word is taught and practiced, and class members are encouraged to share the Word with others.

Through a variety of programs, Sunday school growth is emphasized. One such program is "enrollment plus." In this program, every person with whom contact is made or who visits the church is enrolled in Sunday school. Followup occurs routinely, and many of those so enrolled eventually become active members of the Sunday school.

In the area of men's and boys' ministries, we operate a number of viable programs, among them Royal Rangers and Kingsmen International. Royal Rangers is a program for boys. In some aspects it is similar to scouting programs—uniforms, badges and awards, campouts—but it is different in that each meeting also involves Bible study, application of Bible principles, and opportunities to lead boys to Christ as Savior. Thousands of boys find Christ through this program each year.

Kingsmen International is a men's program for reaching unsaved men. By inviting friends and neighbors to a banquet featuring a well-known Christian speaker or musician, the sharing of the gospel message at the banquet, and subsequent followup, hundreds of men have found Christ as Savior through this program.

Women's ministries include Joy Fellowship for adults and Missionette programs for girls. Local women's ministries groups host Joy Fellowships and invite other women from the community to attend the meetings. A meeting may involve a speaker, special music, sharing of a unique testimony, and a time for fellowship and personal sharing over a cup of tea or coffee. In this manner, thousands of women are evangelized for Christ.

Missionettes, with several age groupings, is a girls' program similar in purpose to the boys' Royal Rangers program. It achieves similar evangelistic results.

Youth programs include Youth Alive, an intense evangelistic

program among junior high and high school youth; Speed-the-Light, a program of fund-raising by youth to purchase missions equipment for overseas evangelism; and Chi Alpha, a college campus ministries and evangelism program. Ambassadors in Mission, a youth missionary program, focuses on evangelism, and the Bible Quiz program aims at discipling youth through a concentrated study of God's Word.

We also engage in a variety of evangelistic efforts using communications. "Revivaltime" is a half-hour weekly radio broadcast with more than 550 releases worldwide. "Every Day with Jesus" is a fifteen-minute, five-days-a-week radio Bible study.

Television ministry began in the late 1970s with a series of interview programs with well-known Christians. In the late 1970s we developed radio and television spots also aimed at evangelism and reaching those outside the churches. In 1983 the Assemblies became the first to telecast a national church meeting live via satellite and several cable TV networks to the general public. Hundreds of people responded to the TV altar call and indicated that they had accepted Christ as Savior. Further similar programs are being planned. In December 1983 we launched Church Satellite Network, a narrowcast programming to our churches to assist in their evangelism and discipling efforts.

The *Pentecostal Evangel,* official weekly publication of the church, has a circulation of some 300,000 and reaches nearly a million readers weekly. Articles often deal with evangelistic themes, and testimonies of miracles, healings, and God's provision are regularly recounted. Response coupons are routinely included offering literature and helps to people who want to know more about Christ, the church, and various doctrines. Through these efforts, hundreds of people find Christ as Savior annually.

Many local churches also print their own newspapers, produce radio or TV programs, or even own radio stations. Many churches also sponsor multimedia campaigns, materials for which are produced by the church headquarters.

Dr. Thomas Zimmerman is the General Superintendent of the Assemblies of God, which has grown in membership 70 percent over the past ten years. Now the fastest-growing denomination in the United States, obviously it represents a plan that works.

Dr. Zimmerman is a favorite speaker at the Billy Graham Schools of Evangelism as well as author of several books on evangelization. He may be reached at The Assemblies of God, Executive Offices, 1445 Boonville Avenue, Springfield, MO 65802.

# THE SALVATION ARMY
## COMMISSIONER NORMAN S. MARSHALL, NATIONAL COMMANDER
## THE SALVATION ARMY IS COMMITTED TO EVANGELISM

THE Salvation Army was born as an evangelistic movement. It was a child of the passion of William and Catherine Booth for the lost. William Booth, the Army's founder, was first and foremost a soul-winner.

Evangelism was the swaddling clothes of the infant movement, even before it was "christened" with its name, which would designate its purpose: "The Salvation Army." Mile End Waste of London, with its destitute and down-and-outs, was the Bethlehem of the Salvation Army.

Our evangelical mission is emblazoned on our flag with the words, "Blood and Fire." The red color represents the shed blood of our Lord for sinners. Evangelism is woven into the very warp and woof of the Salvation Army.

Evangelism is incorporated in our songbook with major sections on *Christ's Atoning Work, The News of Salvation—Invitation and Repentance, Response and Forgiveness, Experience and Testimony.*

Evangelism is incorporated in the legal deed poll of our

movement. Salvation is a major tenet as stated in our sixth doctrine: "We believe that the Lord Jesus Christ by His suffering and death made an atonement for the whole world that whosoever will may be saved."

The Salvationist in song, doctrine, and personal experience does go on to the deeper Christian life, to holiness and communion with God, and to its practical outworking in life and service. But evangelism is interwoven throughout the total tapestry of all we are and all we do.

Our *mission statement* articulates evangelism as a continued purpose of our movement:

> The motivation of the organization is the love of God and a practical concern for the needs of humanity. This is expressed by a spiritual ministry, the purposes of which are to preach the Gospel, disseminate Christian truths, supply basic human necessities, provide personal counseling and undertake the spiritual and moral regeneration and physical rehabilitation of all persons in need who come within its sphere of influence regardless of race, color, creed, sex or age.

Our current international theme is "Christ Is the Hope of the World." Some preceding themes included "Christ Is the Answer," "Witness and Win," and others which articulate the Army's worldwide evangelical mission.

## MANY AVENUES OF EVANGELISM

Today evangelism in the Salvation Army has many avenues of expression. It has an internal emphasis with our new generation of Salvationists, and as a part of our worship experience. Every corps, which is our equivalent term for "church," has a "mercy seat." It is the place where the Salvationist and those seeking a Savior make sacred decisions and dedications.

The Salvationist is expected to be an evangelist, to witness on a person-to-person basis to his family, to his associates, and to those in the world about him. Each summer the Salvation Army conducts a National Soldiers' Seminar on Evangelism at the Navigators' Headquarters in Glen Eyrie, Colorado, for the purpose of training an elite corps of lay members in evangelism. Evangelistic outreach is a major emphasis of our organization.

## THE HALLMARK OF THE SALVATION ARMY

But let me deal with a somewhat unique expression of the Salvation Army's evangelism. It is a quality that has become the hallmark of the Salvation Army. Billy Graham once described our movement as having "a cup of cold water in one hand and the Bible in the other."

We have never known any artificial polarization between the sacred and the secular. The motto of our founder was: "Soap, Soup and Salvation." William Booth believed you could not talk to a hungry man about his soul. You had to feed him first, help him to become clean, and have his dire physical need met, and then you could talk to him about salvation. In his last public appearance he flung out his spiritual gauntlet, which became the battle cry of succeeding generations of warriors in the ranks of God's Army:

While women weep as they do now, I'll fight!
While little children go hungry as they do now,
    I'll fight!
While men go to prison, in and out, in and out,
    I'll fight!
While there yet remains one dark soul without the
    light of God, I'll fight—
I'll fight to the very end!

Metaphorically speaking, for the Salvationist, the horizontal beam of the cross points him toward his fellowman for whom he has responsibility, and the vertical beam points him to God and the ultimate claim on his devotion. Human services and evangelism are the obverse and reverse sides of the coin of the Salvationist.

## MULTIPLE MINISTRIES

There was to ensue from the Army's humble beginnings of "Soap, Soup and Salvation," a prolific expression of ministries to the total man. These ministries represent the hands of Christ extended in practical help, the heart of Christ in compassionate ministries. It is our mandate and privilege to reach the desperate, destitute, and distressed in institutions, prisons, hospitals, rehabilitation centers, and with programs of crisis intervention. Our parish includes both the prominent and the prostitute, the ghetto resident and the suburbanite, the down-and-out and "up-and-in." Our outreach and ministry cross all cultural, racial, and socioeconomic lines.

One cannot approach a ghetto resident on his crumbling porch where inside his family lives in a rat-infested house and in poverty, and unsheathe his "King James sword" and say, "God loves you." Some people have been shot for less effrontery than that. Rather, we must demonstrate that we care about the person, his family, his destitute circumstances. We must link arms with him to do something about his needs. Then perhaps, if we have truly represented Christ, his spirit, his compassion, if we have served with integrity, then maybe we have established a relationship and a credibility that will give us the right and the opportunity of sharing our faith.

After we have done something about the hunger of the body, then we may present the Bread of Life. After we have tendered the cup of cold water, then we can share the One who satisfies the deepest thirst of life that no earthly spring can quench.

## HUMAN DOCUMENTARIES

A testimony is often better than a treatise. Let me share with you some human documentaries that illustrate the life-changing experiences in Christ that come through ministry to the total man. We remind our readers that the Salvation Army works primarily, not with large numbers of people, but rather with the individual on a one-to-one basis.

The *Miami Herald* reported that he was "the most arrested drunk in Miami in 1969." After six years on skid row, in and out of jail many times, Frank Dyer was brought before one more judge. He recalls the remarks of the judge that day: "Frank Dyer, you are sixty-one years of age and I and the courts find that the stockade does you no good. I believe that you have reached the point of no return. However, I am sentencing you to the custody of the Salvation Army at the Men's Social Service Center to see if they can do anything for you."

Frank went to the "center" where he was given shelter, meaningful employment, and an atmosphere of Christian faith and love. The administrator read his court record and said to him, "Mr. Dyer, you have tried everything else, why not try God? I know he can help if you will let him." In Sunday morning chapel service at the center, Frank knelt at the mercy seat, confessed his need of God, and Christ became his Savior and Lord. On Easter Sunday he was enrolled as a soldier of the Salvation Army and he himself became a counselor at the Army's Center, helping others with similar problems.

Frank testifies, "God reached down into the gutters of Miami and picked up Frank Dyer in his mysterious way, put this lost sheep on his shoulder, and carried me into his fold. I became a new person in Christ. From that time my desire has been to share with others what Christ has done for me."

Frank Dyer is an example of how we needed to relate to deep personal needs of a chronic alcoholic who had gone to the dregs on skid row. The modern counterpart of "soap and soup" became a rehabilitation center with counseling, work therapy, and opportunity to achieve self-esteem. Then there came the opportunity of "salvation."

Sometimes the very reputation of the Salvation Army becomes a gateway for helping a person find Christ. Such was the case in the story of a teenage girl who was seen sitting by the entrance of our Salvation Army Headquarters on 14th Street in New York City. The Salvation Army leader who observed her noticed when he returned from dinner in the evening that she was still sitting there. He went over to her and asked if there was any way he could be of help. She shared how she had just arrived in New York the day before from New Hampshire, had been robbed of her suitcase and money while still in the bus station, and did not know where she could go from there. She had spent the night in terror, worrying that someone would assault her, as the area was not safe. She had missed six meals.

The Army leader called our emergency lodge and arranged for her to be taken that evening to the shelter, have a good meal, clean-up, and made to feel more comfortable. Later she responded to the invitation to share in the Christian faith of the Army. Before she left, she was asked how she came to sit by the Army building. She replied, "As long as I was sitting under the Salvation Army light, I didn't think anyone could hurt me." What a challenge to us to always keep that light shining! Not merely the electric lights on our buildings, but the Light which was the Light in Galilee, the Light that shines in the darkness of sin, Jesus—the Light of the World.

Another story from the Midwest concerns a young man who was given the name "Jehovah" by his gang. He tells the story: "One day we came over to wreck the Salvation Army gym, and the Salvationists and the Salvation Army woman in charge came out to meet us. She said, 'Oh, I am so glad you came, this gymnasium is for you. Bring your friends and make good use of it.' No one ever spoke to us like that before. Usually they ordered us away. We soon saw that this woman really loved us."

Then he told how one day she took him to the chapel, pointed to the mercy seat, and told him what that place of prayer was all about. "Jehovah" knelt and rose to testify, "God changed me at that place and it would not have happened if that woman hadn't loved us. I have brought four of my guys to this place tonight and they're going to find what I found. My name's not Jehovah anymore, it's Mike!" Jehovah who became Mike is representative of many young men and women whom the Salvation Army attracts from the subculture of violence and crime in the streets, to an atmosphere of love and faith where they can find the deeper meaning of life.

## GOD'S INFANTRY

Christ has called the Salvation Army to a privileged ministry. We are to be the infantry of the militant Christian church, serving out in the trenches of life. It is a sacred privilege, and it is a sacred responsibility.

When visiting our Salvation Army Multi-Purpose Center in the Hough ghetto of Cleveland, Billy Graham said to its director at that time, Major Henry Gariepy, as he observed the galaxy of meaningful ministries serving over a thousand people a day: "Truly, this is Christianity in action!" That expresses the mission of the Salvation Army. It is evangelism in action. It is being the instruments of the compassion of Christ to troubled lives and to a tortured world. May God keep us faithful to the calling he has vouchsafed to us.

# THE CATHOLIC DIOCESE OF SIOUX FALLS, SOUTH DAKOTA
## JERRY AND NANCY ANDREWS
## A CITYWIDE OUTREACH TO THE INACTIVES

CHAPTER

21

WHAT happens when seven parishes within the same city decide to reach out to those who have left the regular practice of their faith, and those who have become alienated over the years? Here is the story of what the Diocese of Sioux Falls in South Dakota was able to do when their bishop and two lay people worked together. The seven city parishes united in a common cause and were able to locate over one thousand families, train up special visitation teams, and make personal contact with over eight hundred of these families.

The results were that not only did several hundred families return to their church, but the parishes themselves experienced a revival among the regular membership, and developed ongoing outreach programs.

Here is proof that visitation works.

How do we reach out to others to tell them about Christ? How do we find those who once went to church but no longer go and bring them back to active membership? How, especially in the

Catholic Church where congregations are usually so large that we often lose sight of the individuals who make up the people of God?

As a lay couple in the Catholic Church we had been asking ourselves these questions for some time and had been actively looking for a practical way of doing this. We had heard a lot of idealistic talk about evangelization and read even more, but what we needed was a down-to-earth way to reach out and bring Catholics back to church and back to Christ.

The 100,000 scattered souls in this rural diocese of Sioux Falls, South Dakota, are noted for their insistence on practicality and for their independence. The very word "evangelization" smacked to them of an intrusion into the private lives of people. We knew that our first proposal needed to be one that had a high likelihood of success in order for evangelization to spread.

In August 1981 we found what we were looking for at the Catholic Lay Celebration of Evangelization in St. Louis, Missouri, in an approach outlined by Dr. Glenn Smith of the National Catholic Office of Evangelization. Dr. Smith outlined a home visitation program consisting of the following steps:

1. Create the atmosphere—make your parish a warm, friendly community where all feel they belong and are welcome.
2. Gather the names of inactive Catholics within your parish boundaries.
3. Prepare the materials; for example, parish information booklets for those visited, letters, training materials.
4. Establish an initial contact with inactives by mail.
5. Recruit and train visitation teams.
6. Make home visits to invite the inactive Catholics back to the church.
7. Welcome them back in some special way.
8. Follow up on the visits with additional contacts.

Here were eight *practical* steps which, when accompanied by much prayer, sounded very workable. We were excited and could hardly wait to get back to our bishop, Bishop Paul V. Dudley of Sioux Falls, and tell him what we had found.

Bishop Dudley shared our enthusiasm and assigned us to work

out the program with a Franciscan priest who was the diocesan director of evangelization, Father Earl Jennings. We decided on a pilot citywide reachout to include the six parishes of Sioux Falls and one in Brandon, a neighboring town, and to begin with a eucharistic celebration in January 1982, led by Bishop Dudley and calling people to be evangelists.

At this celebration held in one of the parish churches, more than 500 active Catholics heard Bishop Dudley issue the call to prepare themselves and their church to reach out in love to alienated Catholics and bring them home. He challenged them to create warm, welcoming, and participating congregations. More than half of those present committed themselves to a specific evangelization effort in their own parishes in a special anointing ceremony at the end of the Mass.

On the day of this special celebration our diocesan director, Father Jennings, suffered a mild heart attack and was no longer able to work with the program, so we became the diocesan coordinators for evangelization.

Twelve months later, 739 Catholic households had been visited by trained two-person teams and invited to active participation in church life. Nearly half, 45 percent of those visited, indicated some degree of interest in being reunited into the Catholic community. Many came back right away, many were put in touch with inquiry classes, some began the process to have marriages blessed and children baptized, and, unfortunately, we are sure most did nothing—at least not right away.

The most important result of our outreach was not the number of bodies now back at Sunday Mass, although that was important too, but that 160 active, committed Catholics knocked on the doors of 739 inactive Catholics, out of love, to listen without judgment and to say, "We care. We love you. We miss you. Please come home." That is Christ's mystical body functioning as he would have it function. We decided at the beginning that we would let the Lord count the noses.

We began the actual work of evangelization in the spring of 1982 with the formation of leadership groups in each of the seven parishes, followed by recruitment of parishioners to fill such roles as greeters, handwriters, and prayer team members, as well as visitors. Dr. Glenn Smith came out to our diocese and put on a two-day orientation for the priests and parishioners. Greeters were organized in each of the parishes to meet people at the church doors and welcome them to each Mass—part of "creating the atmosphere."

On Pentecost Sunday each pastor in the seven parishes asked parishioners to fill out cards with names of inactive Catholics they knew. The names of 1,125 area Catholics were gathered. A letter from Bishop Dudley was sent to each one along with a booklet, "We're Family," about the church. The bishop's letter said, in part, "I do want you to know that you are missed and we do have a loving and caring concern for you." His letter was followed by a letter from each pastor to the inactives in his parish area expressing love and concern for them.

Each parish spent the summer months recruiting potential visitors and preparing parish information booklets.

In early October Dr. Glenn Smith again spent a weekend with us training visitors and sending them off on their first visits. After spending Saturday learning Dr. Smith's simple, low-key visitation technique and practicing it in simulated visits, on Sunday all the visitation teams and all the prayer teams gathered for benediction and a sendoff by Dr. Smith. Then, with the special blessing of their respective pastors, the teams went out and made one visit each while the prayer teams stayed behind to ask God's blessings on their visits. When the teams returned after the visits to share their experiences, many moving stories were related. "I miss the church so much," said one of those visited. "I'd really like to get back." And then her eyes filled with tears. And from another, "I've been waiting for you!"

One of the followups to the visits, and a highlight of the reachout, was a series of three seminars on topics dealing with frequently expressed problems of the alienated—changes in the church; marriage, divorce, and annulments; and the church and the Bible. When an inactive shared a problem relating to one of these topics, the visitor invited him to come to the seminar. The parish information booklet also provided a means of followup, as a week after the visit, our visitors were to call those visited and answer any questions they might have about parish activities and then offer rides if there was interest in attending an activity.

In the course of completing this year-long pilot effort, we experienced discouragement, antagonism, apathy, ignorance, rivalries, and factions, as well as heroic levels of commitment, love, and hard work. We witnessed miracles of reconciliation and the constant harassment of Satan. We discovered anew that the imperfect human nature of Christians has not changed since the church of Acts. As we began to put the reports together for the bishop, we realized we had learned some important lessons— lessons that can be of value to any reachout effort. We realized that what would have been most valuable for us at the outset would have been some advice in retrospect from someone who had gone through the effort from start to finish. Rather than a "recipe for evangelization" then, we want to share the lessons we learned.

UNDERGIRD YOUR EFFORT WITH PRAYER.
Nothing new in this lesson, is there? Yet we didn't do enough, even though we knew better. We are convinced that evangelization is going to be ineffectual without as much effort spent on prayer as on all the rest of the work put together. As St. Paul asked of the church at Ephesus, "Do all this in prayer, asking for God's help. Pray on every occasion, as the Spirit leads. For this reason keep alert and never give up; pray always for all God's people" (Ephesians 6:18, TEV).

Organize prayer teams and prayer chains whose members will make a priority commitment to pray for the success of the outreach. All those who work on the evangelization must make a special commitment to prayer, to fasting and penance. Every gathering, every committee meeting, every visit, ought to be preceded and followed by prayer. And not the perfunctory, bowed-head, eyes-closed, fifteen-second variety either, but deep-down, Spirit-led encounters with the Christ whose Kingdom is being built up.

If your effort is not characterized by prayer of this sort, wait until you have this type of prayer going. While our program was termed "successful" by most observers, we believe the relative secondary importance our prayer effort was given limited the good intentions and effort of many.

HAVE A PRACTICAL AND TESTED PROGRAM TO ADAPT.
The old saying, "Don't reinvent the wheel," has never been more true than with a Catholic reachout effort. All around the country, Catholic parishes and dioceses have developed effective evan-

gelization programs. We were blessed to have Dr. Smith's practical, step-by-step approach to begin with, and we can recommend it to anyone. Had we tried to create our own program from the beginning, we would have multiplied our mistakes unnecessarily.

The important aspect of this lesson is to adapt any program to local needs and conditions. Avoid the recipe mentality. Your own common sense will tell you what is workable for your area and what isn't.

### INSIST ON FULL, VISIBLE, VOCAL PASTORAL SUPPORT.

Some pastors are reluctant, for various reasons that are important to them, to support an evangelization effort from the pulpit. One of the most direct cause-and-effect relationships we observed was that, where the pastors held nothing back from the visible and vocal support of the program, the program prospered. Workers were abundant and the cooperation was outstanding. However, in those parishes in which the pastor felt the pulpit was not the place for such support, the work languished and apathy on the part of the average Catholic prevailed.

As a people, Catholics follow their shepherds. If the shepherd will not give sincere and full support from the pulpit, perhaps the time is not right.

### SPARE NO EFFORT
### PREPARING THE ATMOSPHERE IN THE LOCAL PARISH.

At one of the first meetings of our local parish leadership group, one member felt we should hold off any reachout effort to inactive Catholics until we had made a more concerted effort to renew the active members of the parish. Because we were involved in a multiparish program with a goal of reaching all inactives by Christmas, we didn't feel we could "get out of step" with our neighboring parishes. Dr. Smith's first step was to create the atmosphere. With the benefit of hindsight, we believe that at least a year of parish preparation should go into an evangelization effort before any organized reachout is attempted.

Such preparation would have several beneficial effects. The church home to which you welcome new and old members should be one of warmth and welcome. It should be a church in which sincere and meaningful participation in the liturgy is practiced by all, not just those occupying the front third of the pews. With the preparation of the congregation for evangelization, a general readiness to be open and welcome could be built. Also, the recruitment of workers and visitors would be made easier in a parish that spent a year preparing for the event.

We confess that we were so eager to get started, we neglected somewhat this lesson. No one knows for certain what the cost of that neglect was.

## TOO MUCH COMMUNICATION IS IMPOSSIBLE.

As part of the preparation of the atmosphere of the local parish, constant communication about what is planned, what is happening, and what the results are is vital. Parish evangelization must be a total family effort. Everyone has a part to play. Communication makes everyone a partner. We would recommend that someone with communications skills be recruited to keep a constant flow of information going out to parishioners, to the local press, and to other churches. As mentioned previously, one of the earliest steps in our outreach effort was a letter from the bishop, followed shortly by a letter from the local pastors. These communications alone were all that a few needed to come back. Hundreds of households welcomed their guests readily because the communications effort had prepared them.

## RECRUITMENT AND TRAINING
## OF THE RIGHT VISITORS IS CRITICAL.

Recruitment of visitors works best when done personally on a one-to-one basis. The principle qualification to be a visitor should be a high degree of commitment to the church and to evangelization—a quality that is difficult to measure. No one considering becoming a visiting evangelist should be made to feel badly for not having that commitment. We believe a full year of parish preparation of the atmosphere for evangelization will help develop a high level of commitment among potential visitor volunteers.

We learned that in a city- or parish-wide evangelization program, we had to offer potential visitors solid, practical training, equipping them with an adequate expectation of what might happen on a visit, how to handle the situations that might arise, what to say to get in the door, how to get down to the purpose of the visit, etc. This was one of the special strong points of Dr. Smith's assistance. He had trained literally hundreds of visitors and was able to teach the simple, straightforward techniques in a manner that was clear and easy to apply.

One of the early hurdles to overcome in preparing visitors was to convince them that they were being sent to listen and to welcome, not to judge, argue theology, or discuss canon law. Even though we were told by Dr. Smith that the overwhelming majority of households visited just wanted someone to listen and be sympathetic, we were still amazed at the number of homes in which that actually was true.

When it came right down to making an actual visit, reluctance to make the call was a problem for many potential visitors. They were not sure what would happen on a visit, how they would be received, what they would say—so they procrastinated and avoided making their visits. We learned that two-person visitation teams—one to talk and one to pray, as Dr. Smith recommends—were most effective in this regard. The support of a companion made the visit much easier. Also, much practice of visiting techniques is important—enough practice so that visitors feel fairly comfortable with many plausible situations. And, most important, visitors must learn to be open to the Holy Spirit and rely on him to work through them.

## THE REACHOUT IS JUST THE BEGINNING; FOLLOW-THROUGH IS THE PROOF OF THE PROGRAM.

A parish-level evangelization effort is very like a sales program with a full field of sales people. It requires management and support. A well-planned and organized evangelization effort must have this vision of the overall effort and ultimate impact. Such programs need to avoid the "drive" mentality, as if the reachout were for the money to build the new auditorium. Pope Paul VI, in his Apostolic Exhortation *Evangelii Nuntiandi*, written in 1975, declared that evangelization is the *essential mission* of the church. A reachout to inactive Catholics is just the beginning.

Someone has observed, "The Catholic Church has been dominated in this century by an 'aquarium' mentality—we keep it clean, we put food in it, we keep it the right temperature, but the only growth that occurs in it is what is born in it." Christ directed his followers to be his witnesses to the ends of the earth, and that certainly includes everyone within the boundaries of our parishes. Since over 95 percent of the people in this country reside within a thirty-minute drive of a Catholic Church, we have plenty of fields to harvest without going "to the ends of the earth."

If we Catholics can continue to learn from the first halting steps of these early attempts to break out of the "aquarium" mentality, then the "sleeping giant," as the Catholic Church has been called, will not only awaken but become a powerful force for extending the Kingdom.

PART THREE

# Nine Outstanding Parachurch Organizations

# THE MOODY BIBLE INSTITUTE
## CHICAGO, ILLINOIS
## DR. GEORGE SWEETING, PRESIDENT
## THE CHURCH AND THE MEDIA—
## PARTNERS IN EVANGELIZATION

## THE MOODY BIBLE INSTITUTE—
## GOD'S WEST POINT OF EVANGELISM

Founded almost one hundred years ago, MBI stands in the heart of Chicago, training evangelists, printing evangelism materials, broadcasting evangelism, and motivating thousands of pastors and lay leaders from various denominations to do evangelism. Communicating the gospel of Jesus Christ is MBI's very reason for existence.

More than 105,000 students each year study under its ministry with some 2,000 students living on campus who pay no tuition. Its staff of teachers and full-time employees number over 600 and its outreach is worldwide. Under the direction of its sixth president, Dr. George Sweeting, the Moody Bible Institute is truly America's West Point of evangelism. President Sweeting presents a vision for the future evangelization of all America through the use of media—radio and television. He states that his vision, and that of the Moody Bible Institute, is to expand and become a strong instrument in God's plan in fulfilling the task of world evangelization in this very generation. Here is how they plan to do just that.

In 1973, the Moody Institute of Science produced a film titled, "Empty Cities." The film attempts to answer the question, "Why do civilizations die?"

One of the civilizations examined was the Mayan culture of over 1,000 years ago in the Yucatan Peninsula of Central America. The Mayas excelled in astronomy, architecture, and mathematics.

But the Mayan civilization declined.

John W. Gardner in his book, *No Easy Victories,* writes:

> In Guatemala and southern Mexico one can observe the Indians who are without doubt the lineal descendants of those who created the Mayan civilization. Today they are a humble people, not asking much of themselves or the world, and not getting much. A light went out.

While in the jungles of Yucatan, I was also forcefully reminded of the power of the media. Walking down a remote jungle trail, I saw a thatched roof hut with a TV aerial. They were actually receiving telecasts from Merida, eighty miles away. As I gazed in amazement at the aerial, I wondered, "Could this be the method to rekindle the light again?"

If nations fall because they forget God, then the cure is found in a return to God and his Word.

The theme of this article is "The Church and the Media— Partners in Evangelization."

World evangelization is our *commission.* Establishing and building local churches is our *method.* And the media is an *instrument* given to us to carry out the Great Commission.

## FIRST . . . CONSIDER THE CHURCH

What is the church? Theologian Augustus Strong says, "It is the body of Jesus Christ." The local church is a group of regenerated people in a specific place who have joined together, accepting the Bible as their rule of faith.

While Jesus was here on earth, he promised in Matthew 16:18,

"I will build my church; and the gates of hell shall not prevail against it." Jesus called the church "my church." He guaranteed its future. Jesus never wrote a book; he never built a college; but he did found the church. Nothing on earth is more important to Jesus Christ than the church.

The book of Acts tells us *how* the church began. In Acts 1:4, Jesus said, "Wait for the promise." In Acts 1:14, 15, 120 believers waited in one accord and prayer.

In Acts 2:1-4, the promise was fulfilled: 120 believers were empowered.

In Acts 2:6, the 120 began to witness, ". . . every man heard them speak in his own language." Parthians and Medes and Elamites and others heard the "wonderful works of God" in their own tongues.

After this saturation program of witnessing, Acts 2:14 reports, "Peter, standing up with the eleven, lifted up his voice . . ." and preached. Peter was the speaker. What did Peter say?

Acts 2:22, ". . . Jesus of Nazareth, a man approved of God among you. . . ."

v. 23, ". . . ye have taken, and by wicked hands have crucified and slain."

v. 24, "Whom God hath raised up. . . ."

v. 36, "Therefore let all the house of Israel know assuredly that God hath made that same Jesus . . . Lord and Christ."

Peter was the speaker; Christ crucified and risen was his message.

What was the response? Acts 2:37, "Now when they heard this they were pricked in their heart, and said unto Peter and to the rest of the apostles, 'Men and brethren, what shall we do?' "

Peter answered, v. 38, ". . . Repent and be baptized every one of you. . . . Then they that gladly received his word were baptized: and the same day there were added unto them about three thousand souls" (v. 41).

Immediately these new believers began to evangelize. "And they, continuing daily with one accord in the temple, and breaking bread from house to house, did eat their meat with gladness and singleness of heart" (Acts 2:46).

These believers had a drink at Joel's place. They were Holy Spirit intoxicated. They were praising God and having favor with all the people. In Acts 4:4, 5,000 men alone were added to Jesus

Christ and the church. "And daily in the temple, and in every house, they ceased not to teach and preach Jesus Christ" (Acts 5:42).

World evangelization was their passion. Starting in Jerusalem, Judea, Samaria, and going to the uttermost part of the earth, they proclaimed the Good News.

Luther L. Grubb states, "The reason for the existence of the church is *missions*." It is my conviction that establishing and building local churches is the Bible way of evangelization.

In the technical sense, the church has no partners. All of us, church and parachurch, are members of one body serving Jesus Christ and serving his body, the church. A healthy local church, preaching the gospel, is the best way to world evangelization.

At this juncture, may I recognize other agencies of Christian ministry outside the local church, called parachurch organizations.

The word "para" means "alongside of." Parachurch organizations to a degree have always existed, but not in the numbers and strength of today.

The Sunday school began as a parachurch movement and then it became part of the church. We are told that there are some 6,500 parachurch organizations among Protestants and Catholics. Merely to illustrate, we have Youth For Christ, Young Life, and Word of Life for high schoolers; Campus Crusade, Inter-Varsity, and Navigators for collegians; Christian Businessmen's Committee for men; Christian Women's Club for women; Christian Medical Society for doctors; and on and on and on.

But parachurch groups have grown so strong that some are asking, "Is the tail wagging the dog?" Is the arm leading and controlling the body? For example, the media often quotes parachurch leaders rather than pastors. Parachurch groups aggressively raise millions of dollars through direct mail, radio, and television. Only 50 percent of seminary and Bible college graduates are going into local churches.

Can anything be done to balance the situation? How can we have greater cooperation? How can we more effectively evangelize?

In a new way, we need to recognize the place of the local church in world evangelization. Some look at the church with disdain. This is sinful. Others ignore the church. This is equally wrong. Though the church has many critics, it has no rival. The local church is God's central agency working on earth.

Dr. James Engel of Wheaton Graduate School in his article, "Local Churches: The Missing Link in Evangelism," says, "Some on the parachurch side publicly proclaim they are an arm of the Body but in reality attempt to control the Body."

We who are parachurch organizations need to ask, "What difference would it make to the church if our organization stopped ministering today?"

It is my personal conviction that parachurch groups are to serve the local church and be accountable to them.

Dr. Wesley Willis of Scripture Press believes that any parachurch ministry must always make the assumption it is working itself out of a job. We need to call for a recovery of the centrality of the local church, a call to be churchmen in every sense of the word. This would be a giant step forward in promoting the gospel rather than personalities, programs, and institutions.

Let us resolve to "keep close to the local church." Jesus did not say, "I will build my parachurch." Rather, Jesus said, "I will build my church."

## SECOND . . . CONSIDER THE MEDIA

What are the media? The Random House Dictionary defines the word "media" as an instrument, an agency, or a tool.

For example, two graduates of the Moody Bible Institute, John and Elaine Beekman, labored among the Chol Indians of Southern Mexico for twenty-five years. Along with others, they succeeded in translating the entire New Testament into the Chol language. Through the media of the printed page, that tiny church has grown to over 18,000 souls and it is totally self-supporting.

Some time ago, I heard James Johnson of Wheaton Graduate School tell of a missionary flying from Sao Paulo, Brazil, to Miami, Florida. The missionary sat next to a seventeen-year-old Brazilian man. After considerable conversation, the missionary asked the excited seventeen-year-old what he wanted to see most when he arrived in Miami.

The young man displayed a full-page color ad of a TV dinner.

"When I get to Miami, I want one of these." Well, I'm sure he was disappointed. Needless to say, they had painted the picture and written the copy so well that he was in a hurry to eat a TV dinner.

Habakkuk 2:2 reads, "And the Lord answered me, and said, Write the vision, and make it plain upon tables, that he may run that readeth it."

Brothers and sisters, our challenge is to present the message in such a Spirit-filled way that people will be quick to obey the gospel.

Christian books are expanding and selling as never before. From our own Moody Press publishing house, we ship out 40,000 books a day.

Christian radio is more popular today than ever before. Ben Armstrong, Executive Director of National Religious Broadcasters and author of the book, *The Electric Church*, writes, "Today more than sixty Christian organizations operate international radio stations and hundreds of organizations on every continent produce programs for them."

Armstrong continues, "Far East Broadcasting Company has the potential to reach half of the world's 4 billion people. Every day 28 stations beam 300 program hours in 72 major languages and dialects" (p. 70).

Armstrong writes, "With stations in Monte Carlo, Bonaire, Cyprus, Swaziland, Guam, and Sri Lanka, Trans World Radio actually encircles the globe with the gospel. This worldwide network utilizes the combined talents of 400 radio missionaries and a total of 5 million watts of power to proclaim the Good News in 70 languages."

Ben Armstrong concludes chapter 5 of his book with these words, "Missionary radio stations large and small are a 20th century embodiment of the prophecy of Romans 10:18 . . . 'their sound went into all the earth, and their words unto the ends of the world' " (p. 80).

And what about television? Sherwood Wirt predicts in *Evangelism and the Media*, "Christian television operations will expand a hundredfold. With satellite communication, program packaging, home videotaping, and a dozen other 'breakthroughs,' the 1980's will see the growth of electronic evangelism on a scale unimaginable."

The opportunities are mind-boggling. But there are also dangers!

Tools are instruments for construction or destruction. A shovel can be used to build a hospital or a church, but also to dig potholes on a super highway.

Malcolm Muggeridge in his book, *Christ and the Media,* portrays what he calls "the fourth temptation of Jesus." In his imagination, Muggeridge has Satan offer Jesus prime time on television so that he can preach his gospel to the whole world. But Jesus refuses the offer.

"Our Lord's reason for refusing is that in all of his teaching, Jesus concerns himself with truth and reality, whereas television bases its whole existence on images and fantasy." So writes Muggeridge.

But he could be wrong. No one knows what Jesus would do. Let us always remember that the "Word of God is not bound." "With God all things are possible."

What are the dangers we face? Keep in mind I am not shooting at anyone in particular, but at all of us.

## 1. ADDING TO OR SUBTRACTING FROM THE GOSPEL

There is the danger in adding our culture to the gospel. For example, in June, while in Japan, I saw an American gospel telecast. I was inspired. The Asians I was with were offended.

Some promote self-improvement with the gospel. Some mix politics with the gospel. Others accent the Good News, but the Cross is omitted. It is a serious matter to confuse the gospel. Galatians 1:8 is serious: "Though we or an angel from heaven preach any other gospel, let him be accursed."

## 2. SUBSTITUTING ENTERTAINMENT FOR THE WORD OF GOD

Sherwood Wirt warns, "To satisfy the restless 'religious' market and to raise funds, many Christian television producers have added the syrup of entertainment to the evangelistic message." Wirt continues, "Sometimes it becomes difficult to determine whether a 'testimony' beamed to 50 million people is aimed at convicting the heart or merely titillating the senses."

Perhaps some are experts in communication and TV, but amateurs in the Bible and in Christian experience. There is the temptation to pick participants because of looks rather than their character and ability. We dare not copy secular radio and television which are aimed at entertainment and popular acceptance.

### 3. THE DANGER OF BIGNESS
The Moody Bible Institute is not small. We are not opposed to bigness, but "big" is not necessarily "best." It is possible to build an ever-growing giant that demands more and more dollars—which drives us to unwise methods of fund-raising.

One of the curses of secular education is gigantism—students who are lonely in the crowd—Behemoth University.

For example, recently I made a long-distance phone call. I said, "My name is. . . ." The operator said, "I don't care what your name is. I want your credit card number."

May we strive and pray to be a "caring community."

### 4. THE DANGER OF EXTRAVAGANT SPENDING
### AND AN EXCESSIVE LIFE STYLE
Each day a billion people go to sleep hungry . . . a thousand million people. My Asian friends were offended by the elaborate TV background, rich appearance, and fifty-dollar hairdos. Wasting money is as much an act of violence against the poor as refusing to feed the hungry. Jesus is our model; though rich, he became poor.

As I have visited some churches, campuses, and TV centers, I have thought of Luke 9:58: ". . . Foxes have holes, and birds of the air have nests; but the Son of man hath not where to lay his head."

The love of Jesus Christ working in and through us should move us with compassion for the whole world. When we learn that what we have is all out of proportion to what other people have, it should make us ill at ease, uncomfortable, motivated to take action.

We must retrain our self-desires. As the children of light, we must reach out in Christian compassion to the whole world.

## THIRD . . . CONSIDER WORLD EVANGELIZATION
This is the church's assignment directly from Jesus himself. This is our goal! If the means hinder our goal, they must be corrected.

When the means achieve the end, we persevere in grace.

David Ben Gurion, former prime minister of Israel, was asked what it would take to establish his new nation firmly. He laughed and replied, "All I need starts with the letter A—*a* lot of planes, *a* lot of guns, *a* lot of money, *a* lot of men."

All *we* need also starts with the letter A—a lot of love, a lot of humility, a lot of vision, a lot of perseverance.

Jesus stated our mission in Matthew 28:19, 20, "Go ye therefore and teach all nations, baptizing them in the name of the Father, and of the Son, and of the Holy Ghost: Teaching them to observe all things whatsoever I have commanded you: and, lo, I am with you alway, even unto the end of the world."

The action of the New Testament is concentrated on the word "go." The direction is "out" to the "uttermost part" of the earth. The procedure of the New Testament is addition and multiplication. "The Lord added to the church daily" (Acts 2:47). "The number of the disciples was multiplied" (Acts 6:1).

## WHY EVANGELIZE?

1. Because, according to Romans 1:14, we are debtors. (To have is to owe.)
2. Because, according to Ezekiel 33:8, we have knowledge. (To know is to owe.)
3. Because our blessings make us responsible (2 Kings 7:6-9).
4. Because Mark 16:15 is still in the Bible.
5. Because God's love constrains us (2 Corinthians 4:14).
6. Because of our position as ambassadors (2 Corinthians 5:20).

## WHY WORLD EVANGELIZATION?

First, second, and third—because Jesus *told us* to evangelize. He commissioned the church to evangelize.

I have four sons whom I love dearly. Just suppose our lawn needed to be cut. I could say, "Boys, can you see the need? The grass is high. It's above my knees. Soon I will not be able to get to the garage. Don't you see the desperate need?"

But in the final analysis, they mow the grass because their father says, "Mow the grass!"

World evangelization is an imperative because Jesus *said so.*

During the reign of Oliver Cromwell, there was a shortage of currency in the British Empire. Representatives carefully searched the nation in hope of finding silver to meet the emergency. After one month, the committee returned with its findings. "We have searched the empire in vain seeking to find silver. To our dismay, we found none anywhere except in the cathedrals where the saints are carved from choice silver."

To this, Oliver Cromwell eloquently answered, "Let's melt down the saints and put them into circulation." Why not ask the Lord to melt *us* down for greater spiritual circulation?

## THE MINISTRIES OF MOODY BIBLE INSTITUTE

Moody Bible Institute: A group of ministries God has stretched around the world, touching lives for Jesus Christ. From education to publishing, from broadcasting to Bible conferences, MBI pursues a threefold purpose of education, edification, and evangelism.

Under a board of dedicated trustees, the Institute is guided by Dr. George Sweeting, the sixth president since MBI's inception in 1886.

"It is our vision that Moody Bible Institute expands as a strong instrument in fulfilling the task of world evangelization in this generation," says Dr. Sweeting.

MBI's distinctive stance is rooted in its history and a unique foundation in Bible fundamentals and financial support. The ministries are based on the Bible as God's authoritative, inerrant, inspired, and complete revelation to man. The Institute is a faith ministry supported by God's people.

In partnership with these donors, more than 600 employees direct and operate the ministries of Moody Bible Institute.

These pages are designed to give you a glimpse of what Christ is doing through their lives and through the tool of Moody Bible Institute.

EDUCATION
Founded as a school, the Institute commits the largest portion of its resources to the preparation of men and women for communicating the gospel of Jesus Christ.

Education at MBI is centered on the philosophy that teaching and learning are processes directed by the Holy Spirit. Through these processes, students become more conformed to the purposes of God and to the character of Jesus Christ.

From kindergarten through older adults, more than 105,000 students are in training each year. The four basic programs are:

1. Day and summer collegiate programs in Chicago.
2. Evening School on college and popular level in eight cities across five states.
3. Worldwide Correspondence School offering popular and college-level courses.
4. Kindergarten through twelfth grade Christian school in St. Petersburg, Florida.

In addition to classroom training, students in the Day, Summer, and Evening Schools participate in Christian service. Some work one-to-one with inner-city children, others at bedsides in hospitals, in mission pulpits, and elsewhere as a total of 2,600 hours each week are spent using classroom training to reach souls for Christ.

Institute founder Dwight Lyman Moody dreamed of mass publishing of Christian literature. His vision has become a reality through the Moody Press, Moody Literature Ministries, and *Moody Monthly* magazine.

Moody Press pioneered in Christian book publishing and continues as a major publisher today, releasing over 100 new titles each year with over 1,000 active titles in circulation. It operates two large Chicago area bookstores and ships to over 8,500 bookstores around the world. The cross-cultural ministry of Moody Press brings people of more than 100 different languages in contact with 500 Christian book titles.

Tracts and Gospel portions touch an estimated 12 million lives each year through Moody Literature Ministries' global distribution. Public schools, libraries, military bases, and nursing homes are provided books on a free or subsidized basis. MLM cooperates with missions and national churches in more than 120 countries to fund local printing and distribution of foreign translations.

Seeking to provide spiritual input for the vast Christian public, MBI publishes *Moody Monthly* magazine. Oriented to the family, the magazine seeks to build up its readers through inspiration, edification, and information. *Moody Monthly* has become the largest magazine of its type with circulation nearing 300,000. It has served as a model for other publications and provides a voice for leading evangelical spokesmen.

PROCLAMATION
D. L. Moody was said to have a "proclamation theology" because he spent his life finding new ways to proclaim the gospel of Jesus Christ. His innovative spirit pervades the proclamation outreaches of the Institute today.

*Broadcasting.* Radio broadcasting emerged in the United States in the early 1920s and at Moody Bible Institute in 1926. A leader in Christian radio, MBI owns and operates eleven commercial-free radio stations:

WMBI-AM (1110) Chicago, IL
WMBI-FM (90.1) Chicago, IL
WMBW-FM (88.9) Chattanooga, TN
KMBI-AM (1330) Spokane, WA
KMBI-FM (107.9) Spokane, WA
WCRF-FM (103.3) Cleveland, OH
WKES-FM (102) St. Petersburg, FL
WGNB-AM (1520) St. Petersburg, FL
WRMB-FM (89.3) Boynton Beach, FL
WDLM-AM (960) Moline, IL
WDLM-FM (89.3) Moline, IL

On the fringes of these stations, twenty-four translators in ten states pick up the originating station's signal and rebroadcast it to a local community, thereby expanding the outreach of the station.

MBI also produces programs aired on more than three hundred stations worldwide.

In 1982, MBI began a satellite programming service—Moody Broadcasting Network—linking its owned and operated stations, and available to other existing stations, cable systems, and translators. The MBN signal can be received in the Continental United States, Alaska, and Canada.

*Extension.* The local church receives support and strength

through pulpit supply, Bible, and prophecy conferences, and family seminars sponsored by MBI's Extension Department. On the Chicago campus, an aggregate of 40,000 attend the annual Founder's Week.

In 1972, MBI established an annual Pastor's Conference, designed to draw pastors and key laymen for a time of spiritual teaching and refreshment. The conference hosts more than 1,000 in attendance each year.

In 1980 Sonlife Ministries was added to the work of the Extension Department. Its purpose is to train youth pastors through Sonlife Strategy Seminars, and lay and teen leaders through Youth Discipleship Institutes. Annually Sonlife conducts a four-day Christmas Teen Conference.

*Moody Institute of Science.* The Moody Institute of Science, begun in 1943, is an example of the innovation and creativity of MBI. It produces "Sermons from Science" films, educational films, filmstrips, and audiovisual products from its headquarters in Whittier, California. More than twenty sermons from Science films have been released, and many have been translated into eleven different languages.

*Moody-Keswick.* In 1977, Southern Keswick, Inc., donated its thirty-five acres of conference grounds and other facilities to MBI. It's open to the public with guest rooms and meals available. From January to April, outstanding men from around the world come to minister the Word of God at the Bible Conference, where the motto is "Life . . . More Abundant."

Although its impact spans the nation and the world, MBI's distinctive strength comes from its unified leadership in the Chicago headquarters. We pray the innovation and creativity which have characterized MBI's history will continue.

As the Lord wills, MBI will stride forward into the 1980s, preparing, publishing, and proclaiming the gospel of our Lord Jesus Christ.

# ETERNAL WORD TELEVISION NETWORK
## BIRMINGHAM, ALABAMA
## MOTHER ANGELICA, DIRECTOR
## A NUN BEAMS THE GOOD NEWS

*C H A P T E R*

# 23

LOCATED in Alabama, near the city of Birmingham, stands a monument to the faith of one great lady working for the Lord. Her very life seems more miracle than natural. As you view the Monastery of Our Lady of the Angels, you can come to believe in miracles. She began at twenty-one when she left her job in Ohio as an ad writer and joined the Franciscan sisters in Cleveland. After an accident with a commercial scrubbing machine, she prayed that "If the Lord would let me walk, I'd build a monastery of cloistered sisters in the Southland." She still wears a leg brace, but in thanks for God's healing, she did as she had promised, and in 1961, she and eleven other sisters moved into their brand new monastery. Besides the miracle of healing, she enjoyed the miracle of building.

The monastery is one of the finest in contemporary style, with a fantastic chapel and beautiful grounds where stand statues of various angels as described in Scripture, surrounded by spouting fountains. Between the chapel and the sisters' quarters is an Olympic swimming pool. It seems that the builders became so interested in Mother Angelica and her devoted sisters that they wanted to donate something and suggested tennis courts. But the sisters suggested a swimming pool—a swimming pool they got, free of charge. Mother Angelica writes it all off as just another miracle.

Miracles abound in the monastery. When their packaged peanut business began to fail (this was the first way they supported themselves), Mother Angelica got in the car and drove down to the local factory that sold printing presses, and with only $200 in total assets, ordered $13,000 worth of printing equipment. The salesman asked Mother Angelica if she knew how to use the machines, to which she replied, "Not yet, but be sure to include the manual of instructions."

On the way home to the monastery, one of the sisters asked Mother Angelica, "But what will we print?" "Books" was Mother Angelica's answer. When the sister asked, "But whose books will we print?" Mother Angelica simply answered, "We'll have to write our own."

And write they did. From Mother Angelica's pen came a flood of spiritual books. Sister Raphael learned how to do the artwork, and the rest of the sisters began reading the manuals and setting up the presses. They now own and operate one of the largest and finest printing press operations in the entire South. Working six days a week, ten hours a day, the sisters now produce four million books a year, written in dozens of languages, and ship them into forty-eight countries.

All this is done behind the cloistered walls of the monastery, and the sisters have learned to use special lifting machines to move the tons of paper, ink, and cartons that such a large operation requires.

The most amazed people in Birmingham these days are the truck drivers, who drive up to the warehouse each morning to find, all lined up in impeccable order, the neatly packed cartons of books labeled to go throughout the world. Since the packers are cloistered nuns, the drivers never see them. They simply sign the waybills, load up the trucks, and drive away with cartons of books that will reach millions of people around the world.

Another miracle takes place with each carton of books—not only their production, but the fact that they are free of charge. No invoices are mailed, and no money is expected. But somehow God moves the hearts of those who receive them, because from the investment of $13,000 for that first press, a multimillion-dollar printing operation continues to flourish. This author has personally walked through that printry, and your mother's kitchen isn't as spotless as the nuns keep their favored presses.

With a miracle like that taking place, it wasn't long before Mother Angelica received an invitation to appear on Jim Bakker's PTL television program.

Mother Angelica was impressed with the possibilities of television, and while she appeared on various programs she was seen to carry a pencil and pad. She took notes of everything she saw; she asked the cost of everything. She jotted down descriptions and layouts and, before long, she had a model of a television station—her own. With plenty of prayer power behind her dream, the Eternal Word Television Network was born.

A sign was placed up in her office which read, "WE DON'T KNOW WHAT WE'RE DOING, BUT WE'RE GETTING GOOD AT IT." And good at it they got. When she was in a Chicago television studio, Mother Angelica looked around at all the equipment in the studio and simply prayed out loud, "Lord, we have got to have one of these!" Almost instantly her prayer was answered, when a major network offered her their old equipment after they purchased new equipment for their studio.

A group of interested laypeople donated a traveling van complete with all the equipment to work with—and their network was ready for action.

The sisters began small, making a few video tapes and peddling them to various stations around the nation. They were instant hits, and off they went into their own production of religious programs.

As with the books, the sisters worked up their own materials. Miracle after miracle followed. There is really no other word to describe their operation. How else do you explain eleven cloistered sisters under the direction of Mother Angelica, operating a multimillion-dollar book printing each year; and then, with the bills paid in full, turning on their own satellite switch to beam out over thirty-one states—the "Eternal Word of God"?

"Our mission," says Mother Angelica, "is to portray spirituality in a way that gives hope to Catholics and non-Catholics alike." To that end, she programs four hours each evening, including a church-sanctioned drama, *Westbrook Hospital;* sitcom reruns such as *My Little Margie;* wholesome old movies such as *It's a Wonderful Life*—and they are all free of commercials. The nuns intersperse their programs with prayer spots. By far the most popular show is Mother Angelica's own twice-weekly half hour, *Mother Angelica Talks It Over.*

One of the greater miracles about Eternal Word Network is the matter of finance. With a monthly overhead of more than $200,000 and a secular staff of some seventeen people, Mother Angelica flatly refuses to ask for funds. She says, "The Gospel should be free," and free to her viewers it is. While it is free to her viewers, it isn't free to her. She comments, "RCA does not accept love of God for payment." So Mother Angelica needs to use guest performances and promotional crusades to raise funds for her costly evangelization efforts.

"Unless you are willing to do the ridiculous, God will not do the miraculous," quips the Franciscan abbess. And it appears that God continues to allow the miraculous to flow within and through the Monastery of Our Lady of the Angels, as eleven sisters and their abbess continue to obey the divine commission of their Lord and Savior Jesus Christ. As cloistered nuns, they cannot go out personally, so from their printing press and their television network, they beam the Good News of the gospel to countless millions, reaching forty-eight nations with their books and thirty-one states with their television. To top it all, the sisters simply say, "We have just begun!"

So that the reader will understand these sisters better, and the source of their power, it is important to recognize that they are indeed cloistered sisters. They live a life of prayer, praise, and work. Their daily Mass is a joy to behold—their recitation of the daily office a time of real spiritual growth. Their prayers touch the very throne of God, and their time of work exhibits a real dedication to excellence and productivity.

Reaching souls for Jesus Christ and his church is their mission. When you get one of those rare opportunities to see one of these sisters, you'll see the joyful face of a happy child of God—one who knows she is in tune with the Eternal Word of God.

For information as to how to obtain a listing of the sisters'
books on evangelization, write to:

Sister Mary Raphael
Our Lady of the Angels Monastery
5817 Old Leeds Road
Birmingham, AL 35210

# THE BILLY GRAHAM CENTER
## WHEATON, ILLINOIS
## DR. MELVIN E. LORENTZEN,
## ASSOCIATE DIRECTOR
## TO BEAR WITNESS TO THE LIGHT

CHAPTER

24

MODERN evangelicalism, unlike the great liturgical traditions, suffers from a degree of myopia when it comes to its own sense of church history. At the dedication of the Billy Graham Center in Wheaton, Illinois, in 1980, Ambassador Charles Malik of Lebanon observed in his address:

"There are . . . some who affect to think that nothing really worth knowing happened in the Christian world between Saint Paul and Billy Graham. I know Billy Graham is a landmark, but not a landmark to the extent that everything between him and St. Paul has been a total blank."

One might think it audacious for a former President of the United Nations General Assembly and leader in the Orthodox Church to make such a statement in the very presence of the world-renowned evangelist, while dedicating a building that bears his name. But Dr. Malik knew that the Center represents a breakthrough in evangelical self-understanding and creates a new kind of base for promoting world evangelization.

Physically, the Billy Graham Center is a 200,000-square-foot

Georgian colonial building on the campus of 125-year-old Wheaton College. Yet, as Dr. Graham himself says, "A building is only a tool, an instrument. This building represents a major investment, but it is more than an investment in bricks and mortar; it is an investment in people and programs which will affect lives around the world for Christ. The important thing is not this building, but what will take place here."

What *does* take place at the Center?

Researchers from around the world probe previously unexplored primary source materials on evangelism and missions. Graduate students study a range of courses from Audience Research to Wilderness Learning, from Hebrew Exegesis to Community Psychology. University and seminary scholars confer on subjects such as Christian higher education and on personalities such as Jonathan Edwards. Executives from mission organizations map strategies for creative, cooperative advancement of the gospel to the world's billion Chinese. Pastors submit their preaching to constructive criticism during intensive workshops. And tens of thousands of men, women, and children annually "walk through the gospel" in the Center's dynamic museum.

Obviously, then, the Billy Graham Center is a service agency to help the people of God better understand their heritage and mandate for proclaiming the saving gospel of the Lord Jesus Christ to the uttermost parts of the earth.

The mission statement reads: "The Billy Graham Center is a division of Wheaton College dedicated to the study and promotion of world evangelization. The Center exists to work with Christian leaders around the world in developing strategies and skills for communicating the Gospel."

## FACILITIES AND RESOURCES

Born out of a vision for collecting and preserving the records of Dr. Graham's decades of evangelistic ministry, the Center's resources have been developed extensively around that core of materials. Three departments house varied research collections.

The Archives collects primary resources, documents, and unpublished material including diaries, correspondence, business records, photographs, slides, posters, scrapbooks, audio and video tapes, films, microforms, and maps.

Holdings of this division fall into three categories: (a) documents of Protestant evangelists and evangelistic organizations; (b) records and papers of missionaries, interdenominational mission boards and support organizations; and (c) materials of evangelical congresses, conferences, leaders, and important institutions.

Among the more than 300 current collections in the Archives, for example, are literally tons of materials related to the ministries of the Billy Graham Evangelistic Association; records of such diverse organizations as Youth For Christ International and Evangelicals for Social Action; and ephemera of key lay persons such as Herbert J. Taylor and evangelists Billy Sunday and Paul Rader. A tape library of oral history interviews is growing constantly.

Use of the archival resources by evangelists, teachers, pastors, scholars, and church or parachurch leaders provides insight into widely diverse ways of telling and showing how the grace of God in Christ transforms individuals and impacts on cultures. Because the bulk of the material has never before been so concentrated or accessible, the Center Archives constitutes a unique research reservoir.

The second department, the Library, is also a special collection that focuses on historical and contemporary information on world evangelization. Its nearly 200,000 printed and microform sources include works by and about evangelists, about evangelistic endeavors, and about their beneficial results for society.

There are also materials on the history of religious revivals, those occasions when the work of God in the lives of people was unusually evident. Another principal segment of the collection encompasses materials relating to world missions, the transmission of the Christian message across geographic and cultural boundaries. A specialized reference collection is geared to undergirding research on the propagation of the gospel, and a basic theological collection aids analysis and evaluation.

Several kinds of materials fall within the evangelism collection. For example, there are published works from the pens of evangelists, among which are doctrinal essays and sermons, correspondence, memoirs, autobiographies, and devotional literature. Historical materials include biographies, works treating particular evangelistic movements or specific periods of revival, and select denominational histories. Another category is methodological studies that relate to Christian evangelism, including personal evangelism, mass evangelism, and media evangelism. Additional materials include studies relating to psychology of religion and conversion, hymnals associated with evangelistic activity, and training materials used as a means to evangelize or to follow up personal decisions for Christ.

The Library is a major reference base for Wheaton College graduate and undergraduate students, and is completely open to the public with lending privileges for qualified persons.

Most public of the Center's resource departments is the Museum. Contrary to any myth that it exhibits "stuffed apostles under glass," its galleries disclose the considerable impact of evangelical religion on American society from earliest colonial times to the present.

The collections and exhibits of the Museum are valuable in showing contemporary Christians the triumphs and failures of past efforts to evangelize America, thereby helping to establish directions for new strategies in evangelism. As with any museum, there is much more to the resources than meets the eye. Only a small percentage of the holdings can be exhibited permanently, or in the temporary galleries. Behind the scenes is a wealth of materials available for researchers and other interested persons. Especially valuable are the visual materials documenting the influential frontier phenomenon of the camp meeting. Noteworthy, also, is the Gast Collection of American religious lithographs with 785 items, over 40 percent of which are from Currier and Ives.

In the galleries, visitors to the Museum not only can trace the unfolding of American life in religious perspective, but can become acquainted with the diversities of modern evangelistic outreach as represented in the multifaceted ministry of the Billy Graham Evangelistic Association. The Center has a theater where mixed media presentations document the organization, preparation, conduct, and followup of a citywide evangelistic crusade.

Climaxing a visit to the Museum is the "walk through the gospel," where text and dramatic architecture combine to tell the "old, old story" of the Cross, the tomb, and the heavenly splendor of the resurrection. In a small chapel, visitors can meditate on the experience, and even record their own personal commitment to Christ.

Understandably, the Archives, Library, and Museum are in regular use. Among their most constant patrons are the several hundred students in the Wheaton College Graduate School, which, though a separate division of the College, is housed on the second floor of the Graham Center.

Founded in 1937, the Graduate School currently offers the Master of Arts degree through four major programs, each with its several concentrations: Communications (including Mass Media and Missions/Cross-Cultural); Educational Ministries (with special emphases in religious education curriculum studies and in Christian camping); Psychological Studies, focusing on counseling psychology; and Theological Studies (including Biblical Studies and Christian History/Theology).

All course work in the school is fully accredited by the North Central Association, and the full faculty, study resource, and cultural benefit advantages of Wheaton College are available to graduate students.

One wing of the Center building is the 474-seat Barrows Auditorium, used for academic and extracurricular activities, for Center conferences and workshops, and for various public gatherings that do not require the 2500-seat capacity of the College's main chapel/auditorium.

The other wing of the building contains a campus visitors' center, and space dedicated to development of television studios and journalism lab facilities. In the latter area, as the installation becomes operational, both instruction and production purposes will be served.

## PROGRAMS AND ACTIVITIES

The Billy Graham Center not only *serves* through the resources of its distinctive collections on evangelism and missions, but it also *functions* through an ever-enlarging variety of its own programs.

Since its first year of operation, the Center has conducted workshops for the continuing education enrichment of pastors and lay leaders in the churches. The Preaching for Commitment workshop each summer has drawn registrants from North America and overseas representing more than fifty denominations. Attention is given, of course, to the improvement of sermon preparation and delivery—not only through discussion of sound theory by leading clergymen, but also through "practice preaching" in a clinic situation where video instant replay helps the person in the pulpit to see objectively from the pew perspective.

The preaching workshop frequently includes presentations by Wheaton College faculty members outside the field of religion—such as sociology, psychology, biology, art—that help preachers to update their own knowledge and gain insights into contemporary issues and trends that may find a place in their sermonic ministry.

An Evangelism Strategy Workshop each summer focuses sharply on helping pastors and lay persons to evaluate their local community situation so as to apply and adapt suggested principles and methods in the most fruitful way. The basic premise of the evangelism workshop is that the laity must be mobilized for marketplace witness if the mission of the church in society is to advance. Pastors are not "hired hands" to do the congregation's job in evangelism. Rather, they are the motivators and managers of every-member outreach.

The evangelism workshop, therefore, encourages pastors and lay persons to attend together, not simply to share the inspiration of the experience, but to lay the groundwork mutually for an evangelism strategy appropriate to their church and community dynamics. Numerous lectures, seminars, and lab sessions are designed to promote fuller understanding of the task, more creative approaches, and larger congregational participation.

The Missions Impact Workshop, like the other two, has special concerns. It is not simply to provide "missionary education" or to generate enthusiasm for world mission. Again, the practical need for skills is emphasized, with briefing sessions on a wide variety of mission-related topics.

Even beyond that, however, the Graham Center designs a workshop in missions that will activate a whole congregation's concern and participation. It is not enough to secure a member's pledge to the missions and benevolence budget of the church. It is not enough even to enlist a member to pray for the missionaries and their work. In times like these, with the internationalizing of American society, from Manhattan to Minot, American Christians have direct daily contacts with foreign-born neighbors representing vastly divergent traditions, perspectives, and beliefs. It is no longer "missions" just to travel thousands of miles to a remote continent to evangelize a "heathen" population. It is a matter of Christian friendliness, helpfulness, and hope extended to the Muslim we shop with in the local supermarket, to the Hindu dentist who fixes our teeth, to the unregistered Hispanic worker and the displaced Cambodian refugee—all here among us!

In a word, then, the continuing education workshops at the Graham Center make every effort to be "relevant." There is only one gospel for all time and for all people: "God so loved the world that he gave his only begotten Son." But the perpetual need to *translate* that gospel—by word and deed—into terms that nonbelievers can comprehend and embrace, is the challenge today to *every* Christian, not just to the "full-time" professional worker.

In addition to such workshops, which are short-term, intensive continuing education opportunities for Christian workers, the Billy Graham Center has established certain institutes to concentrate on particular concerns pertinent to evangelism and missions.

An Institute for the Study of American Evangelicals designs programs that capitalize on the Center's historical research potential. One of the tasks of the Graham Center is to communicate to the scholarly community the close relationship between evangelistic and educational concerns. American colleges and universities have newly affirmed the need for values-centered curriculum, but often are adrift in a mistaken brand of humanism that makes ethics "situational" and morals "relative." Evangelicals need to remain firmly anchored to their biblical moorings (within the great Judeo-Christian ethical tradition) and at the same time demonstrate their intellectual respectability as corollary to their evangelistic fervor.

The ISAE at the Graham Center, by convening conferences on topics or persons that integrate faith and learning, is positioned to significantly impact the academic community with an interpretation of the gospel that links head and heart.

Another enterprise is the Institute for Chinese Studies. Graduate-level course offerings, in both English and Chinese, combine with special library resources, professional consultations, and information services, to acquaint American churches and organizations with the massive challenge of evangelizing the one quarter of the world's population that speaks Chinese. In particular, the Institute creates helpful liaisons with Chinese language churches in North America, and with hundreds of Bible study groups among Chinese students on American university campuses. It fulfills a catalytic role in bringing together policy-makers from Christian organizations who can profitably work together in accomplishing their shared goals.

In its formative stages is another institute which addresses yet another challenge to the American Christian community: the evangelizing, discipling, and reestablishing in society of hundreds of thousands of men and women in the nation's prisons. This is a whole "forgotten population" who, especially on their release, are almost forced to remain misfits or to become "repeat offenders" because various establishments, including the church, are not prepared or equipped to minister to their traumatized condition.

The Graham Center believes that there are many kinds of boundaries to cross with the gospel of Jesus Christ: geographical, linguistic, cultural, social, and emotional, among others. While it recognizes its own limitations in becoming directly involved with all needy areas, it also senses its opportunity to be a helper by alerting the people of God and by linking up good efforts by others to apply redemptive truth wherever the tragedy of human lostness from God occurs.

In keeping with the principle that it cannot assume to itself responsibility for all that needs to be done, the Billy Graham Center is dedicated to preparing church leaders worldwide to forge new instruments of ministry and mission for the Spirit of God to use. An international scholarship program annually awards hundreds of thousands of dollars for study at the Wheaton Graduate School. This makes it possible for promising young men and women from the indigenous churches overseas, and for furloughing missionaries or American students committed to mission service, to gain the academic credentials necessary for entree into key positions of leadership. They receive the academic training and professional skills here that will enhance their service at home, as they combine education at Wheaton with Graham Center impetus to evangelize their own people.

Whether it is represented by a busload of senior citizens who have come for a few inspirational hours in the Museum, or by a classroom buzzing with excited interchange between graduate students from many lands and their professor, or by a closed-door strategy-planning consultation among agency heads, or by an auditorium vibrating from the hymn-singing of a few hundred revitalized pastors and lay folk—the Billy Graham Center *is* a people place, where things happen to them that will help them to make things happen for Christ.

In the Rotunda of Witnesses at the entrance to the Center's Museum, nine seventeen-foot tapestry banners command the visitor's attention. They depict leaders in the church of Jesus Christ from nine different centuries: St. Paul the Apostle, Justin Martyr, Gregory the Great, St. Francis of Assisi, John Wycliffe, Martin Luther, Blaise Pascal, Jonathan Edwards, and Oswald Chambers.

How wide a range of differences—in time, in attitudes, in culture, and even in religious expression. But they circle that room together for one common cause: to bear witness to their personal faith in the crucified and risen Christ.

And in the center of the rotunda floor, the symbolic hub around which all the banners hang, glows a luminescent marble disc inscribed with these words:

> I am the light of the world. Whoever follows me will never walk in darkness, but will have the light of life (John 8:12).

With the saints, and martyrs, and ministers, and missionaries, and the people of God in all ages, the Billy Graham Center is in the world "to bear witness to the Light."

It knows that a dying world is desperate for Good News. It knows that there is more work to be done than any one man, or institution, can do. It knows that with God all things are possible.

Therefore, the Billy Graham Center is committed to using all that it has to do all it can do, helping sisters and brothers in the faith to do all they can do, so that together we will behold what the Lord can do.

# THE HOSPITAL CHAPLAIN'S EVANGELISM MINISTRY
## CHAPLAIN FRANK BONNIKE
## EVANGELIZING IN A HOSPITAL

MANY people have the mistaken notion that people in hospital or nursing home settings ought never to be evangelized, thinking that this is too sensitive a time to talk about one's relationship with God, Jesus Christ, and the church. While it is true, that inexperienced pastors and well-meaning fellow Christians can do more harm than good when they visit a sick person, a well-trained counselor or pastor can find such times golden opportunities to truly evangelize.

Chaplain Frank Bonnike brings a host of education and experience to this much-needed area. With graduate degrees from both Northwestern University and The Catholic University of America, he has been chaplain for a good number of years in one of America's largest and most prestigious hospitals, Lutheran General of Park Ridge, Illinois.

His experience will help you develop the evangelization skill to reach people in real need.

# EVANGELIZATION OF THE SICK

The words of Jesus, "Go teach all nations, baptizing them in the name of the Father, of the Son and of the Holy Spirit" (Matthew 28:19, 20), ring in the mind and in the heart of any committed Christian. Indeed, there have been men and women who have responded so completely to this mandate as to sacrifice their very lives. Evangelization has been called "the essential mission of the church." So, although the task, the challenge, the mission to open the door to Christ extends to all believers, how specifically does it apply to those who visit the sick? Specifically, do the words of Jesus, "I must proclaim the Good News of the kingdom of God. . . . That is what I was sent to do" (Luke 4:43, JB), apply in a hospital where Christians and non-Christians alike are primarily in search of and expect physical healing? Do they apply in a nursing home? in a private residence?

There are those who would answer very simply. They would say that such places, especially hospitals, are the *last places* where there should be evangelizing. The place and the time are too sensitive. The sick person is preoccupied with somatic concerns. He or she is too much like crystal, too easily shattered by unwise impact. Attempts at evangelization constitute taking advantage of sick people and could even upset their recovery.

There are others who would say that the sick are *among the very best* persons for evangelization. The total person, body and soul, should be healed. After all, so the argument goes, the early Christian medics very often were clergy, persons who were doctors of both the soul and the body. Proponents even cite medical-ethical codes from as late as thirteenth-century France when medics were told to first give absolution before performing surgery. So too, today if a person ever gives a thought at all to the meaning of life, to the finiteness of worldly existence, to death, to spiritual things, it is a sick-bed setting, away from the ordinary preoccupations and daily routines. I, for one, tend to agree.

I have worked full time in a hospital for ten years. When I moderate a grief group, counsel a nurse whose marriage is on the rocks, assist in the training of student chaplains, or make pre-op visits, am I proclaiming the Good News? How much of what I do is evangelical?

In 1974 the International Synod of Roman Catholic Bishops,

responding to many concerned signs from many quarters, tackled the need for all in the church to work at evangelization, at opening the door to Christ. Two of the four senses of the word which these bishops developed have special bearing for us. In one, the term means "every activity whereby the world is in any way transformed in accordance with the will of God." No one should have any difficulty seeing that almost everything done by almost any one for the sick would fit into this definition of evangelization. Every personal greeting, every gift of flowers, every IV that provides nourishment, and every physical therapy treatment can make this a healthier world. It might also prepare, and could, with due respect for man's freedom and God's undeserved grace, help solicit that first basic and responsible commitment to the gospel of Christ.

The second applicable sense of the word described evangelization as "the activity whereby the gospel is proclaimed and explained, and whereby living faith is awakened in non-Christians and fostered in Christians."

Pope Paul VI received the four definitions. He then wrote one of his own which made evangelization even more explicit and challenging. He said, "If it had to be expressed in one sentence . . . it would be to say that the church evangelizes when she seeks to convert, solely through the divine power of the message she proclaims, both the personal and the collective consciences of people, the activities in which they engage, and the lives and concrete mileaux which are theirs."

And in describing the interior change that is to take place, he spoke of "upsetting through the power of the gospel, mankind's criteria of judgment, determining values, points of interest, lines of thought, sources of inspiration and modes of life, which are in contrast with the Word of God and the plan of salvation."

Notice that word, "upsetting." What are those of us who visit the sick doing and what can we do, with the help of God's grace, to effect this inner conversion, "to upset through the power of the gospel"?

Perhaps before tackling this tough question we might go back to the question I asked myself, "What is specifically pastoral, Frank, in what you do as a hospital chaplain, hospital visitor, clinical pastoral educator, or hospital minister?" Basically, the root question is, "What is pastoral care?" In raising this more basic question, perhaps we can find answers to the more specific one as to what is evangelical in what I do, or in what any caring staff member, friend, or family member does in visiting the sick.

Pastoral care, whether performed by an ordained or non-ordained person, involves the presence and acts of one committed by faith to Jesus Christ, who attempts to help others in whatever ways seem appropriate, meaningful, and relevant to experience the reality and the love of God. In the actual fulfillment of this one role, the pastoral care person can function explicitly or implicitly. Very often these two functions overlap. Not all pastoral care, incidentally, is evangelism; but often evangelism becomes a part of pastoral care. It, too, can be explicit or implicit.

One can begin with an explicit function and end up doing the other, or vice versa. Explicit pastoral care functions such as worship, the administration of the sacraments, prayer, Scripture reading, patient visitation, and counseling that focus directly on one's relationship to God and to his Son, Jesus Christ, can also be explicit evangelization on the part of the pastoral care person. There can be in these acts that clear and decisive proclamation that God is for us—that we are acceptable and have been claimed by him through Jesus Christ. These acts can also be just words, and even counterproductive of faith.

The same can be true of implicit pastoral care acts such as general visiting, general counseling, and helping a bereaved family contact an undertaker. They could constitute evangelization in the broader sense of the word cited earlier.

Some examples of explicit and implicit pastoral care and evangelization could be illustrative. One morning I was summoned to a room to minister to a woman whose thirty-nine-year-old husband had just died of lung cancer. I was asked to pray, which could be an explicit evangelical function. The wife was crying and was embracing her dead husband, speaking to him, and kissing him. I introduced myself and commiserated with her . . . an implicitly evangelical function. I prayed the ritual prayers . . . an explicitly evangelical function. Finally, she said to me and to a female friend who was with her, "We had better get his things together and go." I watched her and deliberately let her put his things into the suitcase in order to face the reality of his death. After putting his slippers, pajamas, and toilet articles into the suitcase, she reached for an open carton of cigarettes on his nightstand. At first she placed it into his suitcase, then she looked at the carton and suddenly hurled it across the room at the bathroom door. Her friend and I were aghast. Then she turned, walked toward the bathroom door, and proceeded to kick at the scattered packs of cigarettes, screaming, "If people who smoke only knew what they do to those whom they have left behind!" She and her husband had three young sons.

I secretly wished I had a video tape recorder so that this demonstration could be shown before smokers at I.Q. clinics! Later, before she left the hospital, I sat down with her and talked about the incident and the meaning of her anger . . . how God could accept it, and how she could make the anger she had for her husband redeemable through Jesus Christ. So, what began as a specifically overt, pastoral, and evangelical function turned out to be even more explicitly evangelical as well as providing an opportunity for some implicitly pastoral functions.

Sometimes it works the other way. A Service Leaguer brought me an elderly lady who had simply walked into the hospital in an apparent daze. The Service Leaguer asked if I would help the lady get home . . . certainly an implicitly pastoral function. After identifying herself, the senior citizen began to tell me that she was so utterly confused and depressed because she had just walked in on her forty-year-old daughter and found her in bed with a divorced man. She wanted to know if God was punishing her for not letting her daughter go out more when she was younger. In helping a person work through emotional and interpersonal conflicts, one may end up dealing with faith issues. What began as implicitly pastoral, or what some would call preevangelical, can end up as explicitly pastoral and even explicitly evangelical.

After all, the Spirit of God is alive everywhere. Who are we to say that there is only one way to bring ourselves or others to Christ?

It is my conviction that evangelization, opening the door to Christ for the sick, requires three things: (1) that we know and love ourselves; (2) that we know and love the patient; and (3) that we know and love Christ.

## KNOWING AND LOVING OURSELVES

First, we must know and love ourselves . . . our gifts and our limitations. It was significant to me that nowhere in the synodal document on evangelization did the assembled prelates deal with the person of the evangelist or his or her personality. The Pope, however, definitely stressed the person of the evangelizer. He spoke both generically and specifically. In general terms he said that the evangelizer must act in union with the mission of the church and in the name of Christ; he must be formed in the Word of God; he must rely on the action of the Holy Spirit who stirs up the "new humanity of which evangelization is to be the result."

But he also said some specific things about the evangelizer which I would like to apply.

## 1. THE EVANGELIST IS TO BE EVANGELIZED.
To me this means that I must have a spirit of openness, a readiness to learn, a listening ear, a humble spirit, a recognition in myself of my need to be converted. If I see the spiritual and physical weaknesses and strengths in others, really see them, I see my own need for a Savior, a liberator. One sees the personal need for Jesus. One becomes aware of one's own struggles. Like Paul, "We see no answer to our problems" (2 Corinthians 4:8, 9, JB); and "In my inmost self I dearly love God's Law, but I can see that my body follows a different law" (Romans 7:22, 23, JB). In our ministry to others, we can see the need for our own conversion.

Intrinsic to our healing ministry is the sobering fact from Hebrews 5:2-9 which enables us to deal gently with the ignorant and wayward because we are beset with weakness, and "bound to offer sacrifice for our own sins." Thus, it is essential that we make peace with our own humanity. If we can see the tears of others and have nothing to say and can just barely "hang in there," then through our weakness God can reconcile.

What harm can be done if we are not in touch with our own gifts or lack of them, our own psychological needs, hostilities, and fears, to say nothing of knowing our motives for evangelizing!

The purpose of this self-knowledge is not merely psychological health for its own sake, but rather it is necessary in order to open the door to Christ. For example, can we trust others? Do we feel our problems are so unique that no one can help us? Have we really forgiven ourselves for our own mistakes and sins? Do we look for real help or only sympathy and support in seeing our difficulties more clearly? Are we better at giving advice than support, more given to denial than simple reassurance, more given to thinking through a patient's problem than feeling what the patient feels? Do we always appear to be in a hurry or to be too busy? Are we willing to give our time and our psychic energy?

## 2. THE EVANGELIZER MUST BE AUTHENTIC.

Every pastoral care person can testify to "horror stories" told by former churchgoers and no-longer-committed Christians about clergy, religious, and laity who simply were not authentic. Do we really believe when we tell the bereaved they will see their loved ones again because Jesus Christ has conquered death? If faith flows from our hearts, we will be effective evangelizers simply by sharing the person of Jesus with others and by sharing with them our own faith.

## 3. WE ARE TO HAVE A REVERENCE FOR REVEALED TRUTH.

We are to impart solid truths, truths anchored in the Word of God and presented in such a way as to make one's commitment of faith ever more loving, conscious, and active. Good catechesis is required in the hospital, as it is elsewhere, if evangelization is to be the result.

The rituals serve as a good example. Some hospital chaplains fail in their use of ritual and waste opportunities for evangelism by making them sound like an intellectual exercise, a Bible class on Job, or a theology class on the anointing of the sick. Although such an approach informs, it does not seriously prepare for or call forth or deepen a commitment of faith. What really counts is the evangelizing dimension of religious instruction. Evangelization and catechesis have to accompany and complement each other.

## 4. THE EVANGELIZER IS TO HAVE
## A ZEALOUS FERVOR IN PROCLAIMING THE MESSAGE.

The message *is not* to be *imposed;* it *is* to be *exposed.* We are not to proselytize in the perjorative sense. The code of ethics of the College of Chaplains states, "Witness can always be given but coercion is irresponsible." However, the message is to be opportunely and appropriately exposed. The respectful presentation of Christ and his Kingdom is more than the evangelizer's right, it is his duty; and it is the *patient's* right to receive it. We may know the patient, even interiorly; but his hidden yearnings for truth, love, and faith will remain untouched without our invitation and challenge. So, in seeking to know ourselves in order to open the door to Christ for others, we have to see if we have through negligence or fear or shame, as St. Paul put it, "blushed for the Gospel" (Romans 1:16), and thus failed to proclaim the message.

## KNOWING AND LOVING THE PATIENT

The second requirement for an evangelizing pastoral care person is a knowledge of the patient. This means to be more in his or her body and heart and mind and feelings than in our own. The evangelizer is to have the love of a father or a mother, of a brother or a sister, for the sick person.

More specifically, this love *demands* that we have respect for the physical, the religious, and the spiritual situation of those being evangelized, respect for their tempo and pace. We must respect their conscience and convictions. Evangelization is a delicate matter. It will lose much of its force and effectiveness if it does not take into consideration the actual people to whom it is addressed, and if it does not answer the questions they ask and have an impact on their life.

So, for us, this means to accept people where they are, to respect non-Christians and Christians, believers and non-believers, skeptics and born-agains, homosexuals and heterosexuals, the angry and the resigned, alike. It is understood that we accept everyone as made in God's image, not necessarily accepting their beliefs.

Dietrich Bonhoffer put it this way: "The first service one owes to others . . . consists in listening. He who can no longer listen to his brother will soon be no longer listening to God either."

So, what I would like to do is to make some general observations about knowing patients.

A general factor of importance would be to make some type of spiritual assessment of the sick person visited. This would be most helpful with longer-term patients. Such an inquiry would seek to assess the patient's relationship to God, to self, to a community of faith, to others, and to specific life events in terms of their spiritual significance and human values. Is the one I visit:

(a) in need of being prepared indirectly or implicitly for a first commitment of faith; (b) in need of being solicited for that commitment; (c) ready to be solicited for that commitment; or (d) a committed believer whose faith simply needs consolidation or deepening?

One can never remain satisfied with a first-time commitment of faith, no matter how sincere or deep. It needs conscious renewal and deepening, as you and I can testify. We should provide the message to everyone as if it is news, the Good News. Faith, even that of a devout Christian, often fluctuates in a time of illness. Where there are questions of doubt and/or guilt one must move very carefully, and only after one has really allowed the patient to articulate and release this doubt and/or guilt.

Another general guideline is to realize we are going to try to do something *with* the patient. We are going to empathize. My view of evangelization is *not* to do something *for* the patient: e.g., read the Scriptures; *nor* is it to do something *to* the patient: e.g., give answers.

Having said all this and presuming that a relationship beyond bridge-party chatter already exists with a patient, and that we have dissipated our mutual anxiety about each other; and furthermore, presuming at least one of us realizes that being together itself is a valuable and healing force and also somewhat of a religious phenomenon, what next? We have shared as humans, we have been present to each other; we have shared some feelings and are now ready to move on to some deeper sharing, some theological reflection. What can we who are ministers to the sick say that might elicit a discussion on explicitly religious or spiritual matters?

I would like to share some one-liners that I have used:

1. For a presurgical patient or his family . . . "I am sure you have prayed about this."
2. For any patient . . . "Lying here probably makes you think about life and its meaning" or "Where do you see God fitting into your illness and your stay here?"
3. For orthopedic patients . . . "Are you having any words with God about all this pain you are having?" or "I am sure this experience has tested your faith."
4. For believers . . . "Does being a believer help you in this

situation? Have you had any sense of God's presence or thoughts about God in this experience?"

5. For students . . . "Right now I am interested in spirituality. If you don't mind, I would like to ask you what spirituality means to you."

6. For an alcoholic patient . . . "Have you ever heard of the fifth step?"

7. For a cardiac patient . . . "Realizing what has happened, it probably is very hard to sort out values as you lie here."

8. For a new mother . . . "Do you ever wonder what God has planned for this little child?"

9. For a soon-to-be-discharged patient . . . "What will you remember spiritually about your stay here?"

10. For a patient experiencing difficulty in reconciling God with his suffering . . . "As I hear your situation, I find myself thinking about how hard and yet how important it is for me to believe" . . . or "We are both having some problems as to where God is at work in your situation."

11. For a depressed, lonely patient . . . "Maybe Jesus wants to fill that empty space."

When a patient says in response to my one-liner, "It really is snowing out there," I know I have struck out! Knowing and loving the patient also involves knowing and accepting the fact that some patients don't want us.

Patients are all individuals. We cannot stress this enough. To know one patient is not to know another with the very same illness. The words or non-words we use with patients are symbols. What they symbolize will be determined not only by us or by the message, but even more by the experiences, the associations, and the present perceptions of the patient. The message we send is not always the message received. Each patient then is a human document, a living person, involved in a lifelong process.

My experience also suggests that there often are certain spiritual issues the sick must deal with. They may or may not be part of the personal experience of the person you visit. These issues are: anger (with self, with God, at seeing others do what they cannot physically do); control (not trusting others or God);

perfectionism; depression; guilt (connecting illness with sin and God's punishment); denial; the "failure" of God to intercede; the mystery of suffering and death; hopelessness; inability to accept limits; priorities in terms of affection, allocation of time and financial resources; sexual needs; feelings of loneliness, of uselessness; loss of privacy, security, self-esteem; the need for a life's review; the need for integration, for meaning, for "getting one's act together."

It is important to come to know the needs, psychodynamics, and motivation of patients to effectively minister to them. We may miss on all counts. That is a human limitation we face. Also, the patient may not be ready to move to any spiritual depth. That is a limitation in any pastoral or spiritual relationship. Finally, we can never fully evaluate the meaning or impact of any visit. If we believe in God's Spirit, we must believe that that same Spirit works through us, in spite of us, and without us. There comes a time when we must "let go" and "let God" do the work within the sick person.

## KNOWING AND LOVING JESUS CHRIST

Lastly, true evangelization requires that we know and love Jesus . . . to know his humanity, his suffering, his loneliness and anxiety, as well as his power and divinity. Without knowing and loving Christ, our ministry may be effective humanism—of value, but not spiritual care.

How then can we share that knowledge and love of Christ? There are means by which Christ has chosen to reveal himself:

1. THE BIBLE
Successful evangelization requires more than reading or even meditating on the sacred Scriptures with patients. It is necessary to know a little of the medical, psychological, and social conditions in which the Word of God is to be presented in the hospital if it is to appear truly as Good News. Even an introduction as homely as this would help: "Everyone else here is probably going to bring you a pill or give you a test. Even the language they use will probably be strange. But I am here to bring you something simple, something familiar, something which I enjoy and helps me, something which I think you will

enjoy and perhaps can help you. Would you like to have me read to you about Jesus?"

## 2. PRAYER

As a prelude to prayer, as implicit evangelization, a very clear point of reference and contact in visiting patients is to engage them in conversations about their family. Praying with the patient is so much easier and more meaningful when one has a source of reference such as the family to refer to in prayer. We can also ask the patient what he or she would like to have us pray for or about. If we pray well, we can teach others the art of personal prayer; but we can also evangelize through our prayers. For example: "Janet, let us recommit ourselves to the Lord Jesus who suffered much more than we will ever suffer, yet believed and trusted unfailingly in his Father." We could also pray with the patient that faith in Jesus might be spread in the hospital.

## 3. HEALING

The laying on of hands or the proper touch at the proper time is such a powerful sign of God's healing. Patients wish to be healed. We can help patients realize that both religious and medical language speak of being healed as the moment between two different states, the one evil and other good. Isaiah encountered God, was touched by the Spirit and healed. He was then able to proclaim healing for others: "The Spirit of the Lord God is upon me . . . to bind up the brokenhearted" (Isaiah 61:1). We can help patients view their healing as a moment of grace in which God, acting freely and out of his love covenant, has through other persons brought them back into the right relationship with him as Lord, as Parent, and as Friend. We succeed with our evangelizing in the very measure as Christ means ever more in the patient's life, in the very measure that faith in him becomes more mature and authentic. Even though it is not difficult to find passages in the Gospels in which Jesus himself says to someone, "Thy faith hath made thee whole" (Matthew 9:22) or "Thy faith hath saved thee" (Luke 7:50), it was not and is not faith that heals or saves. It is Jesus Christ who heals. The healed in the New Testament had faith in the power of Jesus to heal. It is always he who does the healing, not faith.

## 4. THE EUCHARIST

The two fundamental aspects of faith are its content and its commitment. The central idea of Christian revelation is that God's saving love for us is manifested in the paschal mystery of his Son, that he suffered and died but is here for us to know, to love, and to communicate with in the Eucharist. True faith in one's identity with the Man of Sorrows can afford a solace without illusion and can truly put one's troubled heart to rest. Something like this could be said to patients: "Christ said he would be with us always. Here he is. He suffered as you are suffering. His body which suffered will now touch yours. Listen to him. Speak with him. He loves you."

It is in the Eucharist that the patient can find renewed hope and courage through faith in Jesus, who conquered sin, suffering, and even death. So close is the tie between Christ and those who suffer that the weak and suffering who choose to unite themselves with Christ and his suffering have been referred to as the "aristocracy of the Kingdom of God."

For any who feel they are no longer capable of significant relationships, communion with Jesus can put them into the most significant relationship of their life.

At the same time, we recognize that Holy Communion can be received with little or no commitment of faith. This is why preference must always be given to evangelizing catechesis and not ritualistic sacramentalism. The former is hard work, but authentic evangelism will lead to the true appreciation, reception, and realization of the sacrament. Otherwise, the patient will return home and see no more purpose or value in the reception of the sacrament than before hospitalization.

It is my hope and my prayer that this modest effort at depicting the possibilities for evangelization of the sick will help each of us open the door to Christ for others and for ourselves.

# THE PRISON CHAPLAIN'S EVANGELISM MINISTRY
## PRISON FELLOWSHIP
## CHARLES COLSON
## CHRISTIANS BELONG IN JAIL

"TOUGH GUY COLSON HAS TURNED RELIGIOUS." The headlines were openly mocking. And why not; wasn't Charles Colson the Watergate hatchet man who represented President Nixon in one of the nastiest scandals ever to hit Washington? Yes, he was known as the White House hatchet man, the dirty tricks specialist, the man who had supposedly vowed to walk over his grandmother to get the President reelected.

Who could blame people for laughing when Charles Colson spoke of a newfound faith in Jesus Christ? It had to be a gimmick. But ten years later, with the bitterness of Watergate fading in the memory, Charles Colson was proving the skeptics wrong. His conversion has not only stood the test of time, but it has borne fruit in a remarkable ministry to some of the most desperate and forsaken people in our society—the 400,000 men and women in American prisons.

Chuck Colson's one-man project to reach his fellow inmates in prison has grown to incorporate over 12,000 volunteers who each day march into our nation's prisons to bring the gospel message, to teach new Christians, and to provide support to those men and women who wish to change their lives. It has been heralded as one of the most dynamic, fastest growing movements to reform both prisoners and prisons yet to be seen.

## NO EASY MINISTRY

"Prison is a hard place to minister," Chuck Colson says. "It is a spiritual battlefield. When a group of Christians enter a prison to minister to the inmates, you can almost feel the spiritual warfare going on. Prisons have been such an exclusive territory for the devil for so long, you can feel the sapping effect it has on the people who both work and live there."

Chuck says, "It's the front lines—a tough place to be."

Like most Americans, including most government officials, Chuck Colson had never seen the inside of a prison. He was shocked at what he found there—not just the violence and bad conditions, but the wasted lives. "What was most painful for me was to see the human degradation that takes place in prison," he says. "The people there have nothing to live for and no place to go and nothing to care about. If you spend any time inside, it becomes very obvious that no one is being rehabilitated. Psychologically and spiritually, and in every other way, the people are headed down."

While in prison, Colson saw one ray of hope: the fellowship Christians had with other Christians. As they encouraged one another, prayed together, and simply expressed their brotherhood and support, he was able to see the change in their lives. While in prison, Colson vowed somehow to help other prisoners once he was outside again. "I really didn't plan to organize Prison Fellowship when I got out—and I had no idea the troubles I would have when I decided to do something. If I had, I doubt if I would have had courage to begin."

Among the problems that Colson did not see was the recent explosive growth in the prison population. The number of prisoners doubled between 1970 and 1982; at the present rate of growth it will double again by 1988. The prisons throughout our nation are packed. The tensions are explosive. Murder, beatings, homosexual rape, and stabbings are all part of the daily routine.

Citizens outside merely say "good." After all, criminals are in prison to be punished, not to enjoy themselves.

Colson agrees that crime is serious business, and he believes people who break the law should be punished. But he does not think that what happens to prisoners in our current system helps anyone.

"To begin with," he says, "it's a real misconception to think prisons are filled with murderers and rapists. Nearly 50 percent of people in prisons are there for nonviolent crimes—things such as business fraud, forgery, and theft—in which no weapons were used and no bodily harm was done." He recalls the guy in the bunk next to him who was doing three years for $3,000 income-tax evasion. Another fellow had cashed a bad check for eighty-four dollars. And then there was one guy who had murdered twenty-eight people.

"We throw all these people together into the prisons and forget about them. We say 'good enough for them' if they get beaten and raped and shoved around and their families break up. 'Good enough for them, they're being punished.' We forget that when they get out of prison they're going to be back on the streets. The behavior they've learned in prison and the scars from that kind of encounter stay with them."

The results?

"Seventy-four percent of the people who get out of prison are arrested within four years, according to the F.B.I. Eighty percent of the crimes are committed by people who have been in prison before. Our prisons are not working. They have really become the training grounds for the breakdown of order in our society."

## A CHRISTIAN ATTITUDE TOWARD PRISONERS

Colson adds that Christians should be among the last to clamor for other people's punishment. "We all deserve to be punished," he points out. "Our faith tells us that we are sinners, we need to be forgiven. Christ marched up the hill of Golgotha to hang on the cross as much for the guy in prison as for anyone in any church anywhere. Most people get self-righteous when they start thinking about prisons, but if you really understand the nature of sin there are no grounds for the Christian to feel self-righteous."

Colson points out that, as Christians, we have a duty to perform, a direct command from the Bible. Hebrews 13:3 says, "Remember the prisoners as if chained with them." There is no way that any Christian who reads the Bible can avoid being convicted about his duty to care for people in need, including prisoners. So, according to Colson, Christians must not have a harsh attitude toward prisoners, even though the rest of the nation has that attitude. Indeed, Colson says, "Our job is to challenge that attitude." He believes that the only single force to change the prison situation is the Christian. We alone hold the solution to the current crisis. "Something has to change within a prisoner's heart to make him want to change," he says. "You can give people education in prison, you can give them vocational training, you can give them all sorts of things. And when you release them from prison, basically what you have are educated criminals. What's needed is a change in their heart if you want the criminal to change. The only thing I know that will do that is Jesus Christ."

## HERE'S WHERE THE CHURCH COMES IN

Colson emphasizes, however, that for a change of heart really to take hold, the newly converted prisoner needs many other types of support. "Someone can have a genuine conversion experience in prison, but if we toss him out on the streets with nothing but twenty-five dollars and a bus ticket—no job, no money, no church to involve him in Christian life—he's going to be back in trouble. That doesn't reflect on the sincerity of the conversion; it reflects on the church that didn't offer him a helping hand. If you are dealing with the individual's total needs—his spiritual hunger and his physical hunger—you simply are not going to be able to cope with his criminal conduct."

The Prison Fellowship is trying to establish a network of Christians across the country who really care about these people, not only about their spiritual needs but their human needs as well.

The term "network" describes well how Prison Fellowship works. Although a staff of nearly 100 work at the office in Washington, their primary job is to assist the 12,000 volunteers who carry out the real ministry. These volunteers represent all denominations and walks of life: they include Catholic nuns, Baptist pastors, doctors, truck drivers, police officers, and even one ninety-seven-year-old widow. They evangelize in the prisons, write letters to prison pen pals, lead Bible studies, help newly released prisoners find jobs and homes, provide help for prisoners' families, or simply pray for the ministry.

## HOW YOUR CHURCH CAN PARTICIPATE

Through the leadership of Prison Fellowship, volunteers are organized into Community Care Committees. The committees pool the resources of volunteers, churches, and local agencies to serve prisoners in their area. They send people into the prisons to lead special seminars, worship services, and Bible studies. Prisoners may even be allowed to attend special programs held outside the prisons. The purpose of the seminars is to train the prisoners to minister to their fellow inmates. There is a program of volunteer/inmate matchups so that the volunteer can reach an individual in a special way. Care committees are also organized, and in 1983 more than 2,000 families were assisted. They were able to help the offenders coming out of prison find jobs and a new home.

Preparation is all important. It isn't just a matter of coming into a prison to sing a few hymns and preach a sermon or two. What's needed is specialized training. This is where Prison Fellowship comes in. The organization has put together a guidebook for those who wish to help. The basic handbook is called *Prison People*, and can be obtained from the Washington offices.

Evangelization behind the walls of our nation's prisons has begun in a very special way. In 1977 there were a total of 103 volunteer workers, and in 1982 there were 12,334. Again in 1977 some 674 inmates received specialized training; but by 1982 that number had increased to 25,179. The volunteer matchup program with inmates in 1977 involved some 175 people; but by 1982 the number had reached 8,109. The budget alone has reached over 4 million dollars.

When asked how churches can help, Colson said, "Local church involvement can be as varied as the churches themselves. In Columbia, South Carolina, three members of the Forest Drive

Baptist Church serve on our Care Committee. But that's just the beginning. Three of their four pastors minister regularly in the nearby prison. Other church members grade Bible school lessons completed by inmates; some lead or attend Bible studies in prison."

One member is in prison as many as six days a week. He arranged for one pastor to teach a twelve-week Christian doctrine course for inmates, and has organized softball games between inmate and church teams. Several church families have "adopted" inmates, and one family shares their home with a recently released ex-offender.

In Fort Wayne, volunteers from the Waynedale United Methodist Church collect clothing for inmates on work-release programs. The inmates participate in Sunday worship and fellowship groups.

The youth choir at Kendall Presbyterian Church in Miami goes into prison to sing for inmates and to take part in their worship service.

Often local congregations are first exposed to Prison Fellowship when it sponsors a seminar in their community. Once they meet Christian inmates and learn to care about them as brothers and sisters in Christ, their concern and commitment lead them into further ministry involvement.

## HOW WILL ALL THIS INVOLVEMENT MAKE A DIFFERENCE?

It proves that someone really cares. It is faith in action. It is, for the prisoner, a friend on the outside. One such church involvement led to the start of the Agape House in Jefferson City, Missouri. Without a penny to begin with, a group of concerned Christians opened a house in which the families of inmates could be housed overnight. With four prisons in the community, and over 4,000 inmates, their families were unable to visit because they could not find housing. Sister Ruth Heaney, a Roman Catholic nun, and Janice Webb, a Southern Baptist laywoman, organized a home to offer hospitality to these inmates' families. They were able to raise $46,000 to purchase and furnish an old rooming house, and to date they have welcomed nearly 7,000 people into their Agape House. At a recent White House luncheon, President Reagan commended Agape House as a prime example of community volunteer work. When asked why they serve in this ministry, the volunteers said, "We want to show God's unconditional love to the prisoners and to their families. It's a love expressed in action. But more important, it's the spirit we are called to demonstrate to the 'least of these,' as members of the family of God."

## A PROGRAM FOR BOTH CATHOLICS AND PROTESTANTS

Prison Fellowship has no denominational ties. Catholic priests and nuns work alongside of and together with Baptist and Methodist pastors, and all those interested in evangelizing in prisons. Father John Scott, chaplain at Indiana's state prison, has a well-developed Prison Fellowship program with over 120 inmates attending each session and attending the six weekly Masses he holds. He has been able to get prisoners to write people, and Christians to write back as pen pals. To get involved in such a ministry simply takes a telephone call to your local prison chaplain's office. Father Scott said, "Inmates gladly welcome visits or letters from people they don't know. It's especially important to have a Christian contact when they are trying to live a Christian life here on the inside."

At the Jefferson County Jail in Steubenville, Ohio, students from the university, under the direction of Father Dennis Gang, visit male and female inmates every Thursday evening. "It is explicit evangelism," Father Gang said, "and the students are able to reach prisoners that professional clergymen usually can't get to. The prisoners know the students don't have to come to the jail. They know it's a free decision, and so they are open to talking."

Father Gang said the students meet for fifteen minutes of prayer before going into the jail. Then they share what Jesus means to them with the prisoners and explain how they too can enjoy a personal relationship with Christ the Lord.

"It is exciting to see what God can do with a college student and a prisoner," Father Gang said. "The Lord really anoints these students, and the results are often amazing."

One of the most remarkable stories coming out of Prison Fellowship is the American nun, Sister Antonia, who not only works in the prison, but lives there as well. The prison is La Mesa Penitentiary located in Tijuana, Mexico. There are over 2,000 inmates. She entered the religious life late, after raising seven children, and now she serves the convicted murderers and drug smugglers who call her "Mama." In the four years that Sister Antonia has served the prisoners of La Mesa, things have changed. She has found ways to bring dignity and the love of Jesus to people who have otherwise been abandoned. It is one of the most fantastic Christian ministries one can imagine. And it is a ministry that we can all share in.

## HOW YOU CAN GET INVOLVED

Prison Fellowship is a ministry for every church, both the young and the old. If your church desires to participate, all you need to do is to write to:

Charles Colson, President
Prison Fellowship
Post Office Box 40562
Washington, DC 20016

and ask for a copy of the annual report. It will outline the work of the ministry and how you can participate. Start up a volunteer organization and have one of the Prison Fellowship people get you started. The possibilities are endless. The need is urgent.

Don't be afraid to get started; there are manuals available, people to guide and help you, and seminars held to instruct you and your church on how to evangelize in a prison setting.

Write today: there are thousands waiting for your help.

# GARDEN GROVE MINISTRIES
# THE REV. BILL STEVENS
# PRISONERS FIND HOPE

## EVANGELIZING BEHIND THOSE PRISON WALLS

There is no place in all the world that possibility thinking can have more of an impact than behind those prison walls. The Rev. Bill Stevens is director of the Garden Grove Community Church's Prison Outreach Program. For the past several years he's been helping inmates discover God's possibilities for their lives.

It all began when Stevens visited a battered woman in the hospital. He was asked by the woman to go visit her husband who was responsible for her condition. He was in prison serving time for the beating. Before Stevens left the prison that day, the chaplain told him, "Your church ought to get involved here. Your people could do so much good for these prisoners."

About a year later, the church began a prison ministry and Stevens began visiting the prisoners, forming friendships with the inmates and the chaplains. Now he takes volunteers with him three times a week and leads several Bible studies with the inmates. But the biggest event of the year is at Christmas.

In 1979, the year the church began the ministry, Pastor Stevens took along 450 Christmas packages made by church members to the prison inmates. The packages seemed so meager that he was almost embarrassed to take them in. But the response was so great that it began a yearly ministry that continues to grow. To the men and women who received them, the gifts were luxuries; the inmates really felt loved!

The following Christmas Stevens told the congregation, "I want 6,000 dozen cookies!" "Bill, don't you mean 6,000 cookies?" But he meant what he said. That year they delivered 6,000 packages, each including one dozen cookies. And each year the number increases.

This year, decorating Christmas packages began in mid-October for about 1,000 parish families who have joined Stevens in his outreach program. They hope to deliver more than 10,000 care packages to five state prisons in Chino, California.

The love expressed in each of these gifts has changed lives. One woman, Cherie Seilhan, received the support and hope she needed to wait for her release. She recently married Joe Ayla, another ex-convict. They've both met Jesus Christ and are doing well. Joe also had received a package while in prison. When the prisoners were released, Stevens' staff of volunteers supplied them with clothing and furniture and assisted them in finding jobs and homes. Other staff members provided them with the regular counseling.

On February 11, 1984, a seminar on prison ministry was conducted at the Crystal Cathedral. Stevens said, "We hope we have begun to draw people from within and from without the prison walls—church members, chaplains, and correctional officers—in order to build awareness of the need for prison ministry. Volunteers need to know how to help. And we need to support the prison chaplain, because state institutions often don't realize his vital role."

Here is a ministry of evangelization every church can enter into. Along with the cookies, Bibles and other religious reading can be sent. Members can learn how to send cheerful cards and letters to encourage the inmates that they are loved and prayed for.

If you are interested in such a ministry, why not contact the Rev. Bill Stevens at Crystal Cathedral Prison Ministry, 4201 West Chapman, Orange, CA 92668; or, better yet, why not send for a free folder describing next year's Prison Ministry Seminar.

# THE BILLY GRAHAM EVANGELISTIC ASSOCIATION
## DR. STERLING W. HUSTON, EXECUTIVE DIRECTOR
## ORGANIZING A BILLY GRAHAM CRUSADE

*CHAPTER*

# 27

## CITYWIDE EVANGELISM

Billy Graham has preached face to face to over 100 million people in almost every country on the globe. At his invitation to come to Christ, more than one million have responded as inquirers seeking spiritual help. Although Billy Graham's methods of sharing the Good News have varied from one-on-one personal witnessing, to addressing 1,120,000 persons in one service at Seoul, Korea, he is best known for his citywide Crusades which are often tele-recorded and rebroadcast across North America and in many parts of the world. To best understand his method, one must look at citywide Crusade evangelism in perspective.

## PERSPECTIVE

Evangelizing through citywide Crusades is a mission whose scope encompasses an entire city or metropolitan area and employs a variety of methods based on biblical principles. The term "mass evangelism" is a misnomer. People can't come to Christ "en masse"; each person responds individually. And, in fact, Crusade evangelism is based on personal evangelism. Crusade evangelism is not different in kind from other methods, but merely different in degree. Scores and even hundreds of faith communities across an entire city or metropolitan area cooperate to do the work of witness and proclamation of the gospel for their city.

## PURPOSE

A mandate for evangelism was given by Jesus Christ when he said, "Therefore go and make disciples of all nations, baptizing them in the name of the Father and of the Son and of the Holy Spirit, and teaching them to obey everything I have commanded you. And surely I will be with you always, to the very end of the age" (Matthew 28:19, 20, NIV). Jesus spoke the Good News to individuals, to small groups, in synagogues, and to the masses. Citywide evangelism is merely one way of fulfilling this mandate, and its goal should go beyond "decisions" to the making of "disciples." Two objectives necessary to reach this goal are:

1. *To evangelize the community.* The primary objective is to proclaim the gospel of Jesus Christ and the power of the Holy Spirit, to invite men and women to commit their lives to Christ, and to refer those who respond to a local faith community for continuing nurture and discipleship. Citywide evangelism involves many methods, including person-to-person, small-group, literature, radio, television, youth, music, and visitation evangelism. Evangelism begins before the public meetings are held and continues long afterward. Billy Graham has emphasized that personal evangelism is the most effective form and that a large evangelistic meeting is effective only when substantial personal evangelism has taken place in advance.

2. *To strengthen the church for continuing witness and discipleship.* Archbishop William Temple said, "The evangelization of those without cannot be separated from the rekindling of devotion of those within." Equipping the church through training, prayer, and emphasis on witness results in a motivated and renewed congregation which

not only serves to reach the goals of citywide evangelism, but remains following a Crusade to serve the church under the leadership of local clergy. Following one Crusade a clergyman wrote that from the time his church first began to prepare for the meetings, to the followup afterward, their stewardship had increased by 300 percent, their attendance by 150 percent, and the number of first-time commitments to Christ by 100 percent.

## PREREQUISITES

Three prerequisites determine (help assess) whether or not a city is prepared for multiple-church cooperative evangelism:

1. Concerned praying people, who are burdened for lost mankind, must pray and depend on the power of the Holy Spirit to reach them.
2. Adequate numbers must be represented in the involved churches to make this method work. Citywide evangelism, because of its sheer size and visibility, requires greater numbers than other methods of evangelism.
3. Suitable facilities of the right size should be available at the right time to extend the outreach to that particular community.

## PRINCIPLES

Effective citywide evangelism is not built around a public personality, but rather upon biblical principles. These principles can be adapted to larger or smaller meetings and apply whether you are dealing with a well-known evangelist or relatively unknown proclaimer.

1. *Evangelism is the work of the Holy Spirit.* Thus the primary dependence for everything that is done in preparation must be on the work of the Spirit. In light of this, prayer is the most critical element in evangelism. The amount of prayer will determine the amount of blessing.

2. *Reaping requires sowing.* St. Paul pointed out that one person sows, another waters, but God brings the increase. To reap well, there must be adequate sowing of witness and watering through love and prayer. The gift of an evangelist can be exercised effectively only when others in the church have been sowing and watering.

3. *Evangelism is built on relationships.* "Mass evangelism" actually is personal evangelism in an aggregate setting. Only as you have individuals sowing and watering in the lives of others can you expect to see results in a Crusade. Research has shown that at least 80 percent of the unchurched who respond for counseling in Billy Graham Crusades have been brought personally by someone else. In light of this, Christians need to be challenged to set specific goals to pray for others and to bring them to the meetings.

4. *Involvement produces commitment.* Although the spiritual key to successful evangelism is prayer, the human key is involvement. This determines participation and commitment. When a man or woman agrees to a place of service in a Crusade, it involves his/her family, friends, and neighbors. It determines his/her priorities and focuses his/her prayers on the coming events. In citywide evangelism we seek to involve as many people as possible in every form of meaningful activity to capitalize on this principle of commitment. This requires extensive organization, recruitment, and communications. Churches who involve their people report the greatest blessing. The bigger the circle of involvement the greater the surrounding circle of people who are touched and influenced to attend the Crusade.

5. *Integrity is essential.* Integrity needs to be exercised in the policies of a citywide Crusade in organizational responsibility, finances, and followup. Integrity also must be exercised regarding promises that are made about the results of a Crusade, in the procedures (which should be church-centered), and in the preaching (which should be biblical and Christ-centered).

Three factors are important in obtaining maximum participation in citywide evangelism:

1. *Involve others from the beginning.* When exploring the prospects of a citywide Crusade, it is important that as many people as possible with a concern for evangelism be involved with the initial plans. Making plans with a small group and then inviting others to join the program after it is set will have a negative effect on the scope of participation. The question of which churches participate can best be settled by letting them decide this for themselves. If you make clear the message, the methods, the materials, and the men and women who will be utilized in the Crusade, churches can then decide whether this is a program they want to support.

2. *Committee organization.* It is recommended that a broadly based committee be formed. Its members should

## ORGANIZATION OF A CONGREGATIONAL COMMITTEE

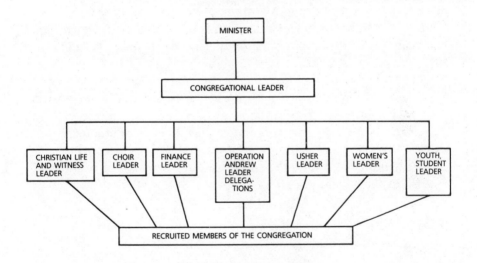

meet certain basic criteria such as commitment to Christ, concern for evangelism, representation of historic denominations, and significant peer-group influence. This committee is responsible for guiding all aspects of the Crusade. Usually, the evangelist's staff members function in an advisory relationship with the local committee.

3. *Involve the local church.* Local churches need to view the Crusade as though they are responsible for it. They are requested to form their own congregational committee within the church to work with the citywide Crusade committee. This congregational committee will assist the pastor in ensuring maximum participation and involvement at the local level.

## PRODUCT

Although more than one million persons have responded publicly as spiritual inquirers under Billy Graham's ministry, and hundreds of thousands through the ministry of his associate evangelists, questions still arise about the benefits of citywide evangelism and the enduring results. As part of a doctoral dissertation, pastors in the Memphis area were surveyed following a Billy Graham Crusade in that city. They listed in the following order the benefits they experienced from a Crusade.

1. *Preparatory training.* Pastors indicated that their people were better trained and motivated to serve in evangelism and in leadership in the local church following the Crusade. Some pastors noted that they were able to involve church members in the citywide project who would not attend the same training program if conducted in their local parish.

2. *Unity of Christians.* The united witness of churches coming together had an effective impact on the unchurched in the local community. Christians experienced a new unity of the body of Christ across denominational lines.

3. *Emphasis on evangelism.* The emphasis on evangelism gives a new motivation to personal evangelism, especially

as a result of the witness training classes. It also encourages churches to actively engage in programs of outreach. In addition, it is a reminder to the unchurched and the lapsed church member of his or her need for a commitment or a recommitment to Christ and his church. A minister in Milwaukee told of six people who started attending his church several weeks following the Crusade meetings. Although they had not attended the Crusade services, they were conscience-stricken about their spiritual needs because of all the publicity.

4. *Spiritual renewal.* Ministers have often commented that a renewed and rededicated laity was a direct result of their involvement in a Crusade. A survey of one Crusade by a Vanderbilt sociologist indicated that three out of four lay leaders felt the Crusade was an effective spiritual renewal effort for the local church. Also, six out of ten saw it as helping the local congregations prepare for the discipling of new Christians.

5. *New additions.* A Crusade in Cincinnati in the fall of 1977 recorded 160,572 in attendance with 7,075 inquirers. A post-Crusade telephone survey of these inquirers was conducted five weeks after the effort. In response to the question: "Are you attending church regularly?" 83 percent answered "yes" and 17 percent answered "no." Of those answering "no" to the question, 47 percent indicated a desire and plan to attend more regularly and 42 percent requested and were given help in their church relationship. The Cincinnati statistics indicate that a very high percentage of the inquirers were attending a church, and half of the remainder wanted to be related to a local church.

## POTENTIAL

Jesus' mandate to "make disciples of all nations" was to his church. In a world that is growing daily in numbers, the church needs to grow in order to fulfill this commission. Jesus never gave a command that could not be fulfilled with the power of the Holy Spirit. Among the gifts given to the church is the gift of an evangelist, which is intended to be used not only to proclaim the Good News but to call people to faith in Christ. That gift can be applied to one-on-one, in small groups, in local parishes, and across an entire city. Whenever it is applied, it should be done in light of biblical principles which are necessary for effective evangelism. During more than thirty years of Crusade activity, Billy Graham and his team have sought to apply these principles and use them to strengthen the church of Jesus Christ by going "everywhere preaching the gospel." For all that God has been pleased to do through this ministry in its limited scope and duration, we give him all praise and glory.

Note: This chapter is excerpted largely from the book, *The Billy Graham Crusade Handbook* by Dr. Sterling W. Huston, published by World Wide Publications, 1303 Hennepin Avenue, Minneapolis, MN 55403.

# THE NATIONAL CATHOLIC EVANGELIZATION ASSOCIATION
## WASHINGTON, D.C.
## FATHER ALVIN ILLIG, EXECUTIVE DIRECTOR
## REACHING AMERICA'S UNCHURCHED MILLIONS

CHAPTER

28

RENEWAL and evangelization are intimately associated one with the other.

Evangelization without renewal can be hypocrisy. Renewal without evangelization can be disobedience to the Lord.

When Pope John XXIII announced his renewal council on the feast of the conversion of St. Paul, January 25, 1959, he laid out four great objectives or challenges for the council: identity, renewal, ecumenism, and evangelization.

The fourth objective, evangelization or mission, was to give purpose and meaning to the struggles involved in achieving the first three objectives. By working our way through the agony and the ecstasy of identity, renewal, and ecumenism, the Pope said that we would be putting our house in order so we could reach out with new vigor and enthusiasm to the whole world with the good news of salvation in Jesus Christ.

The turmoil that followed the end of Vatican II in 1965 was so great, however, that for nine long years Pope Paul VI, who had made his own the four objectives of Pope John, knew that little could be done in terms of a new Catholic awareness of evangelization or mission.

Then, in 1974, despite a worldwide lack of enthusiasm for the theme, Pope Paul held a synod on evangelization. Two hundred bishops came to Rome from around the world, many of whom were from mission countries. Pope Paul felt that the time had come for the Catholic world to "discover" the fourth great objective that Pope John had envisioned and that Pope Paul saw beginning to emerge from the renewal which had then been underway for the better part of fifteen years.

On December 8, 1975, fourteen months after the synod and ten years to the day from the closing of the Second Vatican Council, Pope Paul issued his apostolic exhortation, *Evangelii Nuntiandi (Evangelization in the Modern World)*, boldly declaring, "The gospel must be proclaimed!"

*Evangelii Nuntiandi* is the Magna Carta for Catholic evangelization in the modern world, the ground rules that guide the thinking, the planning, and the programming for Catholic evangelizers for the rest of this century. Steeped in Scripture, it is a ringing 23,000-word affirmation of our 2,000-year-old heritage as an evangelizing people, a clear call for the Catholic community today to imitate Jesus of Nazareth, the greatest Evangelizer. In *Evangelii Nuntiandi* Pope Paul lays out a twenty-five-year plan and vision "as we prepare for the third millennium of Christianity."

As one of its responses to the call of Pope Paul, the National Conference of Catholic Bishops in the fall of 1976 set evangelization as a major priority for the United States Catholic community.

Following the leadership of the Holy Father and the American bishops, the Paulist Fathers—the first religious community of men to be founded in the United States in 1858 as a home mission group—established in July 1977, the Paulist National Catholic Evangelization Association, an action-oriented association to wrestle with these challenges:

a. To stimulate prayerful concern among the clergy, the religious, and the laity to minister spiritually to inactive Catholics and to all Americans who have no church family to call their own.

b. To train clergy, religious, and laity to engage in primary evangelization.

c. To develop, test, and document contemporary ways in which Catholic dioceses and parishes can evangelize the inactive and the unchurched in a post-Vatican II ecclesial community of faith.

d. To distribute model programs on what is now being done in dioceses and in parishes to serve the religious needs of the inactive and the unchurched.

e. To design and help conduct workshops and conventions on primary evangelization for dioceses, religious communities of men and women, and for national Catholic Church organizations.

f. To provide the clergy, the religious, and the laity with one location where contemporary resource materials can be obtained for the evangelization of the inactive Catholic and the unchurched.

Today the Paulist National Catholic Evangelization Association is the largest Catholic evangelization organization in America, an organization with well over 200,000 members. Sensitive to the ecumenical and interreligious dimensions of evangelization, the Paulist Evangelization Association focuses its energies on bringing the good news of salvation in Jesus Christ to the 15,000,000 inactive Catholics and to the 65,000,000 unchurched Americans.

In the effort to reach these 80,000,000 people, the director of the Association has given workshops on evangelization to over 20,000 Catholic clergymen who pastor many of the 19,000 Catholic parish communities that dot the United States. These pastors have heard that the 52,000,000 active Catholics who are their parishioners are the best hope that the Catholic Church has for the evangelization of the unchurched of America.

Among its many activities, there are seven programs that best reflect the purposes of the Paulist Evangelization Association.

1. "Share the Word" is a program of regular home Bible-study in magazine format. It is designed to help men and women share Christ with others by reaching out in a spirit of love and friendship through small neighborhood prayer groups. Share the Word includes a study and discussion guide for the Sunday readings along with a daily Bible reading guide. The Sunday readings are taken from a lectionary that is not only common to all Catholics, but is in use in most of the Lutheran, the Episcopal,

the Presbyterian, the Methodist, and the Church of Christ communities. So that everyone, including the poor and those on fixed incomes, can be enriched by Share the Word, individual subscriptions are offered free of charge. Share the Word in turn is supported by the free will offerings of its generous readers.

A weekly thirty-minute television version of Share the Word is now being aired in many American cities to introduce millions more to the sacred Scriptures. Through a wedding of the printed word with the electronic word, viewers are invited to subscribe to Share the Word so that the viewer can follow up the television presentation with a discussion on Scripture with a group of friends in the viewer's home.

2. "Another Look" is a national program ministry to reach inactive Catholics. It has five major purposes.

a. To raise public awareness and interest among active Catholics to pray and work for the return of their inactive relatives, friends, and neighbors out of a deep love and concern for their spiritual well-being.

b. To produce information and materials that will give consolation and hope to the families and friends of those who have left the active practice of the faith.

c. To challenge the inactive to review their faith and decide what their response to that faith is going to be.

d. To assist Catholic parishes in establishing a special ministry for the inactive. Such unique parish ministry would be run by lay ministers who, for the most part, experienced a period of two years or more in their own lives when they were counted among the inactive, but who are active today. As the parish surfaces the names and the addresses of the inactive, these ministers meet with them to share their personal story of a journey out of the church and back again. They help the inactive in their return to the practice of the faith.

e. To mail four times the first year, and three times each year thereafter, to the names and addresses of the inactive Catholics sent to the Paulist Evangelization Association, a cordial invitation to come back with an expression of apology if we have hurt them.

Presently the Diocese of St. Petersburg, Florida, with 350,000 active Catholics, is adapting this program in a year-long, diocesan-wide effort to invite the 80,000 to 100,000 inactive Catholics in that mid-central, west coast area of Florida to be reconciled with God and the church. This experiment is being carefully watched by many of the 181 dioceses in the United States and may well become a model program for large, organized, diocesan-wide evangelization efforts for the inactive Catholic.

3. National Catholic Lay Celebrations of Evangelization are conducted to inspire and to train Catholic lay persons to be evangelizers. Eleven of these four-day celebrations have been conducted in cities such as Los Angeles, St. Louis, Minneapolis, New Orleans, Hartford, and Miami.

The specific goals of the Lay Celebration are to emphasize the role of the laity as Catholic evangelizers; to recognize the good work that is already being done in the area of evangelization; and to feature successful program models. In addition to general presentations on evangelizing the active Catholic, on evangelizing the inactive Catholic, on evangelizing the unchurched, and on the ecumenical and interreligious aspects of evangelization, an array of workshops conducted by lay people highlight these prayerful events. Well over 17,000 people have participated, thousands of whom are today working in their home parishes as Catholic lay evangelizers.

4. "Invitation: A Catholic Learning Guide for Adults" is a new twenty-six-chapter program for the unchurched adult. Offered free of charge through secular newspaper and magazine advertising, Invitation is designed for those who are searching for self, for God, and for friends, and who would like to investigate the Catholic community of believers in their search. A three-ring binder with a descriptive summary of the twenty-six chapters, chapter one of the adult learning guide, and a complete index of the total learning guide is sent immediately to those who write. The inquirer then receives one chapter per month for twenty-five months, slowly building his or her own catechism. Toward the end of the two-year process the inquirer is introduced to a Catholic priest living in the immediate area of the inquirer, with the hope that the inquirer will want to be enriched through Word, sacrament, and community as a member of the local Catholic parish family.

5. The RCIA Training Institute is a national training facility for Catholics seeking the most effective way in which to initiate new members into the full Catholic way of life. For one full month,

representatives from parishes across the nation gather in Washington, D.C., under the leadership of an expert in the Rite of Christian Initiation of Adults (RCIA). The trainer presents the students, most of whom are laity selected by their pastors, with the intellectual content as well as the process that is so important in helping the adult inquirer become an active member of a Catholic parish community.

The Rite of Christian Initiation of Adults is a process developed in the early ages of Christianity. Unfortunately, it was ignored for many centuries, but now revised for today's church as one of the fruits of the Vatican Council. The RCIA is parish based, usually runs from the fall of the year to Pentecost Sunday, and uses many of the contemporary insights of the behavioral sciences as well as the time-honored heritage of the church. The inquirer studies the Scriptures, participates in the prayer life of the community, learns the basic message of Christ as enshrined in the teachings and the moral code of the Catholic community, begins practicing justice and charity, and is presented to the Catholic community at Sunday Masses by a sponsor, all the while building a network of friends in the parish who will sustain the new Catholic after baptism and reception into the Catholic Church.

The RCIA Training Institute has developed and field-tested a team manual that contains both the content of the instructions as well as the process of formation which graduating students adapt to their local situation when they return to their home parishes.

6. A Film Training Program has been produced for pastors who wish to introduce their parishioners to the basic principles and practices of evangelization. Four thirty-minute, 16mm color films or three-quarter-inch video cassettes, along with an assortment of printed materials to enhance the films and to generate group discussion, are available for rent. The titles of the four films that come as a unit are: *Catholic Evangelization Today, The Five Groups in America Most Enriched by Evangelization, Fourteen Basic Principles to Assist Catholic Lay Evangelizers, Contemporary Methods and Materials to Help Laity Evangelize.*

7. *Evangelization and Initiation* is a national newsletter on Catholic evangelization in America that reports on outreach programs for the inactive Catholic and the unchurched American, and highlights successful efforts to help interested persons enter the Catholic Church. In addition, it publishes commentaries and

the results of scientific studies as it documents the emerging movement of Catholic evangelization within the American community. *Evangelization and Initiation* is published six times per year and is available free of charge.

Should the reader desire to receive the newsletter, *Evangelization and Initiation,* or information on developments within the Paulist National Catholic Evangelization Association, simply send your name and address to: National Catholic Evangelization Association / 3031 Fourth Street, N.E. / Washington, DC 20017. There is no charge for this service.

# THE CHRISTIAN BROADCASTING NETWORK
## PORTSMOUTH, VIRGINIA
## PAT ROBERTSON, DIRECTOR
## THE 700 CLUB

IT was October 1, 1961, in the city of Portsmouth, Virginia, that a young preacher by the name of Pat Robertson first stepped before a television camera. From this tiny UHF station began one of the most outstanding outreaches to unchurched America that has ever been accomplished. It had very humble beginnings. Pat and his wife Dede had come from New York City just two years before with total financial resources of $70.00. Robertson's vision was to create a television ministry to the Tidewater area of Virginia, and that's just what he did. He called the station WYAH, which is taken from the Hebrew word for God, YAHWEH. Tidewater Christians now had their television ministry where Pat and his associates loudly proclaimed, "Jesus is Lord!"

It has been a rapid growth for which Pat credits God's special blessings. In August of 1962 he began a radio station, WXRI-FM, and within a few weeks it rose to fifth place out of twenty local stations. In two years the station had a larger transmitter which gave it the most powerful signal in the area.

With such resources to work with, a revival broke out throughout the listening area and the team called it "a channel for God's miracles and blessings to flow through and reach mankind."

The Christian Broadcasting Network was now a reality, and God began to multiply the outreach of this one station into a network of six stations throughout North America, one radio station in South America, one color television station in Portsmouth, and a television permit granted for future use in Atlanta. CBN had now reached a potential audience of some 10 million Americans twenty-four hours a day with the Good News of Jesus Christ.

The term "700 Club" came when CBN began its first telethon fund-raising program. They asked 700 viewers to come forward with a ten-dollar-per-month pledge to help meet their $7,000-per-month operating expenses.

By 1972 the outreach had a potential of 50 million people, which grew to 110 million by 1975. The programs went international that year, reaching out to Canada, Mexico, and the Bahamas. Not only radio and television, but some thirty-four counseling centers were opened throughout the area to follow up on people who were seeking Christ through CBN's ministries.

By October 1976, a two-hundred-acre piece of land in Virginia Beach was purchased, and on this site has been built an international communications center, as well as a school for training people for evangelism. The ministry has had an impact upon America that no other religious broadcasting program has ever enjoyed. The station ran a nationwide special called, "It's Time to Pray, America," which brought together the nation's leaders to urge restoration of America to its historical religious perspective. Since that date they have reached out to Taiwan, then to Japan.

During this time, the new CBN University opened its doors and students began learning skills in radio/television, journalism, advertising/public relations, communications studies, and visual methods of communication—all with a Christian dimension for the eventual reaching of every American with the gospel of Jesus Christ.

The ministry was not all "tell and no show." A real concern for

God's needy ones arose, and counseling centers were established across the nation. By 1980 some seventy counseling centers were in operation with trained professionals available to give guidance for life's problems, but with a sound Christian dimension. Over 2 million telephone calls per year were being received asking for both spiritual and emotional assistance.

The plight of Cambodia's refugees touched the hearts of CBN listeners and some $800,000 was donated to help alleviate suffering and misery in Southwest Asia.

It was a real highlight of CBN's ministry when, on April 29, 1980, more than 400,000 Christians of all denominations gathered together in Washington, D.C., to pray for America's spiritual health.

It was a month later that the CBN University graduated its first class of professional communicators. These graduates have been placed throughout the United States to begin their roles as communicators of the gospel message. Already their effect is being felt in critical places throughout the nation's communications business.

In Japan, where the Christian population is less than 1 percent, exactly what it was in the seventeenth century, through the daily telecasts of CBN, Japanese students are now purchasing special Japanese editions of the Bible and an all-out media blitz in every major Japanese city is being mounted. A skilled media evangelism project will reach out to Japan's millions as no other previous outreach has ever been dreamed of before.

The secular news hits most Americans every morning with the woes of our times, and CBN thought it was time to introduce early morning Americans with a upbeat, Christian outlook. As a result, "U.S.a.m." began broadcasting in the summer of 1981. We can now wake up to a bright, fresh blend of news, views, interviews, and positive, inspirational features.

CBN is reaching people who never go to church and people who were once church members, but no longer attend. Some 80 million Americans have never crossed the threshold of anyone's church, and without the "700 Club," they might never learn of the gospel of Jesus Christ. In the quiet of their homes, they listen to interesting programs, talk shows, and news reports that all lead to the message of Jesus Christ. People who would never read a Christian book, open the Bible, or even allow a friend to tell them about Jesus Christ now are able to sit and listen to the presentation of Christ's saving gospel message.

According to CBN's management, this is not enough. It is only the beginning. They say, "Our hearts yearn to reach out to the world's millions—even billions—of lost souls for Jesus Christ."

No question about it, God has taken a small, difficult beginning and placed his special anointing and blessing upon it, which has caused CBN to become the leading outreach ministry in the world today. No other ministry is reaching so many, so often, in so many places.

All this success comes from God, according to the director, Pat Robertson, and his staff, who received a mighty prophecy in 1976. They claim God told them:

> Was it not my hand that led from England those settlers who came to these shores? Has it not been my ear that heard their prayer, and my heart that remembered? Are you not walking in fulfillment of the prayer that has been prayed years before you? . . . I have called you to a ministry beyond anything that you can conceive . . . your thoughts cannot comprehend what I have called you to. . . .

Those words reinforce Pat and his team, and they claim God has chosen them to usher in the coming of the Lord himself.

Beginning their third decade of evangelistic outreach, they say, "There is a great vision to be seen. There is a world to be reached. There is work to be done." Whatever the case, the 700 Club is preaching the gospel to millions, and God is blessing their work beyond their fondest hopes.

# SOUTHERN CALIFORNIA RENEWAL COMMUNITIES

## DOMINIC BERNARDINO

## PRAYER—THE MISSING ELEMENT IN EVANGELIZATION

TODAY it is exciting to see more and more Christians escalating their efforts to carry out the Lord's mandate to bring the Good News to all peoples. At the same time it is no mere coincidence that a tremendous awakening of prayer is also on the upsurge within the Christian churches. Evangelization and prayer share a very special affinity. They are two allies bonded closely in unison to carry out a most sacred mission. Evangelization calls us to enter into a whole new relationship with God, and prayer calls us to continue on in that hallowed relationship. Oneness with our Creator is a mutual goal of both prayer and evangelization.

It is often the case that before God does something marvelous there is some form of prayer going out and preparing the way. Throughout the history of God's people there have been countless occurrences of the Spirit of God prompting certain individuals to intercede in prayer for some very specific situations to transpire. Augustine of Hippo wrote: "Without God, we cannot; but without us, God will not!" John Wesley remarked that "God does not make a move until there is prevailing prayer!"

Prayer should always be an integral part of our labors for God's Kingdom. Jesus said: "I am the vine, you are the branches. He who abides in me, and I in him, he it is that bears much fruit, for apart from me you can do nothing" (John 15:5, RSV). The Christian servant who prayerfully abides in Christ Jesus discovers the reality of the scriptural promise: "They who wait for the Lord shall renew their strength, they shall mount up with wings like eagles, they shall run and not be weary, they shall walk and not faint" (Isaiah 40:31, RSV). Prayer is our declaration of dependence and trust in theAlmighty. In prayer we acknowledge God as the ultimate source and substance of our being.

Prayer acts very much like an electrical outlet. In itself the outlet is not the source of power but rather serves as a point of contact between the electrical current and whatever appliance we wish to have activated. Prayer is the plug through which we have access to the divine current of God's power. We ask God if we may come into his presence, and upon entering we discover that God's presence has also come into us!

Everyone engaged in the work of evangelization is called into particularly close contact with the infinite and omnipotent love God has for all people. Truly "God's love has been poured into our hearts through the Holy Spirit which has been given to us" (Romans 5:5, RSV). Prayer enables us to see with the Father's eyes the dignity inherent within each and every person created in God's image. In prayer we can feel with the Father's heart the painful separation of his wayward sons and daughters. Through prayer we can hear with the Father's ears the cries of restless and unfulfilled hearts longing to taste real life. It is as we tune in to God that he imparts unto us a portion of his immense desire, wanting "all men to be saved and to come to the knowledge of the truth" (1 Timothy 2:4, RSV).

Through prayer God the Father's design becomes more discernibly clear: to sweep the entire earth with an epidemic of love boundless in magnitude. The manifestation of this love is God's own Son Jesus whom he sent into the world. This divine infection of unconditional love has since come to be known as Christianity. All who invite Jesus Christ to enter as "true God and true man" into the entirety of their beings will become the carriers of God's infectious love: "Therefore, if any one is in Christ, he is a new creation; the old has passed away, behold, the new has come. All this is from God, who through Christ reconciled us to himself and gave us the ministry of reconciliation; . . . So we are ambassadors for Christ, God making his appeal through us" (2 Corinthians 5:17, 18, 20, RSV).

This divine infection of love that we are to transmit to others must also continue its spread throughout the whole of our being. As Paul's prayer for the Ephesians so aptly declares: ". . . according to the riches of his glory he may grant you to be strengthened with might through his Spirit in the inner man, and that Christ may dwell in your hearts through faith; that you, being rooted and grounded in love, may have power to comprehend with all the saints what is the breadth and length and height and depth, and to know the love of Christ which surpasses knowledge, that you may be filled with all the fulness of God" (Ephesians 3:16-19, RSV).

It has been said that prayer is the breathing of the soul. Prayer serves as a spiritual umbilical cord channeling God's nourishment and oxygen to us. Our transformation into the fullness of Christ progresses as we maintain prayerful union with him. In the words of John Chrysostom: "A fish taken out of water cannot live. In a very short time, it dies. Neither can the soul of man exist without prayer: it gradually will grow languid, it will die. Let us be convinced that not to pray and to lose the life of the soul—that is, the Grace of God—is one and the same thing."

In this same vein Teresa of Avila wrote: "Souls which have no habit of prayer are like a lame and paralytic body, which, though it has hands and feet, cannot use them. Therefore: to abandon prayer seems to me the same thing as to lose the straight road; for as prayer is the gate through which all the Graces of God come to us, when this is closed, I do not know how we can have any."

If prayer is this essential to the Christian life then it is of the utmost importance in the lives of all who serve in the work of evangelization. Paul realized that his divine calling to be an evangelist was not in itself a guarantee of always being in God's grace: ". . . lest after preaching to others I myself should be disqualified" (1 Corinthians 9:27, RSV).

Prayer helps bring us to an inner scrutiny, a sort of self-evangelization necessary for all who promote God's truth. "Take heed to yourself and to your teaching; hold to that, for by so doing you will save both yourself and your hearers" (1 Timothy 4:16, RSV). We mustn't allow ourselves to be deluded into viewing prayer as a means of escape from unpleasant realities. In prayer we receive the grace of God to face any situation through Christ who strengthens us. Prayer is not a place where we can run and hide from the shadow side of our personalities. On the contrary, prayer can sometimes (perhaps oftentimes) become extremely uncomfortable because our real selves must stand alone, naked and vulnerable before God.

What God is doing when prayer becomes this unsettling is breaking down and decomposing our own self-made righteousness—the custom-made piety each of us personally designs to fit our own particular biases, tastes, and opinions. Perhaps this is part of what is meant by the Scripture verse: "For the time has come for judgment to begin with the household of God; and if it begins with us, what will be the end of those who do not obey the gospel of God?" (1 Peter 4:17, RSV). For everyone who chooses to be one with Christ, fear gives way to love, and thus this judgment becomes a source of unsurpassable joy, as Paul did discover: "But whatever gain I had, I counted as loss for the sake of Christ. Indeed I count everything as loss because of the surpassing worth of knowing Christ Jesus my Lord. For his sake I have suffered the loss of all things, and count them as refuse, in order that I may gain Christ and be found in him, not having a righteousness of my own, based on law, but that which is through faith in Christ, the righteousness from God that depends on faith" (Philippians 3:7-9, RSV).

Realizing that apart from God we are nothing and can do nothing helps bring us to the threshold of surrender to God. It is indeed a paradox how submission to a higher power beyond ourselves can unshackle and liberate us from the limiting confinement of our own smallness. Such yieldedness to God will be reflected in our prayer life when we no longer try to persuade God to do what we think would be best, but instead trustfully assent to his plan, saying: "Not my will but yours be done." We can then learn to cooperate when the Holy Spirit prompts us from the innermost depths of our being to pray in accordance with our Father's intentions.

Prayer awakens us to innumerable spiritual realities. The discovery that "God is at work in you, both to will and to work for his good pleasure" (Philippians 2:13, RSV), leads us to a whole new perception of divine gifts and graces. The Trinity of God dwelling inside us creates within us our very capacity to even desire and receive the spiritual resources necessary to carry out our labors. Such humble awareness leads us to the throne of grace and moves us to pray with open hands ". . . to him who by the power at work within us is able to do far more abundantly than all that we ask or think" (Ephesians 3:20, RSV).

Sooner or later those who are called to active duty at the "front line" of ministry perceive a need to have stronger spiritual backbone. Paul exhorted Timothy: "Always be steady, endure suffering, do the work of an evangelist, fulfil your ministry" (2 Timothy 4:5, RSV). The onslaughts of resistance to the advancing of God's Kingdom are indeed many and require the Christian servant's prayerful preparation. It is our duty to put on the full armor of God (Ephesians 6:13-18) and be ready for battle. It would be a definite drawback to attempt to put on this armor once a battle is already underway!

Most of us perhaps expected to be hurt in the line of duty for the church, but few of us were very prepared when we were hurt by the church! It is a painful thing to be personally hurt either by those to whom you minister or by others who also minister. I think maybe what hurts the most is that you never even imagined such injury could come from the same place where you expected to receive love and support. If this should occur we may easily become severely discouraged and disillusioned enough to wash our hands totally of such involvement. Here we face the crucible of prayer within our own Gethsemane.

Only in prayer can our heartaches and pains be subjugated to the higher purposes of God. Only in prayer can we make a renewed decision to continue following the Good Shepherd who said: "A servant is not greater than his master. If they persecuted me, they will persecute you" (John 15:20, RSV). We are accustomed to focusing on the physical agony of our Lord during his passion. Seldom do we think about the emotional anguish Jesus had to be experiencing at the same time: being abandoned, denied, and betrayed by his very own friends was surely an inner crucifixion of the heart. The hurts which can lead us to estrangement from others will indeed take place throughout our lifetime. By following the example set by Jesus we can do our part to circumvent any potential alienation by extending and accepting forgiveness and mercy.

Perhaps the Lord allows us to experience such woundedness not only to purify our motives for ministry but also to help us pray with greater compassion for the millions of hurt and alienated unchurched people in existence. It has been said that: "Before we go to men about God, we must go to God about men." It is part of our duty to pray for everyone whom we evangelize plus those we have evangelized in the past. We see reference to this in some of Paul's letters to churches he had evangelized: "I do not cease to give thanks for you, remembering you in my prayers" (Ephesians 1:16, RSV). "We always thank God, the Father of our Lord Jesus Christ, when we pray for you . . . we have not ceased to pray for you, asking that you may be filled with the knowledge of his will in all spiritual wisdom and understanding" (Colossians 1:3, 9, RSV).

In this era of growing ecumenical awareness, Christians from different traditions and backgrounds have a greater opportunity to learn much from one another about the abundance of ways there are to pray. God is big enough to be communed with through more modes of prayer than we can ever imagine! Prayer can be private, communal, silent, vocal, mental, contemplative, auscultative, conversational, charismatic, liturgical—and much, much more!

Realizing that the essence of prayer is communion with God, we should not belittle any type of prayer form others employ just because it may have no meaning to us. True ecumenism involves maintaining a positive respect for the spiritual practices of others. In my own life I have found that my personal relationship with God blossoms the more I avail myself to different expressions of prayer. The core of what really matters is that the reality of the prayer be truly alive within the heart. Otherwise any method of prayer can be in danger of becoming lifeless and superficial.

I believe that during our earthly sojourn, the Spirit of God will unceasingly try to lead us to the many rich deposits of spiritual treasure which are available to us on this side of Glory. Of course, it is imperative that we acquire proper discernment in order to test the true and authentic value of what proceeds from our prayers. Tragic stories abound of sincere people being misled by false illumination. There are safeguards in the church which God provides for us to help protect us from spiritual deception. The ultimate criteria for rightly discerning any spiritual gleanings will always be by judging how well they help us to grow into greater love and thankfulness toward Christ, the "Pearl of great price" whom we already have come to possess!

To disconnect prayer from evangelization, indeed from any aspect of ministry, would be to risk separating God from God's work. The Lord did not just call us to work and then leave us to do the job alone. Jesus promised to be with us always, and he also sent the Paraclete to be our Helper. Let us not fail through presumption to heed the words of the psalmist: "Unless the Lord builds the house, they labor in vain who build it" (Psalm 127:1, NASB).

## SOUTHERN CALIFORNIA RENEWAL COMMUNITIES—HELPING EVANGELIZATION THROUGH PRAYER AND RENEWAL

In the wake of Vatican Council II, during the late 1960s and early 1970s, the American Catholic Church witnessed in the lives of many of its members a remarkable emergence of the Holy Spirit's gifts and graces. Very quickly this charismatic renewal became a movement of major proportion in the Catholic Church throughout the entire world! For such a burgeoning renewal movement to develop properly and make a significant and lasting contribution to the church, it had to have proper guidance, sound teaching, and effective communication. For this purpose Southern California Renewal Communities (S.C.R.C.) came into being.

Under the brilliant and visionary direction of the late Fr. Ralph Tichenor, S.J., a pastoral and theological foundation was built to help this renewal integrate in a positive manner into the context of the local church. S.C.R.C. is basically an association of parish-based prayer groups within the Archdiocese of Los Angeles. In 1972, S.C.R.C. was established as a legal nonprofit religious corporation in the state of California. This paved the way for the establishment of the first diocesan-oriented Renewal Service Center of its kind.

Today the S.C.R.C. Service Center is staffed by twenty hard-working employees and a host of dedicated volunteers. Many services are provided and numerous events are sponsored to aid in the fostering of this renewal. S.C.R.C.'s most major event is the annual Catholic Renewal Convention, drawing over 10,000 participants. The entire operation of S.C.R.C.'s services is a faith ministry dependent upon divine Providence and the charitable financial support of benefactors.

As a corporation, S.C.R.C. is governed by a board of directors consisting of clergy, religious, and laity—all active within the renewal. As a major organization within the Los Angeles Archdiocese, S.C.R.C. is under the full approbation of the Archbishop. Two priests serve in the capacity of liaison between the Archbishop and S.C.R.C.

On numerous occasions Cardinal Timothy Manning has written to the pastors within the archdiocese making known his support of S.C.R.C. and requesting parishes to open their facilities to the renewal. In 1978 Cardinal Manning wrote: "We must be alert to the needs of our people, and from the extraordinary growth of the Charismatic Renewal it is evident that this prayer movement does fill many needs. . . . As more priests become involved, or at least more aware of the meaning of Catholic Charismatic Renewal, its growth along parish lines will be assured and the hoped for renewal of the Church would increase." In his most recent letter the Cardinal stated that: "The Charismatic Renewal enjoys the highest ecclesiastical approval."

Evangelization is an integral aspect of charismatic renewal. In May 1975, Pope Paul VI spoke at the International Conference on Charismatic Renewal in the Catholic Church held in Rome. In the early portion of his address the Pope said: "Alas! God has become a stranger in the lives of so many people, even of those who continue to profess his existence by tradition, and to pay him worship out of duty! For such a world, more and more secularized, nothing is more necessary than the witness of this 'spiritual renewal,' which we see the Holy Spirit stirring today, in such diverse regions and circles."

Prayer groups are a basic element of the charismatic renewal. A charismatic prayer meeting can be a powerful evangelistic tool when it is being faithful to its objectives and authentically following the leading of the Holy Spirit. The promise of Jesus Christ found in Matthew 18:20, KJV, is the basis of a charismatic prayer meeting: "For where two or three are gathered together in my name, there am I in the midst of them." People can best encounter Christ where Christ is present!

A prayer group whose participants maintain sincere openness to the continually renewing and ever transforming power of the risen Lord Jesus, will most definitely be a beacon of light. A loving, sensitive, and mature prayer group can most certainly expect to see the lives of many newcomers being touched and changed as they personally encounter Jesus Christ in their midst. From our experience, the majority of newcomers seem to come to prayer meetings and special events as a result of one-on-one outreach. Even when major publicity and announcements are spread throughout the parish, it is inevitably the peer-to-peer contact that makes a person interested to "come and see."

One of the contributions charismatic renewal is bringing to the church is a new awareness that people who have made a personal commitment to the Lord also need to become aware of the spiritual gifts God bestows upon them. After getting in touch with these gifts, given for ministry, we are more able to serve others: "As each has received a gift, employ it for one another, as good stewards of God's varied grace" (1 Peter 4:10, RSV).

Southern California Renewal Communities is firmly committed to the work of parish renewal. We believe that parishes hold the key to renewal and evangelization in the Catholic Church. That is why the S.C.R.C. service group and its representatives refuse to exercise any authority whatsoever over any prayer group. We maintain that such authority is proper only to the pastor in union with his bishop. To set up any type of "para-authoritarian structure" can incur hidden dangers risking possible setback in furthering the renewal.

A parish prayer group should be designed to serve as a leaven within the local church. People who have experienced a personal renewal of faith should be encouraged by the prayer group to become fully active in their parish. This often poses somewhat of a challenge for members of the clergy to develop a better understanding of religious experiences to help give these people proper spiritual direction.

A prayer group is not considered successful or prosperous just because of large attendance but rather by the amount of people who, because of their involvement with a prayer group, have gone on to become better Christian servants to the entire parish community. The present president of S.C.R.C., Fr. Bill Adams, C.Ss.R., speaking on the subject of parish renewal, has stated that "a renewed parish is one in which each member accepts personal responsibility for the life of the community."

Renewal of Christian life and church life is not something that can happen overnight. Renewal is a process because renewal involves change. Each of us is resistant in some degree to change, probably because we are not always quite certain what the change will produce. But when we are talking about the type of change for the better which God wishes to bring about in us, it is difficult to understand why we resist! Could it be possibly because we are too afraid of letting God love us completely?

God is so tremendously patient with us as we hesitantly peel away the crusty layers of our hardened hearts and draw nearer to his eternal love and glory. Such Good News is meant to be a fountainhead of prayer. Therese of Lisieux wrote: "It is the Gospel above all that is my source of prayer. From it I draw all that is needful for my little soul."

The Good News of the Lord Jesus Christ instills within us the faith necessary to pray. Recently I heard an elderly Italian woman with her heavy accent begin her prayer with utmost confidence and childlike simplicity, saying: "Hey, God! You listened to Abraham, anda you listened to Moses! So pleeza listen to me!" Prayer is the privilege and responsibility of every Christian. Prayer receives its meaning from the gospel, and the gospel advances forward into the world through prayer.

The Scriptures specify a number of things we can pray for in regard to evangelization. Some are to:

- Pray for those Christians in the forefront of evangelization. ". . . pray for us also, that God may open to us a door for the word, to declare the mystery of Christ" (Colossians 4:3, RSV).
- Pray that the veil be removed from the minds of those who have no knowledge of Truth. ". . . a veil lies over their minds; but when a man turns to the Lord the veil is removed" (2 Corinthians 3:15, 16, RSV).
- Pray that church leaders share the same conviction as did

the apostles. "But we will devote ourselves to prayer and to the ministry of the word" (Acts 6:4, RSV).

- Pray for the government leaders of the world (even those who prohibit the freedom of Christianity in their countries). "First of all, then, I urge that supplications, prayers, intercessions, and thanksgivings be made for all men, for kings and all who are in high positions, that we may lead a quiet and peaceable life, godly and respectful in every way" (1 Timothy 2:1, 2, RSV).
- Pray for more laborers in God's Kingdom. "The harvest is plentiful, but the laborers are few; pray therefore the Lord of the harvest to send out laborers into his harvest" (Matthew 9:37, 38, RSV).

And may all Christians everywhere pray and live the words of our Savior: "Thy kingdom come, Thy will be done, On earth as it is in heaven" (Matthew 6:10, RSV). So be it!

Dominic Bernardino, a Catholic layman, is Director of Teaching for Southern California Renewal Communities. He is the author of "Thy Kingdom Come," a seminar designed to help lead Catholics into a more personal relationship with the Trinity of God.

Southern California Renewal Communities Service Center
5730 W. Manchester Avenue, P.O. Box 45594
Los Angeles, CA 90045-0594
Phone: 213-645-1162

# PART FOUR

# Seven Outstanding Resource Agencies

# CHURCHES ALIVE!
## SAN BERNARDINO, CALIFORNIA
## HOWARD BALL, PRESIDENT
## HOW TO CONVERT YOUR MEMBERS
## FROM SPECTATORS INTO MINISTERS

CHAPTER

31

CHURCHES ALIVE is a nonprofit organization serving local churches in the areas of discipleship and evangelism through

1. Materials (printed and cassette tapes)
2. Training conferences
3. Consulting help

Having begun in 1973, the organization now has a staff of nearly fifty working with churches representing more than forty denominational and independent backgrounds. Their ministry extends across North America and overseas.

God established the church for a reason. The church is God's plan for the world. However, to regain our New Testament vitality and effectiveness, we need to reconsider three basic questions and be faithful to the scriptural imperatives that emerge.

## WHY ARE WE HERE? *(What is our purpose?)*

The Scriptures clearly reveal that the *purpose* of the church is to glorify God (Ephesians 3:14-21). After living through 365 days, after conducting all the meetings, after spending the money, after using the facilities, after investing countless leadership hours, the bottom line is not, "Has it filled the calendar?" or "Has it had a good attendance?" The bottom line is, "Has it glorified God?"

## WHERE ARE WE GOING? *(What is our goal?)*

To determine whether or not your church glorifies God, you must translate your purpose into a specific *goal* as the top priority for the church.

In Matthew 28:18-20, Jesus gave to the disciples what is commonly called the Great Commission.

But, as I have traveled the world, it is obvious to me that the majority of churches are suffering from the "Great Omission" in the Great Commission—resulting in a great commotion, but little of our Lord's Great Commission. To underscore this *Great Omission* (which I believe is the cause of the widespread spiritual anemia in the church), I am going to quote our Lord's Great Commission as churches generally interpret it. See if you recognize the *Great Omission*.

Jesus said, "All authority has been given to Me in heaven and on earth. Go therefore and make disciples of all nations, baptizing them in the name of the Father and the Son and the Holy Spirit, teaching them all that I have commanded you; and lo, I am with you always, even to the end of the age" (Matthew 28:18-20, NASB).

Only two words were left out—"to obey." But they are the heart of the Great Commission. Those words have become the Great Omission.

Jesus didn't say, "I want you to go and impart a lot of knowledge about what my will is." He said, "I want you to teach people *to obey* all that I commanded."

The church, in general, places a high priority on knowledge but not on obedience. Too often we produce people who are smart enough to argue about their faith or pass theological examinations—but who are not wise enough to obey God's Word.

By Christ's own definition, you are not making disciples until you teach people *to obey* his commandments.

Inherent in the Great Commission is the concept that every person being discipled must have available to him a reasonably mature Christian who can help him grow in discipleship. That mature Christian ensures that the person being discipled:

- knows and understands the will of God as revealed in his Word.
- is deciding how to adjust his life style accordingly.
- is making progress in obedience to what he knows and understands.

The goal of the church is to make disciples. That goal dictates a far different life style from what the church generally displays.

## HOW ARE WE GOING TO GET THERE?

Some years ago, as one of our church's leaders, I attended our annual planning committees. During our session someone would invariably say, "What are we going to do about _____?" . . . and would describe a long-standing unmet need in our church.

After some interaction, we would always arrive at the same old conclusion; "We really should do something about this need, but we can't. If only we had _____."

Later, the Holy Spirit translated my "if only we had _____" into plain language for me. In my unbelief I was saying, "If only God would quit holding out on the church and give us what we really need, then we could get the job done."

The great majority of churches today have the attitude that God has not yet given them the resources they need to be effective. That attitude rises from the pit of hell.

According to his Word, "God shall supply all your need according to his riches in glory by Christ Jesus" (Philippians 4:19). One look at the Cross reminds us that God has not withheld anything, not even his Son.

Ask yourself, "Is it conceivable that there is a need in any church or its community that God, the Holy Spirit, is ignorant of, indifferent to, or powerless to meet?" Omniscience is not ignorant.

Love is not indifferent. Omnipotence is not powerless.

Churches already possess the resources they need to meet needs. The deficiency lies in our stewardship of the resources already provided by God to the church. Before the foundation of the world, God ordained his plan for his church. The church that gets in harmony with God's plan will realize increasing ability not only to meet present church needs but to expand its ministry to members and become more vital in affecting its community for Christ.

When a person comes to Jesus Christ and by faith receives him as Lord and Savior, Christ gives that person the power to become a child of God. God sends the Spirit of his Son into that person's heart. The Holy Spirit baptizes him into the body of Christ. The Holy Spirit, in his sovereign wisdom, decides what spiritual gift or gifts to impart to the child of God.

Unbelief causes our churches to appear to lack the resources to fulfill our purpose and meet the needs around us. But the Holy Spirit is not unaware of what we need. He gives spiritual gifts so that the needs can be met.

How many packages given to you last Christmas still sit unopened? We quickly open presents because we know who gave them and are confident that the giver has our best interests in mind. We can't wait to see the expression of his love for us.

In your church, how many packages given to you by God the Holy Spirit remain unopened? In my mind's eye, I see packages lined up on the pews of the churches of the world as the body of Christ congregates each week. The great majority sit neatly gift-wrapped in the same condition as when they were given to the church. From the neck of each Christian hangs a gift tag saying, "To the church with love from the Holy Spirit. P.S. I knew you'd need this."

For the most part, church leaders seem to believe there is little of value in the packages the Holy Spirit gives the church. This is evident in how leaders treat them. They are preached to, pleaded with, harangued, and threatened. But usually, little time is spent in opening the packages to find what the Holy Spirit intended when he placed these people in the church with their God-ordained gifts.

Within each church lie all the resources and potential for a great awakening. The harvest is plenteous. But the Christians *reside* in the harvest fields. They do *not labor. We desperately need something to convert Christians into laborers*—instead of residents—in the harvest fields. If our members are not living under Christ's lordship, they will not be obedient. If they are not obedient, they will not exercise their spiritual gifts according to God's plan and, as a result, the needs will continue unmet and the ripe harvest will not be gathered in.

## BECOME A FAITHFUL STEWARD

Typically, a newcomer arrives on the church scene, becomes involved in a program or activity and, ten years later, still participates in the same way—as though ten years in God's church have not altered that person's usability for the Kingdom.

Newcomers should not be handled with, "Well, you're _____ years old, so you belong in that group. . . ." The church must make every evaluation of a person on the basis of:

- Where is this individual now, in relation to God's goal for him as a disciple?
- What are the critical needs that must be met to begin to release this person's potential?

Evaluate your people on the basis of their strengths and needs. Involve them where their needs can be met, but don't leave them there. Monitor their progress. As soon as their participation accomplishes its purpose, move them into new involvements that will further release their potential.

Would you leave money in a 5 percent return account if you knew you could get 10 percent elsewhere? Then why leave people in a low return involvement in the ministry of the church when you can involve them in a higher return for the glory of God?

As a leader, you carry the responsibility of knowing your people and their needs so you can offer them ministry opportunities as varied as their needs and interests. Allow for the Holy Spirit's creativity in designing a variety of ministries for your people with their different spiritual gifts and stages of spiritual development.

Keep in mind that the objective is disciples: increasingly

Christlike Christians. Recognize the God who made the snowflakes—no two alike. He is no less inclined to desire diversity in the church.

So often we approach the church as though it's a bugle corps—everyone playing the same instrument at the same time, in the same way, while God wants a symphony. We offer a single entree to our people. God intended a smorgasbord.

## THE ENEMY'S PLANS

Satan powerfully uses two basic strategies to neutralize the potential of the church: paralysis and polarization.

I call the first "Satan's master strategy for paralysis in the church." He implements it in this way: First, he convinces church leaders that success comes only when all the people in the church move as a convoy.

Then, he slips several people into your convoy who are nonmovers that don't want God's will.

The convoy mentality views the nonmover as the only thing preventing success. As a result, you dissipate your time and energy trying to get the nonmovers to move. In the meantime, the responsive and willing people twiddle their thumbs while you spend your time tied up with the nonmover's problem. Satan paralyzes your church.

When church leaders no longer buy the convoy mentality, Satan switches to his strategy of polarization for the church. It often happens in this way:

Church leaders return to their fellowship from a powerful experience in which they were convicted about the life style of their church. They announce to their people, "You have new leadership in this church. God has really spoken to us about how we've been playing 'church.' Now we're all going to get off our pews and take the Good News about Christ into this community like we should have years ago!"

When I first heard this kind of talk, it sounded good to me. But I began to see that Satan uses these situations to perform an abortion on the embryo of a spiritual awakening.

In their time of new commitment, the leaders are under such conviction about what ought to be done that they lose sight of where their people are. The members suddenly hear a different message from the leaders. They are presented with new demands.

Before, the leaders patted them on the back for years and told them what fine Christians they were because of their faithful attendance and faithful giving. Now, they think the leaders are saying, "To be acceptable around here in the future, you have to be one of God's 'Green Berets.' "

Members realize they don't know how to fulfill these new demands. They feel threatened. They get defensive. From their position of defense they polarize and oppose the person or program that threatens them. When this occurs, whoever or whatever polarizes the church has virtually outlived its usefulness.

In the wake of this polarization, the church leaders say, "I knew it. We never should have tried to do anything until everybody was ready to go." And so, they revert to paralysis.

## CHRIST'S APPROACH

How can we overcome paralysis? How can we avoid polarization? Succeeding over paralysis and polarization requires faith because it requires Christ's approach to calling his disciples. Do you remember how he called them?

Take your cue from Christ's approach to calling people to discipleship. Invite them. Define clearly what they are being called to. Then promise only what you can deliver, and let their motivation to get involved come from the Holy Spirit.

Too many leaders depend on their sales ability to promote people. Instead, put your confidence in God. Present ministry opportunities in such a way that people can say "no" without feeling rejected. If you don't have the confidence that God will move people to become a part of your ministry involvement, then you have a spiritual problem between yourself and God.

The Parable of the Sower contributes another principle that I urge you to follow in a reasonable application.

The sower went forth to sow. The seed fell on the wayside, the rocky soil, the thorny ground, and the good ground. The results in the wayside—nothing. The seed couldn't get through the surface to take root. In the rocky soil it sprang up quickly; but there was no substance to sustain it, and it burned up in the heat. In the thorny ground it was choked off by the cares of the world.

What happened in the good ground? There was a thirty-, a sixty-, and a one-hundred-fold return.

Through the Parable of the Sower the Lord Jesus says to church leaders today, "Stop trying to get your crops out of the wayside, rocks, and thorns. Take time to get to know your people well enough to identify the good soil for your ministry. Concentrate your time and energy with them because they are where the potential of your ministry will be released."

A word of caution—and this is crucial. Remember the difference between us and the Lord Jesus Christ. He is God. Only he can read the hearts of men. Until you have worked in depth with a person, you cannot accurately discern what's inside him. You must avoid labeling people "wayside, rocks, or thorns." Only God is qualified to do that.

I believe God wants us, as leaders, to accept our limitations and find the people who are responsive to us. Concentrate on working with them. As a result of working with *your* "responsive soil," two things will happen:

- You will learn to become more effective in your ministry. People who do not respond initially will begin to respond to your leadership because you have grown.
- The people who respond to you, in turn, will be used by the Holy Spirit to minister effectively to people who do not respond to you.

Since you are limited in time, energy, and ability, good stewardship requires that you concentrate on those who respond to you.

God will work through their responsiveness to release the potential of your ministry.

## APPLYING DISCIPLESHIP PRINCIPLES

As church consultants, we have found that a discipleship approach that is realistic and can lead to steadily increasing volume and variety of ministry must begin with two critical needs:

- short-term followup (ground new believers in Christ)
- long-term followup (equip for ministry by discipling as Christ defined it)

Short-term followup helps ground newly committed Christians in their newfound faith. The orientation provides a bridge to church involvement by first providing for the person's needs at his level.

After effective short-term followup, the new believer is ready for more demanding long-term followup in discipleship.

## *HOW WE CAN HELP*

Our services to churches are so extensive and varied that it is not possible in this space to communicate the details. We offer:

- Materials
  - Printed
  - Cassette tapes
- Conferences for church leaders
  - Introductory seminars
  - Growing by Discipling Seminars (for do-it-yourself churches)
  - Leadership Development Conferences (for those already underway in the Growing by Discipling plan)
- Consulting in three stages
  - Exploratory (one day)
  - Planning (two to three days)
  - Implementing (three years)

If you would like further information about any or all of these services, please write or phone:

Churches Alive International
Box 3800, San Bernardino, CA 92413
Phone: (714) 886-5361

# EVANGELISM EXPLOSION
## FORT LAUDERDALE, FLORIDA
## TIM FLOYD,
## COMMUNICATIONS DIRECTOR
## IT'S BETTER TO TRAIN A SOUL-WINNER
## THAN TO WIN ONE SOUL

CHAPTER

32

EVANGELISM Explosion is a program by means of which local churches may train their people for life style evangelism. It is particularly distinctive in that (1) it utilizes on-the-job training and (2) it works in churches of all sizes, all denominations!

The simple, biblical principle of the ministry is that *evangelism is more caught than taught*. For this reason, a "trainee" in a local program not only hears presentations on how to witness, but actually experiences the activity first hand. He first sees the gospel presented in "live" situations by someone already trained in the EE method. Weeks later, the trainee presents the gospel himself, also in live situations but under the supervision of a trainer.

The ministry is now in use by some of the fastest-growing churches of nearly every evangelical denomination in the U.S. and in many foreign countries. The ministry's goal is trained disciples who can share their faith easily and interestingly; but its by-products are new converts and a healthier church.

# WHY THE MINISTRY ORIGINATED

The training concept was born in 1962 when a young pastor in Fort Lauderdale, Florida, began to despair of ever seeing his lay people share their faith. It was while spending a week in the company of a highly evangelistic fellow pastor that he discovered the excitement of personal evangelism that is never generated amid stale classroom instruction. He returned to his South Florida congregation determined that his people would begin to experience evangelism first hand.

Soon thereafter, young Jim Kennedy built that idea into a personal training ministry. He began to train a few of his members by teaching them a basic gospel outline and carrying them on actual witnessing calls with him. And when they were able to share their faith confidently, they began to make visits on their own, carrying still others with them. Their church, Coral Ridge Presbyterian, soon became the fastest-growing Presbyterian church in the country. The book that explained the local ministry was titled *Evangelism Explosion.* So much interest developed, both in this country and abroad, that in 1973 a separate, interdenominational agency was established and titled Evangelism Explosion III International.

# HOW EE OPERATES

In a local church, the ministry begins small with the pastor or other trained staff member training four other members of the congregation. Dealing with the trainees two at a time, he assists them in memorizing and personalizing a basic gospel outline, complete with illustrations and Scripture references. Over a semester of sixteen weeks, the four trainees gradually expand the outline and flesh it out into a personable and appealing presentation of the gospel.

During each of those sixteen weeks, trainees are responsible not only for listening to lectures, but for outside assignments as well. Each trainee is also assisted by two prayer partners with whom he or she prays weekly.

Central to each week's learning experience is the actual calling situation in which the pastor or leader carries two trainees with him on evangelistic visits. In real-life visits, the trainees see the gospel effectively presented, generally for the first time in their lives. During the weekly on-the-job training, the trainee first observes the gospel being shared; and then he takes a larger share in the presentation himself, under the supervision of an experienced trainer.

After sixteen weeks of such training, each of the four trainees is now qualified to serve as a trainer. During the second semester of EE, each of the four takes on two new trainees, as does the pastor or original leader, bringing the total number of new trainees to ten. This means that by the end of two semesters, generally one year, a congregation is able personally to equip fifteen members for life style evangelism. After semester three, that number grows to forty-five, reaching 135 at the end of the second year.

At the end of each session's on-the-job training, teams return to the church building to share reports of their evening's encounters. Such report sessions not only maximize the learning that stems from the calls, but also allow news of professions to encourage teams who may have had discouraging calls.

## WHAT HAPPENS

The results of Evangelism Explosion in a local church are manifold. First and most obvious is the number of new converts ushered into the church after hearing the gospel presentation. Built into EE training are a series of followup booklets, the persistent use of which has proven effective in folding the new converts into the local church. The first of the series, "Welcome to the Forever Family," explains to the new believer the commitment he has made and is presented on the first evening. As one leading Baptist pastor has put it, however, "Even if [no new Christians] were coming in through EE, I would still want it in my church, and I would still encourage all my people to be involved, simply because of what it does for them."

What EE does for veteran church members is to give them a new spiritual vitality and a priority for life style evangelism. Quickly finding themselves in the midst of spiritual warfare while out sharing their faith, trainees discover a new urgency for the biblical disciplines of prayer, Bible study, and meditation.

Trainers and trainees also come to enjoy a fresh sense of camaraderie which gives a new meaning to the term "fellowship."

And for a local church, EE means new potential for ministry. Pastor and staff quickly discover a new reserve of lay ministers competent to counsel, conduct surveys, or participate in a variety of other ministries, and to do so with enthusiasm! Ongoing evangelism and discipleship can mean renewed health for even the struggling congregation.

Through a process known as *certification*, EE III maintains an advisory relationship with participating congregations around the world. Certification provides basic standards and criteria to insure the highest quality of training in each local program. Further, churches conducting certified programs are able to draw upon twenty years of experience in sharing the gospel and training others to do so.

## HOW TO BEGIN

In order to launch a certified EE ministry in his local church, a pastor or other staff member should first attend a regional EE Leadership Clinic. Such clinics are regularly scheduled in dynamic churches of all denominations across the U.S. and around the world. (A clinic schedule and additional details may be obtained by writing EE III's International Center in Fort Lauderdale, Florida.)

A clinic is a six-day event in which congregational leaders survey EE training materials for the first semester. Teaching technique, underlying principles of EE, and valuable suggestions for administration and troubleshooting are also among the subject matter covered. One other important benefit of a clinic is the ability to observe the ministry being conducted in an exemplary manner by the local church hosting the clinic.

The most unforgettable moments of any clinic come during the last evenings when clinicians accompany trained laymen from the host church on actual witnessing calls. During the first two of the final evenings, the clinicians observe as the laymen present the gospel using the EE presentation. Then on the last evening, the trainers look on as newly trained pastors share their faith. Report sessions following these visits are nothing short of thrilling as pastors are totally taken aback by the proficiency with which laymen can share Christ with others.

Clinic training provides a pastor with the nuts and bolts necessary for returning home, selecting pioneer trainees, and administering Evangelism Explosion training locally. Most churches agree that the most successful training schedules include a fall semester from September to mid-December and a spring semester from mid-January to May. It is generally difficult to conduct EE visitation over the Christmas holidays or to maintain a training schedule during the summer months.

Among the thousands of congregations now implementing successful EE ministries are First Southern Baptist Church of Del City, Oklahoma; St. Louis Catholic Church of Miami, Florida; First United Methodist Church of Carrollton, Texas; St. Stephen's Episcopal Church of Sewickley, Pennsylvania; The Peoples' Church of Fresno, California; and Salem Avenue Church of God in Dayton, Ohio. The ministry is also conducted by churches of some fifty nations beyond the U.S.A., including England, Northern Ireland, Hong Kong, Taiwan, Korea, South Africa, Zimbabwe, Australia, Puerto Rico, and Canada.

In every case, the ministry operates within the local church and is conducted by leaders of the same. Denominational and local church lines of authority are so carefully observed that EE III International only certifies pastors and staff members. Those local leaders must, in turn, certify their lay people by virtue of their own authority.

Evangelism Explosion's motto is *It's better to train a soul-winner than to win one soul; better to train a trainer of soul-winners than to train a soul-winner.* Churches interested in such an equipping program should contact EE III International, P.O. Box 23820, Fort Lauderdale, FL 33307.

# THE INSTITUTE FOR AMERICAN CHURCH GROWTH
## PASADENA, CALIFORNIA
## DR. WIN ARN, EXECUTIVE DIRECTOR
## THE GENIUS BEHIND
## EARLY CHURCH GROWTH CAN BE DISCOVERED IN YOUR CHURCH

CHAPTER

33

OVER the past four decades the good old American slogan "Bigger is better" has crept into the church and done some real damage to our view of evangelism.

We've become preoccupied with big meetings, big crusades, coast-to-coast TV coverage, and mass media campaigns. In the process we've lost sight of the uncomplicated genius behind early church growth.

The unique yet natural process by which the church has grown down through the centuries has been missed by most churches in the late twentieth century. In fact, according to research we have conducted with over 14,000 people, a natural growth process is responsible for 80-95 percent of the lay people now active in American churches today . . . whether we know it or not.

The records of the explosive growth of the early church are recorded in the book of Acts . . . from 12 . . . to 120 . . . to 3,000 . . . to 5,000 . . . from "addition" to "multiplication" in just weeks. And the numbers continued skyrocketing until they reached world-shaking dimensions. But how? How did the gospel travel so fast?

Did the Apostle Peter run off two hundred thousand copies of the *New Jerusalem Herald* headlined "JESUS IS ALIVE!"? And did James start a nationwide telephone campaign? Perhaps John mass-produced gospel tracts and chariot bumper stickers? And maybe later, Paul hit the airways with his first prime-time special, "The Damascus Road"?

Peter, James, John, and even Paul might have been thrilled to have the communication tools that are available to Christians today. But without them, the early church experienced the most dramatic growth period in church history. What was their secret?

The answer is so simple you wonder how we ever got so sidetracked: the church grew as the gospel traveled from person to person to person over the natural bridges of close human relationships. The New Testament word for those close human relationships is *"oikos,"* which means household. And the secret is found time and time again in the New Testament. The word *"oikos"* meant more than the immediate family in the house. It included servants, servants' families, friends, and even business associates. The *oikos* was the sum total of a Christian's friends, relatives, and associates.

Following the resurrection and ascension, the gospel traveled like electricity through these networks of close relationships. That was one of the key secrets that caused the early church to explode.

It happened to Cornelius and his close relations (Acts 10). With Lydia and her friends and relatives (Acts 16). With the Philippian jailer and his family and friends (Acts 16), Zacchaeus (Luke 19), the demoniac (Mark 5), Levi (Mark 2), and so many others.

Noted church historian Kenneth Scott Latourette has observed that "the primary change agents in the spread of the faith . . . were the men and women who earned their livelihood in some purely secular manner, and spoke of their faith to those they met in this natural fashion."

## WHY OIKOS IS EFFECTIVE

Why do people respond so positively to the gospel as it travels through these "webs" of relationships? Here are seven reasons:

1. *OIKOS* RELATIONSHIPS PROVIDE A NATURAL NETWORK FOR SHARING THE GOOD NEWS OF GOD'S REDEMPTIVE LOVE.

The new Christian, who has discovered the genuine joy of experiencing God's grace, is naturally eager to tell others. He wants those closest to him to share in this new freedom and joy. The *oikos* of friends, relatives, and associates is the most natural place for a new Christian to share this newfound joy with people . . . people who mean the most to him.

2. *OIKOS* MEMBERS ARE RECEPTIVE.

There is quite a difference between hearing the witness of a trusted friend and hearing a "religious presentation" from a total stranger. When God's love is discussed with an *oikos* member, that person is usually open and receptive since he or she is listening to the experience of someone he or she knows and trusts.

3. *OIKOS* RELATIONSHIPS ALLOW FOR UNHURRIED AND NATURAL SHARING OF GOD'S LOVE.

Relationships with *oikos* members, by their very nature, are regular and natural. Whether on a social outing or in the comfort of a living room, the relationships are usually easy and relaxed, and so are the places, times, and situations. Communicating the gospel is not squeezed into one short visit or presentation. Being a witness to the life-changing effects of God's love over a period of weeks, months, and even years allows the *oikos* member time for thoughtful consideration about becoming a disciple.

4. *OIKOS* RELATIONSHIPS PROVIDE NATURAL SUPPORT WHEN THE WEB MEMBER COMES TO CHRIST.

When a friend or relative comes to faith, there is a natural source for nurture and encouragement. Since at least one Christian—the original web member—is close to the new convert and eager to see growth in his/her new life, new Christians are not left alone. There is someone to love, care for, and nurture them.

5. *OIKOS* RELATIONSHIPS RESULT IN THE EFFECTIVE ASSIMILATION OF NEW CONVERTS INTO THE CHURCH.

It is natural for the new Christian to begin attending church where his/her friend or family member belongs. Because of the "bridge," the new Christian can much more easily become associated with other Christians in a Sunday school class or fellowship group, and begin to build relationships and new friends within the body.

## 6. *OIKOS* RELATIONSHIPS TEND TO WIN ENTIRE FAMILIES.
When one or two people in a family come to Christ and to the church, it is often the beginning of a process that results in the entire family becoming new disciples. As the entire family grows together in Christ, the family unit is strengthened. On the other hand, if the entire family is not reached, conflict and fragmentation often result. Christians and non-Christians have different goals and priorities. Spiritual growth is more difficult and the new Christian may drop out of an active Christian life due to this lack of family support. An immediate emphasis should be placed on identifying and reaching others in a family, once one member has made a Christian commitment.

## 7. *OIKOS* RELATIONSHIPS PROVIDE A CONSTANTLY ENLARGING SOURCE OF NEW CONTACTS.
Each new person reached for Christ and the church has his/her own group of relatives, friends, and associates who are candidates for the Good News. Research shows that on the average, each new Christian has twelve people in his/her *oikos* who are non-Christian. (Older Christians often have less; the average in most churches is about eight.) In most cases everyone in that new Christian's web is outside of Christ and a local church. The process of identifying receptive people and reaching out is never completed, because with each new Christian there are new contacts and opportunities.

Throughout the 2,000-year history of the church, God has richly blessed its growth through webs of *oikos* relationships. The *oikos* concept is timely, yet timeless. It is planned, yet not contrived. It is founded on solid church growth research, experience, and principles found throughout Scripture. It is the way churches have grown, and continue to grow, as each new *oikos* member who comes to Christ and the church has his/her own web of friends and relatives, and the pattern continues.

# DISCOVERING THE GENIUS IN YOUR CHURCH

To help local churches develop this New Testament strategy for discipleship in their own congregations, Church Growth has developed "The Master's Plan," a powerful rediscovery of the evangelistic strategy found at the heart of the New Testament church.

The Master's Plan combines the often neglected New Testament concept of *oikos* (close relationships) with modern church growth insights. The Master's Plan is specifically designed to help every participating church member have a truly effective living witness among family, friends, and associates.

And the exciting thing is that The Master's Plan allows the local church and its lay members to work as a team—a cohesive, disciple-making unit—working together, holding one another accountable, supporting and encouraging one another in the caring-creative process of reaching out to loved ones and friends. And it works! God gives the increase as church and lay people become intentional and effective and enthusiastic about sharing his love with their own *"oikos"* of friends and relatives.

When your church begins to follow The Master's Plan for Making Disciples, your people and your church will begin growing in ways you always hoped and prayed for. Members discover a new sense of unity and purpose. Their fellowship together will become more meaningful as God's love deliberately yet naturally flows out from laity into the lives of those closest to them. The Master's Plan can help you and your church enter a new dimension of spiritual growth and enrichment. Nothing can match the excitement and personal fulfillment your members will experience as they begin to see their friends and loved ones become Christians and strong members of the body of Christ. If you're looking for an effective approach to disciple-making, one integrated with state-of-the-art research and expertise from the study of church growth strategy, The Master's Plan could be the answer for your church.

# MAKING DISCIPLES

The Master's Plan Church Disciple-making Strategy is a refreshing and effective approach to fulfilling the Great Commission in your community. It was designed to help you apply the insights and principles of the book, *The Master's Plan for Making Disciples*, in your church.

The Master's Plan is an exciting, caring process that can help every member of your church experience the disciple-making way of life found at the heart of the New Testament.

We invite you to join hundreds of churches across America that are rediscovering the contagious enthusiasm of the early church.

The goal of making disciples is the foundation upon which the Institute for American Church Growth has structured its organization and ministry. As the first and foremost group to take world church growth principles and apply them to the American scene, the Institute offers a variety of proven and effective resources for local parishes and regional judicatories.

More information on these effective resources to help your church reach its full potential in disciple-making is what the Institute is all about. For example, The Master's Plan for Making Disciples, using the *oikos* principle, is available in a training seminar for parishes. In this seminar, each active member discovers that the richest and most fruitful opportunities for successful disciple-making can be found in relationships already existing with unchurched loved ones and friends. Members learn how to express their love and care for the people closest to them in ways that build natural disciple-making relationships.

## ABOUT THE INSTITUTE FOR AMERICAN CHURCH GROWTH . . . PIONEERS IN HELPING CHURCHES GROW!

The Institute for American Church Growth is the first organization established in America to help pastors and church leaders understand and apply church growth principles. Founded in 1973 by Dr. Win Arn, the Institute took the concepts of church growth first developed overseas by Dr. Donald McGavran (now Chairman of the Board) and refined them for effective application in North America.

From the first book ever published on American church growth (*How to Grow a Church*, McGavran/Arn), through the first church growth seminars and curriculum for laity, through the only color films on church growth principles, and through continuing "firsts" in state-of-the-art church growth thinking, the Institute has provided ongoing leadership and a standard of quality unmatched by any other group or organization.

Since its beginnings the Institute has been guided by four basic purposes:

1. To motivate and support evangelism and church growth in America through the local church.
2. To enable congregations and regional groups of churches to develop and implement strategies and bold plans for growth.
3. To help pastors and laity understand the things that hinder their church's growth and apply basic growth-producing principles to their church.
4. To serve as an information and consultation resource for the church-at-large in its growth efforts.

Over the past ten years:

- More than 24,000 clergy and 200,000 lay leaders have been involved in training through the Institute's Pastors' Conferences and Church Growth Seminars.
- More than 2.1 million people have seen one or more of the Institute's films on church growth.
- The ministry and services of the Institute for American Church Growth extend to nearly every denomination in America.
- More than 350,000 copies of *Church Growth: America* magazine, published by the Institute, have been distributed.

Is the Institute distinct from other organizations? Yes!

1. The Institute trains laity and professionals in practical applications of church growth. It is not "ivory tower pedagogy," removed from the real world. It is basic, workable, usable training and input that pastors can apply now, in their own situation.
2. The growth resources available to the church, developed by the Institute, are unsurpassed in both quality and

number. Nowhere else is such a wealth of helpful resources for church growth available to the pastor and church that want to grow . . . all based on sound research, thoroughly tested and proven effective.

3. The Institute has credibility established from years of working with churches and regional judicatories. There is no need to worry about unmet commitments or half-baked packages quickly assembled. The Institute is committed to long-term service to support you in every way possible.

4. The Institute is truly a complementary interdenominational resource and service organization. Over fifty denominations are "satisfied customers." Academic credit for seminars and workshops is available through most denominationally affiliated seminaries. The goal of the Institute is to support the structure and goals of the individual church and/or denomination, rather than extricate people from their own system and theological convictions.

5. Because of the commitment to remain the leader in the field, the Institute is continually developing new materials in response to needs of churches. For example, a significant new breakthrough in evangelism for the local parish has recently been developed, based on "state-of-the-art" research and insights from church growth. The Master's Plan for Making Disciples builds on the natural way that churches grow—through friends and relationships of present church members.

If you would like to know more about church growth and the unique variety of films, books, curriculum, and other growth resources, a free copy of the *Church Growth Resource News* is available. There are many helpful resources which you can begin to use at once in your church. Or, give the Institute a call, and they will be happy to talk about your needs.

Dr. Arn is the founder and Executive Director of the Institute for American Church Growth—the leading organization involved in the research and dissemination of church growth principles.

Dr. Arn has published a variety of church growth material. Several of his research studies have been reported in *Time*, *Newsweek*, and the Associated Press. Books he has authored or co-authored include *How to Grow a Church; The Pastor's Church Growth*

*Handbook; Back to Basics in Church Growth; Growth: A New Vision for the Sunday School;* and *The Master's Plan for Making Disciples.*

In addition, Dr. Arn has produced a wide variety of 16mm color films in the area of church growth. Some of these include: "How to Grow a Church," "Reach Out and Grow," ". . . and They Said It Couldn't Be Done!" "Planned Parenthood for Churches," "A Church Is Born," "The Gift of Love," "But I'm Just a Layman," "The Great Commission Sunday School," "For the Love of Pete," and the latest film, "See You Sunday?"

Dr. Arn and the Institute conduct seminars and training sessions for individual churches, consortia of churches, denominations, and continuing education training for pastors in the field of church growth. They are located in Pasadena, California.

# INSTITUTE OF CHURCH GROWTH
## SOUTH BEND, INDIANA
## SETH A. ROHRER, FOUNDER
## "LET THE CHURCH GROW!"
## by Medford H. Jones

*CHAPTER*

**34**

THE cries of nearly one half billion babies born annually certainly indicate the need for rapid church growth in this generation. Yet, in spite of the needs and pressures of this turbulent time, it should be remembered that the prior motivation for church growth has always been the will of God. From before the foundation of the world he planned for the church and constituted it to grow rapidly and to reproduce itself. It is God's intention, then, that his church shall be the prime means of winning the world to himself in Jesus Christ.

If the world is won, it will be because multitudes of churches have been planted and have grown to maturity in every field and social circumstance. Thus, in these times when old line denominations are scarcely holding their own or declining, it is imperative that fresh vigorous thought be given to the issue of church growth. Perhaps, as never before, it is time to "let the church grow."

Church growth is usually thought of in terms of man's own egocentric orientation. Man thinks of himself as the causal factor in growth. He asks the question, "How can I make the church grow?" Or he fabricates organizations and gimmicks to make the church grow. Yet, the church still does not grow as it is assumed it should.

The Scriptures portray the church as a living organism rather than a mere social organization. As a living organism the church should be expected to demonstrate the basic characteristics of living organisms. It should be able to grow and reproduce itself. The Scriptures demonstrate this by showing that the church is endowed by God with all of the necessary elements for its own growth and reproduction. Mark 4:26-28 cites the natural production through seed from the soil, and uses the Greek word for "automatic" to indicate this. It appears that Jesus intended the church to understand its endowment with native ability to grow and multiply. He illustrated growth in the parables of the mustard seed and leaven. The tiny mustard seed in one growing season grows large enough for the birds to nest in its branches. Leaven was cited for its rapid multiplication and expansion.

The church in its natural state fought its way through the Mediterranean world and beyond in ever-widening circles. This was possible because God provided the personnel, organization, purpose, and guidance for growth. Growth was an innate process. Men found ministry as believers naturally within the context of the church as God intended, and the church grew.

While it is evident that we do not "make growth," it is also clear that growth may be influenced. It may be accelerated or slowed or shaped. Many illustrations indicate this in nature. The tiny goldfish in a small bowl will not grow until it is put into a larger bowl. Plants stop growing when they rootbind. Chickens will stop growing before they have reached normal size if the square footage per bird is too small. So, nature illustrates how external factors may influence growth. Thus with the church. Although it is constituted intentionally for rapid growth and reproduction, it can be shaped or retarded in this growth. Men, though well intentioned, through many means have shaped the growth of the church. If what one sees is any evidence, much of this influence has retarded growth.

Man's relationship to the church, then, is simple. He is to align himself within the church to those God-given elements that are designed for the church's growth. Man shares harmoniously within the "whole body," the church, and as part of it, shares in its growth. So man is challenged to "let the church grow!"

## CHURCH GROWTH DISEASES

If the local church does not grow, it is either diseased or strangulated. There are many diseases that prey upon the body of Christ. Malnutrition can be one. If a church is not being nurtured on the Word, it can stop growing. The church can be diseased with an inadequate sense of purpose. If a church forgets it is a garrison of God's army, it will lose its recruitive and revolutionary power and stop growing. A church can lack an adequate will to grow and resist the Holy Spirit. The Holy Spirit can be hindered. If a church deliberately resists or is ignorant of the Spirit's work within it, it can become weak and ineffective. Such diseases are legion.

## CHURCH GROWTH STRANGULATION

Strangulation can stop growth while the church's leadership is unaware of the causes. Scientifically measurable strangulation may occur in leadership, program, property, or social structure. An imbalance creating a stricture in one or more of these factors will stop growth. Inadequate provision among these elements dictates the ultimate size of a congregation. It is a simple fact that regardless of the doctrinal position or the external situation of a church, these four measurable factors usually establish the ceiling for the matured church.

Failure to multiply churches leaves a communion growing old and stagnated. To sustain growth, a communion must constantly start new churches which grow vigorously. If a given communion comes to understand the nature of strangulation, it may well double its membership by permitting the existing congregations to grow to full maturity. Even so, the necessity for planting churches is very urgent if the communion is to sustain continuing growth. Many older communions demonstrate this today with significant growth being experienced only among the new congregations.

The essential question then is how can the growth process be renewed, once slowed or stopped. The following may be mentioned: (1) renew responsiveness to the insistent will of God and the prompting of the Holy Spirit; (2) minimize disease and strangulation; (3) realign with the dynamic factors for growth inherent within the church; (4) pray the "Lord of the Harvest"; (5) seek to have a compelling desire for church growth. It is already tragically late and there must not be delay. The church must be willing to "let the church grow."

The basic strategy for growth is to maintain the state of a dynamic vacuum within the church. The tendency of a vacuum is to fill. When the growth elements are in balance and open for spontaneous growth, the dynamic vacuum is in effect. The action is similar to thirsty fiber which pulls fluid into its structure. So the dynamic vacuum, the state of thirst for growth, must be maintained in the balance of all of the elements God has given for the growth of the church. Thus the Apostle Paul said that in the function of each part the body increases and builds itself up in love. So, if the dynamic vacuum is maintained, the tendency of the church will be to grow spontaneously.

# CRUCIAL FACTORS IN MAINTAINING THE DYNAMIC VACUUM TO "LET THE CHURCH GROW"

ADEQUATE MINISTRY

Maintain a plus factor in ministry to "let the church grow." Adequate ministry within the church must come from application of New Testament teaching. The New Testament word "ministry" means service. Furthermore, anyone who serves in the Christian context is a minister. "The ministry" denotes that body of Christians who serve. "The ministry" is not the exclusive property of a specialized group of servants who may become known as "the ministers." All Christians are to be ministers and a part of "the ministry." In its minimal form New Testament ministry requires each Christian to seek opportunity to lead others to Christ, both through his personal example as a Christian, and through giving the Word to the unbeliever.

There are, of course, gradations of ministry within the New Testament. Besides the ministry in general, there is the specialized ministry of specific functions designated by God in Scripture.

These are for the propagation of the faith and for the equipping of the saints.

When the church brings the ministry of all believers into fruition, the local congregation itself becomes a minister and is its own witness. It is known in its community. Because an individual member is attached to this respected body, he is able to be more fruitful in his witness.

At the realistic level of the local American congregation, paid staff is the key measurable element in ministry. Paid staff is significant because it equips and leads Christians into fruitful service. A study of actual growth patterns shows the church leveling off when a certain staff-to-membership ratio is reached. This holds, as well, for a ratio of Sunday school classes to paid staff. In other words, when the paid staff becomes too loaded with detail work to continue expanding the volunteer ministry, the church stops growing. The staff must be maintained to keep the "equipping of the saints for ministry" progressing adequately. Then classes and other functions will increase with resulting growth.

COMPREHENSIVE RECORDS

Provide adequate records for operational information to "let the church grow." Records must be current, accurate, comprehensive, and structured to activate needed attention with full reporting. These records are concerned with precious people. Concerning its members, the church needs to know the general facts, the spiritual status, and the level of their participation. Concerning potential members, the church needs to know who they are, general information, and the source of contact. The church needs to know the relation people have to its life and program. It must know their needs. The records system must indicate and activate the necessary action.

There is no way the church can grow without being concerned for numbers of precious people. The shepherd who went after the one sheep had to count to miss it. The church that does not know and utilize all that is helpful in the winning and developing of people is not going to grow as it can.

DYNAMIC GROUP LIFE

Provide a plus factor in productive fellowship and Bible study or prayer groups to "let the church grow." Fellowship within the

New Testament implies association, participation, communion, sharing, or partaking. It always involves the interaction of two or more people. Fellowship develops the Christian and holds him in association, which gives meaning to his life. This overflows to pull the non-Christian into the church.

The fellowship is essentially constituted in small homogeneous groups. These become a loose association of interrrelated personal groups. This fellowship is primarily spontaneous and self-sustaining for growth when it is not inhibited. Mutual concern becomes active and the church grows. Care must be taken to provide adequate numbers of such groups and classes so that there is always "room" for more precious people.

## ATTRACTIVE FACILITIES

Provide a plus factor in space and facilities to "let the church grow." Facilities must be attractive, functionally equipped, and adequate. Facilities set an image for the church. They must set a beneficial image.

Strangulation in space is dramatic in reference to the worship services. Worship services level off or decline while people do not recognize the cause. Research[1] shows that when church attendance averages annually 80 percent of its primary seating it is at the point of saturation. It is possible with high motivation or exceptionally favorable external circumstances to average more for a time. However, at the 80 percent level the church begins paying a high price in the loss of nonmembers in the congregation and in the forcing of regular members into irregular attendance. If a church wants to maintain a growing worship service, it will need to be alert to crowding.

To have a growing Sunday school, it will be necessary to provide space for full departmentalization and a ratio of six pupils per class average on a schoolwide basis. Churches characteristically try to maintain impossible Sunday school averages for the number of classes in operation.

It is a fact that a church conforms to its facilities. Thus the importance of careful planning and adequate provision of space and facilities is paramount. Many churches have been doomed to

[1]Dr. Richard Myers has done significant research on this.

mediocrity or to failure because of unwise decisions on facilities. It also may be said categorically that frequently facilities speak so loudly that people cannot hear what the church is saying.

SPECIFIC GEOGRAPHICAL AREA

Identify and attack the specific field and objective to "let the church grow." Any church needs to know what and where its field is. This requires the getting of facts, the eliminating of fiction, myth, and emotional surmise. Facts needed concerning the church require an understanding of its relation in the community regarding the particular need and the social structure in the community. The church needs to face and understand those areas which it is failing to serve within its community. Having recognized these, it must plan to meet whatever characteristic challenge is presented. Within this it is necessary for the church to fix its purpose on a workable area and specific projects. The area must be seen on a map and workably accessible.

The plan of attack in that area must be verbalized and put on paper. Then all of the church's resources must be mobilized and utilized. A church which fails to identify specific contiguous geographical areas and objectives usually just follows its members and has an increasingly scattered field. It finds itself out of touch with the people in the community it should serve. If, however, the church is to remain relevant, it must remain in contact and be engaged with its community. Thus, programming needs to be three-pronged. There will be the continuing general evangelistic thrust within the defined area and services to the scattered members. There will also be periodic projects of limited time and duration.

A church must plan for continuing growth or it plans not to grow. All attack must be planned and programmed. All programming must be evaluated in the light of the results achieved to determine further usage.

Program and methodology are the result of men's efforts to meet given situations. Program and methodology are legitimate and justified exactly in ratio to their effectiveness for God's will. As a specific period of programming closes, immediate evaluation must take place. There will be times when pauses may be necessary for the sake of the work force. These pauses should be with purpose, however. They should give opportunity for planning and evaluation so that the church will be ready to move on after the pause.

## SYSTEMATIC EVALUATION

Stir up the dynamic fires to "let the church grow." Constantly ask of every dynamic factor, method, or idea—is it contributing to growth? Why? Why not? Then adjust these elements to achieve maximum growth. Growth follows preparation.

The whole membership of the congregation must be confronted with the insistent will of God for church growth. The church must never be allowed to drift into a sense of ease or satisfaction with just holding its own. One of the most dramatic forms of the Great Commission in the New Testament is the story of the feast and the householder's will that his house be filled. After the excuses had been made, after the servant had done all that he knew to do, the householder said to the servant, "Go into the highways and hedges and compel them to come in, that my house may be filled." This insistent will of God for the filling of his church is a dramatic, ever-present force within the household of faith. Thus, every inborn desire of each Christian to contribute meaningfully must be utilized. The Holy Spirit must have room to move within the fabric of the church's life. The membership must be immersed in the divine presence and in the essence of his purpose. Certainly the plans of men are of little avail unless they harmonize with the purpose and will of God and are energized by the Holy Spirit.

## CONCLUSION

Thank God in Christ for the growth in the church. Too frequently the church has been more like the nine lepers than the one who returned to thank his benefactor. It is far too easy to forget that the fruitage and growth are the results of the natural power within the church and the grace of God rather than man's own striving and wisdom. So the growing church must keep the elements of its structure in balance; it must maintain the dynamic, open situation and "let the church grow." It must leave room for the influence of the Holy Spirit. It must be constantly thanking God for the victories in growth that are achieved.

Dr. Medford H. Jones is President of Pacific Christian College, Long Beach, California. Previously he was Professor at Milligan College, Tennessee. His teaching career was preceded by training in theology in which he took degrees from Northwest Christian College at Eugene, Oregon, and at Butler University School of Religion, Indianapolis. The Butler Graduate Division granted a master's degree in science and Milligan College conferred the doctor of divinity degree for his work in evangelism and church growth.

Dr. Jones' entire ministry has encompassed evangelism and church growth. He ministered to rural and urban churches. His schooling and research for theses came in this same context. Principles and guidelines thus developed and put to work have proved many times over the vitality of doing God's work in God's way in his church.

# NATIONAL CHURCH GROWTH RESEARCH CENTER
## WASHINGTON, D.C.
## DR. PAUL BENJAMIN, DIRECTOR
## "DO THE WORK OF AN EVANGELIST!"

*Successful professor of evangelism, Dr. Paul Benjamin, is also Director of the National Church Growth Research Center in Washington, D.C., and has spoken about the role of the evangelist to over 50,000 ordained pastors in the past several years. Just as St. Paul spoke to Timothy in days of old, this modern-day Paul speaks to us and says, "Do the work of an evangelist!"*

CHAPTER

35

## THE WORK OF AN EVANGELIST

In 2 Timothy, a veteran missionary reminds his "child in the faith" about his evangelistic responsibilities. Timothy must "preach the word, be urgent in season and out of season, convince, rebuke, and exhort" and "be unfailing in patience and in teaching" (4:2). But regardless of the other demands upon his time, he must not neglect "the work of an evangelist" (4:5).

Why do we have these special instructions to Timothy about the importance of evangelism? Simply because he had to be made to realize the subtle temptation every preacher of the gospel faces. Through his own unflagging efforts, or the work of faithful predecessors, he might be preaching for a large church. Pastoral duties multiply with the growth of the congregation. He had to instruct the young, visit the sick, and take care of administrative details. Soon all his waking hours became absorbed by the membership and their needs. Meanwhile, still in the world were thousands who had never confessed the name of Jesus.

The problem is not new. Richard Baxter mentions it in the seventeenth century. He asks, "If there be a thousand or five hundred ignorant people in your parish, it is a poor discharge of your duty now and then occasionally to speak to some few of them and let the rest alone in their ignorance. Will it satisfy you to deal with one person of twenty or forty and to pass by all the rest?"

The New Testament sets apart a class of servants in the church known as "evangelists." They are some of the "gifts" from the ascended Christ to his church, together with apostles, prophets, pastors, and teachers (Ephesians 4:11). Philip is designated as an "evangelist" (Acts 21:8). His sermon to a high official from Ethiopia may have influenced an entire continent for Christ (Acts 8:27).

In reference to church leadership in the New Testament, Marcus Barth points to the settled work of pastors and teachers. Then he says, "We are justified in inferring that the evangelists, on the contrary, are the missionaries of his own generation, who do not serve any one congregation or area, but move from place to place as they find openings for the proclamation of the gospel."

Unfortunately today, in some Christian circles, the term "evangelist" carries a stigma with it. The minister who preaches from place to place, serving the entire body of Christ rather than one local congregation, is sometimes viewed with suspicion. Sometimes, church members have developed a firm distrust for any Christian leader whose roots are not firmly fixed in one location.

Even though the church has its special class of servants called "evangelists," every member must take responsibility for reaching the lost. The task of evangelism is too large for one set of leaders within the church. In the Ephesian epistle, apostles, prophets, pastors, and teachers are to build "up the body of Christ" (4:12). The body is clearly moving in two directions simultaneously. Every member must strive for "mature manhood, to the measure of the stature of the fulness of Christ" (4:13). Yet at the same time, "when each part is working properly" the body "makes bodily growth" (4:16). The missionary implications of the term "body of Christ" are clear. It is through "the body" that the fullness of Christ, the head, "fills all in all" (1:23).

In American society today, it is very difficult for a minister to function as an evangelist. The preacher may even become "sealed off" from those in the world. He is probably involved with worship services every Sunday and special church meetings the rest of the week. His close friends are committed Christians. He seldom has a conversation with anyone who is not a church member. Here is the old mission compound idea of "missionaries" being fenced off from the unbelieving community.

The work of perfecting the saints is a vital ministry within the body of Christ. Across the centuries, the church has been greatly blessed by its able scholars and pulpit princes. Within its administrative ranks have been those faithful servants whose organizational skills enabled the body to function more effectively. And yet, how much the world has lost because the capabilities of so many able men have been siphoned off to work almost exclusively with those who are already Christians.

The church today must find ways to release the energies of its servants who have special gifts in evangelism. Many ministers, functioning almost exclusively as "pastors," have capabilities for converting hundreds of sinners from the error of their ways. Yet, because of our traditional leadership patterns, many of these workers are practically isolated from the non-Christian world. The God who sent his Son to the "world" is surely not pleased when some of his most capable evangelists become private chaplains to a handful of saints.

I know a minister who felt the poignancy of this problem. He was preaching in a town of seventeen thousand people. Although he had only one full-time secretary to help him with a congregation of 1,200 resident members, he resolved to seek the lost in his community. He started out by visiting the homes and apartments close to the church building. He simply knocked on the door and introduced himself. "We are trying to serve the people in our community," he said. "If we can ever be of any help to you, please let us know." Then he left literature and went on to the next home.

Sometimes he was invited into the home. If he found a family in need of food or clothing, he always notified the deacons. They took the responsibility for discreetly providing help as long as it was necessary. In a few years, this congregation was the largest in town. They averaged one hundred baptisms a year. Dozens of young people entered specialized Christian service. During his thirteen-year stay, he visited every house personally. He called in the last home during the final week of his ministry.

Nothing should keep a minister from doing the work of evangelism. If he has responsibilities for a large congregation, his time for calling may be very limited. Yet his preaching will lack something vital if he is not directly involved in reaching the lost. He may take up some hobby or sport, or perhaps join a club where he has association with those who are outside the Christian faith. While we keep emphasizing the fellowship within the church, we may sometimes forget that Jesus ate with "publicans and sinners."

The problem we face today is critical. Thousands of capable evangelists within the body of Christ are isolated from non-Christians. Our current situation is a denial of the salt-and-light principle. A breakthrough at this point could help release energies and time now being devoted almost exclusively to members of the church. Meanwhile, if the "equipping principle" is employed, their needs can be met also. A concerted effort in evangelism is not intended to create a climate in the church whereby a shallow type of Christianity is either encouraged or develops through default. Rather, it is an attempt to get "the whole body, joined and knit together by every joint with which it is supplied" to become more acutely conscious of the responsibility for "bodily growth" (Ephesians 4:16).

## LIVING IN TWO WORLDS

The effective minister lives in two worlds. It is not enough just to know Christian doctrine. He must also be thoroughly conversant with his contemporary culture. A homiletics professor was complaining about the sermons he heard. "They are either too far on the other side of the Flood," he said, "or too far this side of Pearl Harbor." In short, the minister must be strongly rooted in his own Christian convictions. At the same time, his sermons will miss their mark if they lack application.

The whole "relevancy" era a few years ago was aimed precisely at this problem. So many ministers were preaching sermons which did not reach people where they were living. Consequently, church members were bored. They kept on attending worship because of their faith, but they could hardly wait for the benediction. The pulpit was not touching them at the point of their needs.

The minister who seeks to be evangelistic must also be very sensitive to the "other world" made up of non-Christians. When he uses the Bible to undergird his statements about gambling, drugs, swearing, greed, sexual promiscuity, and the like, his source of authority may be completely disallowed by those with worldly leanings. If he discusses his views with a nonbeliever who refuses to accept his presuppositions, he may find himself out on a limb. He needs to know where the other person is "coming from."

The support for the church from the American intellectual community, especially the leadership in the northeastern corridor of the United States, was lost a generation ago. H. L. Mencken of Baltimore helped to spearhead the revolt. Mencken, a prolific writer who invented words at will, wrote a syndicated column for the "Sunpapers." He also edited two influential magazines, the *Smart Set* and the *American Mercury.* From this vantage point in journalism, he poured buckets of scorn and ridicule over the heads of politicians, preachers, and other "do-gooders."

He was very effective, partly because what he said was on target. Many thinking people, tired of pompous politicians and unloving church people, welcomed his vial of vitriol. His ability to turn a subtle phrase into a machine-gun bullet was amazing. Many Americans laughed while he heaped scorn upon the small-towners who he felt epitomized the "boobousie." He defined a judge as "a law student who marks his own examination papers." He reserved a special scorn for prohibitionists and creationists.

Many of his readers felt Mencken's invectives provided a needed corrective in an overly serious American society. They saw a playful journalistic Jove at work, hurling lightning bolts and clearing the air. Sometimes, they were unconscious of the real bitterness which motivated Mencken. His statement, "I do not admire the general run of American Bible-searchers—Methodists, United Brethren, Baptists, and such vermin," indicated his own personal animosity. He did say that, for the good of society, it might be better to be a lowbrow Methodist than to be an atheist.

Today in the American intellectual society, Mencken's views have fairly well triumphed. They were picked up by a chorus of authors and journalists who felt the time had come for an all-out assault on the biblical foundations of American society. The doors were opened to radical European authors. American boys and girls, coming to the state university from high school and perhaps a small-town Sunday school, are now immersed in an antichurch flood of writings.

Today's "classics" in literature include the works of D. H. Lawrence, F. Scott Fitzgerald, James Joyce, and frequently Henry Miller. Psychology begins with Freud and veers off in a dozen directions. Philosophy courses include ample helpings of Hume, Schopenhauer, Nietzsche, and Sartre. No wonder American young people are so bewildered today. Many of them live in an intellectual no-man's-land. Some may be unwilling to let go of a religious value system they received in childhood. At the same time, they did not get enough help in Sunday school to sustain a Christian faith against a non-Christian onslaught.

Perhaps no institution in our society has a worse misnomer for its name than the American "university." Instead of receiving an integrated approach to knowledge, here the student is offered a plethora of unrelated courses. Even those who take a "major" are not given any means whereby their special emphasis can be consolidated with a larger body of knowledge. No wonder the suicide rate among students is one of the highest in the nation. Many have no real goals in life.

Perhaps, as some have suggested, the best term to describe the American university experience is the word "multiversity." Once we realize the modern university has no unifying core of knowledge, we must also remember its separate units of study are often based on humanistic presuppositions. The Bible is not derided in the average university classroom—it is simply ignored. If a student cites the Bible as an authority, many times the whole classroom becomes a little tense and uncomfortable. The assumption is obvious. With its heavy dose of supernaturalism, what jurisdiction does the Bible have for an enlightened and sophisticated modern society?

Whether we recognize it or not, the intellectual leadership of America today is strongly in the hands of those who discount the credibility of the Bible. Futhermore, many feel it has little relevance for our times and problems. Therefore, the minister must do his work against an indifferent and sometimes hostile backdrop. Church young people may doubt his conclusions because they question his assumptions. They are not opposed to Christianity. They are simply getting an overload of misgivings from the high schools and colleges they attend.

Coupled with doubts about biblical authority is the daily dose of sensualism permeating American culture. Sex sells soaps, perfumes, bath powders, deodorants, automobiles, boats, airplanes, and on and on. As Pitirim Sorokin, the Harvard sociologist said, "We live in a sex-saturated culture." No wonder American young people are facing such struggles today. We must not make the mistake of thinking the battle is lost—that society is too virulent for the gospel to inoculate. It is still not too late to announce, "Let us pray" instead of lamenting, "Let us throw in the sponge."

Obviously, we cannot win the allegiance of vast numbers to the cause of Christ by being constantly on the defensive. The New Testament preachers were "heralds of God." They proclaimed the Good News of the gospel with forthrightness and confidence. The apostles did not hesitate to take on Hedonism and Gnosticism and brand both of them as heresies. They sized up a corrupt pagan society and said, "Thou ailest . . . here and here"!

## APPROACHING A LOST SOCIETY

How do we approach a society that has largely lost its way? The psalmist says, "My eyes shed streams of tears, because men do not keep thy law" (Psalm 119:136). We come to our task on our knees with broken hearts. The "false gospel" of independence from God so effectively communicated by the nonbelievers of a previous generation has left us with a staggering legacy. We do not need to catalog our national sins. We can start with battered children, mention the disintegration of the American family, cite a generation of young people without authority and then stop. We have sown the wind. Now we are reaping the whirlwind (Hosea 8:7).

The American church cannot be exonerated in the process of fixing blame for our growing social ills. The tidal wave of skepticism which carried away the intellectual community also caught the churches woefully unprepared. Basic unbelief in salient Christian doctrines found its way into the upper echelons of

American religious leadership. Some church scholars seemed determined to outdo the followers of Mencken and Bernard Shaw in their shrill criticism of Christianity. Because of their own doubtings, the bugle they played gave forth only "an indistinct sound" (1 Corinthians 14:8). Consequently, outside of a small contingent of Christian soldiers, the rank and file were unprepared for battle.

A democracy can protect its citizenry from spoiled food, but it cannot deliver the populace from tainted ideas. Poisonous and pernicious concepts are being planted in the body politic today from a thousand ruinous sources. If some of these views triumphed, it would spell absolute doom for the nation. Laws have been perpetually ineffective for either developing or changing a mindset. The use of heroin as a legitimate drug only needs enough votes to make it legal in American society.

Opposed to these disruptive and destructive influences must come a stream of Christian ideas which water society and make it blossom. England reached its zenith in the nineteenth century when the political and religious community both upheld a strong biblical authority. If Victorianism carried an overload of prudery, at least it provided a stable kind of employee who showed up for work and took pride in his craft. England's flirtation with the "Age of Reason" was nipped in the bud by the butchery and barbarism of the French Revolution. Thereafter, its political leadership resolved to put a high premium on the value of Christian principles. These ideals laid the groundwork for one of the greatest nations in the history of civilization.

Americans can still repent, but the hour grows shorter every day. We must recognize that millions of Americans will never give allegiance to any religion but themselves. We cannot win them all. And yet, the leavening influence of Christianity could change the course of our own nation and even the entire world. The rediscovery of the Bible by thousands of congregations is indeed heartening. Moreover, many churches are listening with new discernment to the call of Jesus in the Great Commission to take the gospel to the world.

Let us not confuse the church with the world. We are to be "in the world," said Jesus, but not "of the world." Those who consider themselves "strangers and exiles on earth," with their eyes focused on a "heavenly city," will never be understood by people who live as though they are here forever (Hebrews 13). These differences cannot be reconciled outside of a mutual acceptance of the Christian faith.

The true evangelist knows the church, but he also knows about the world of the unbeliever. Perhaps he has recently come over from that side. Regardless of when his pilgrimage was, he should not forget his background. By remaining conscious of his former "worldliness," he will be able to make a more sympathetic approach to those who are still undecided.

Many times, the minister himself sounds so smug and self-righteous, people in the world want nothing to do with him. The evangelist often becomes impatient with outsiders because they cannot see "the truth" immediately. He fishes for men by saying in effect, "bite or go to hell!" Those who are still living in the world may be very defensive. Even if they are thinking about giving up their sins, they resent the person who tries to run roughshod over them. It makes them angry when someone tries to approach them from a higher spiritual plane. If the minister is conscious of his own religious struggles, his awareness will make it easier for him to be understanding toward others who are still groping for truth.

In setting forth the nature of Jesus' ministry, John the Baptist told his audience, "he will not break a bruised reed or quench a smoldering wick" (Matthew 12:20). A "bruised reed" barely stands. It is apt to topple over in the wind at any moment. Yet, when Jesus came along, he did not snap it in two because it was not stronger. The same idea holds true with a "smoldering wick." Here is a candle with only a flickering flame. Jesus does not approach it angrily and say, "Because you are not burning any brighter, I'm going to snuff you out." Rather, he encourages the glimmer of light until it becomes strong enough to illuminate the entire room.

In the Gospels, Jesus encourages even a gleam of faith. He does not dissuade followers because they are weak and immature. Rather, he calls them "disciples" or "learners." "Take my yoke upon you, and learn from me"; he said, "for I am gentle and lowly in heart, and you will find rest for your souls" (Matthew 11:29). Here was an approach which caused the multitudes to seek him out. Not once do we find a harsh and condemnatory word against anyone who was trying. His strongest criticisms are directed against the self-styled religious leaders whose pride and conceit blinded them to the needs of people.

In his portrait of a village preacher, Oliver Goldsmith indicates what personal acceptance and patience can accomplish:

> Pleased with his guests, the
>    good man learned to show,
> And quite forgot their vices in
>    their woe.
>
> Truth from his lips prevailed
>    with double sway,
> And fools, who came to scoff,
>    remained to pray.

If a minister is prejudiced against those who are living in the world, people can feel it "down in their bones." It is not something he says or does, but the result of something he is. If our attitude toward God's lost children is more closely attuned to the elder brother than the waiting Father, we should not expect any great results from our "evangelistic" ministry.

## THE TRAGEDY OF FULFILLED DREAMS

History points to the winds of change blowing across every country. Individuals and nations both have their moods. The minds of a young couple may be virtually closed to the church. For the present moment, tennis and weekend trips to the mountains are more important than worship. Then they become parents. Gradually, their tremendous responsibility for an innocent life breaks over them. They want the very best for that child. In reviewing the value of their own early religious training, they decide to make a renewed commitment to God. The next week, they start to visit the churches of their community in the hopes of finding one where they feel at home.

In times of religious revival, similar changes can sweep over an entire nation. After a while, the life of sensualism begins to pall. Loneliness fills the cities with despair. The tenets of atheism are more palatable in a secure world. When everything nailed down is being ripped up, Christianity often receives another look by those who formerly passed by on the other side.

When these opportunities for "times of refreshing" come along from the Lord, it is very important for the church to stand ready. Unfortunately, the situation is often otherwise. Rather than being prepared, the average congregation suffers from the tragedy of fulfilled dreams. Perhaps a generation ago, a handful of Christians launched a new congregation. They struggled for several years without their own building. It may have been necessary to meet in a school during the early days.

Then they bought property and erected their first house of worship. It was a time of unity and purpose. The members worked faithfully. Their next project was a parsonage. Later they called an associate minister to work with youth and education. When he married, they built another parsonage. The improvements they could not afford when the building was dedicated were added one by one. First came air-conditioning, then the paved parking lot, and finally the new fellowship hall.

It is all paid for now. As one church leader expressed it to me, "We don't owe a dime to anyone." Here we see the misfortune of a church fulfilling its own dreams. Once the goals of an adequate house of worship and a resident preaching ministry have been satisfied, the congregation had no further objectives. Of course, its leaders acknowledge that every church should have a missionary program. Consequently, a few dollars are sent every year. However, there is no throbbing concern for the lost in the community or the multiplied millions around the world who have never heard the gospel.

Across such churches by the tens of thousands, we must write "Ichabod." Truly, the glory has departed. Even the old leadership is vaguely aware now that the church had a better spirit when its members were sacrificing to make building payments. They also had a deeper concern for evangelism. Nowadays, it's only the preacher and one or two deacons who are willing to call on the lost.

The problems started when the foundations of the congregation were being laid. The goals were too small and parochial. The vision of a spacious building, complete with lovely classrooms and paved parking, was constantly discussed. Once these objectives were met, the congregation settled down to "business as usual" and forgot about the Great Commission of Jesus Christ.

When the "settled in" spirit has overtaken a congregation, it is sometimes very difficult to rekindle enthusiasm. If the leadership "burned themselves out" in putting up the building, they will be very reluctant to hear about "more involvement" now. Proper attitudes about the mission of the church must be built in from the very beginning. Otherwise, in order to meet the current budget, a congregation may commit spiritual suicide by excluding missions altogether.

Just as the cathedrals in Europe provide an eloquent testimony to religious devotion, so today, more than three hundred thousand church buildings in America bespeak a concern for God. If we could visualize these places of worship as "training centers" preparing and equipping the saints of Christ for worldwide missionary expeditions, what an exciting picture we would receive. Furthermore, if we see this American effort as a part of a gigantic push in cooperation with Christians from other countries, then our vision becomes even more dramatic.

Faithfully filling the pews in hundreds of American congregations are leadership-type people who have tremendous gifts from God. Some of these Christians should probably remain where they are, witnessing to their faith in their own communities. But others who are seasoned and trained through their years of service in the local congregation should think seriously about the full-time field of evangelism. Perhaps they should consider one or two years in seminary to supplement the education they have already.

After graduation, they could easily join the staff of a congregation as "minister of evangelism." Their recent encounters in the business world would help make them sensitive to the intellectual and emotional barriers which keep the doubting away from Christ. It they did not carry the responsibility for weddings, funerals, and hospital visitation, these added hours could be available for evangelism.

Perhaps their concern may lead them overseas where they still have twenty years of service to give. The congregation that nurtured them might even be strong enough to pay all of their salary and expenses. Consequently, the costly and time-consuming year of deputation would not be necessary in some religious groups. Meanwhile, the congregation must not make the mistake of thinking their missionary dollars eliminate the responsibility they have for their own communities. Taken as a whole, here is a worldwide vision of evangelism, one as large as the New Testament.

Although the Apostle Paul tried for years to reach Rome, we find a very curious mention of Spain in his Roman letter. "I hope to see you in passing as I go to Spain," he wrote, "and to be sped on my journey there by you, once I have enjoyed your company for a little" (15:24). When we think how long it took in the ancient world to travel from Jerusalem to Rome, we wonder how Paul could ever think of going on to Spain.

But here we feel the missionary passion that drove him back and forth across the Mediterranean. Even Rome itself, the Queen City of the ancient world, was not able to satisfy his hopes for the gospel. After preaching the Good News in Rome, he must go on to Spain. Paul never experienced the tragedy of fulfilled dreams.

As F. W. H. Meyers says so poignantly in *St. Paul:*

> Yes, without cheer of sister or of daughter,
> Yes, without stay of father or of son,
> Lone on the land and homeless on the water
> Pass I in patience till the work be done.

> Yet not in solitude if Christ anear me
> Waketh him workers for the great employ,
> Oh not in solitude, if souls that hear me
> Catch from my joyaunce the surprise of joy.

Dr. Paul Benjamin is Director of the National Church Growth Research Center in Washington, D.C., and has worked throughout the United States helping congregations of all denominations learn how to grow. He has published a number of articles on the art of evangelizaton, and is a noted teacher and professor on the subject. One of Dr. Benjamin's recent achievements was to conduct the "Festival of Evangelism" held in Kansas City. Over twenty thousand participants came from every state in the nation as well as from many foreign countries. It was, without question, the largest and the most successful training school in contemporary evangelization ever held. Persons and churches interested in contacting Dr. Benjamin may do so by writing the Center at P.O. Box 17575, Washington, DC 20041.

# INSTITUTE FOR CHURCH GROWTH
## PASADENA, CALIFORNIA
## DR. C. PETER WAGNER,
## PROFESSOR OF CHURCH GROWTH
## EFFECTIVE CHURCH EVANGELISM

*CHAPTER*

# 36

ALTHOUGH the main topic of this presentation is equipping, the way to go about it cannot be profitably discussed until we are clear and precise about what we are equipping ourselves *for*. Our task, of course, is equipping for evangelism. But this is not enough. What does evangelism mean? Many different, and sometimes conflicting, ideas of evangelism have been making the rounds among Christian leaders these days. Which of them is the most satisfactory?

## WHAT IS EVANGELISM?

Evangelism is not simply doing good things in the name of Christ. Healing the sick, liberating the oppressed, and feeding the hungry are good Christian activities. In many cases they actually open new doors for evangelism. But Christian social ministry should not be confused with evangelism. Social ministry heals the hurts of individuals and groups of people. Evangelism is more than this, however. It brings men and women into the Kingdom of God, it moves them from darkness to light, it liberates them from the power of Satan and enfolds them in the loving power of God.

Nor is evangelism simply proclaiming the gospel message. The message must be proclaimed if true evangelism is to take place, but that is only part of evangelism. Many people have heard the message of the gospel on numerous occasions and they are still unevangelized. Here in Pasadena we have a bearded man who stands on a street corner every afternoon, Bible in hand, proclaiming the gospel. He may think that everyone who goes by him is consequently evangelized. But they are not. Scarcely one in a hundred even listens to what he is saying.

Nor is evangelism simply getting people to make "decisions for Christ." Hands raised, or cards signed, or people hitting the sawdust trail, or praying a prayer are not the best indication of how many have been evangelized. It is common knowledge that many who go through those motions are insincere, although many others experience a true work of the Holy Spirit in their hearts when they do so. I believe that making decisions for Christ is an essential part of true evangelism; but just counting every decision is still an inadequate means of reporting evangelistic results.

True biblical evangelism is much more than doing good, or preaching the message, or getting decisions. It is nothing less than fulfilling Christ's Great Commission. The Great Commission appears in Matthew, Mark, Luke, John, and Acts. It is the very last word Jesus said to his disciples when he finished his earthly ministry (see Acts 1:18). The most detailed account of the Great Commission appears in Matthew 28:19, 20. There the imperative verb is to "make disciples." Going, baptizing, teaching, and any number of other Christian activities are evangelistic means or methodologies, but the evangelistic goal is nothing less than to make disciples of Jesus Christ.

What is a disciple of Christ? How do you know when a disciple is made?

Theologically a disciple is made when the Holy Spirit does a sovereign supernatural work of regeneration in the heart of an unbeliever. But, in the final analysis, no human being knows for sure if and when that even takes place in other people. As Jesus said, it is only "by their fruits" that you shall know them. What fruit do we look for? Many answers could be given to this question, but a great deal of research has shown that the most acceptable fruit for measuring evangelistic results is responsible membership in a local church. True disciples are those who "continue steadfastly in the apostles' doctrine and fellowship, and in breaking of bread and in prayers" as Luke described them in Acts 2:42. People can go to heaven without joining a local church, but from the point of view of evangelistic methodology, that is the best single indicator of whether our evangelism has been effective or not.

It is because of this that I myself feel that the best, most concise one-sentence definition of evangelism of all time was coined over sixty years ago by a group of Anglican archbishops. It says it all:

> To evangelize is so to present Christ Jesus in the power of the Holy Spirit, that men and women shall come to put their trust in God through Him, to accept Him as their Savior, and serve Him as their King in the fellowship of His church.

What are some of the most obvious implications of accepting this definition of evangelism?

For one thing, it keeps us from falling into the trap of separating evangelism from so-called "followup." Evangelistic programs which separate the two have built-in failure mechanisms. Evangelism itself involves seeing people, by the power of the Holy Spirit, come to two simultaneous commitments: commitment to Christ and commitment to the body of Christ. It means that Christian discipleship is faulty unless an individual has established bonds of relationship with other flesh-and-blood Christian people. It means that true evangelism results in church growth. As in the book of Acts, when a church is evangelistic, the Lord is "adding to the church daily such as should be saved" (Acts 2:47).

## WHAT IS EQUIPPING?

If evangelism involves adding to the church people who are being saved, then equipping for evangelism needs to focus on the whole church. It is not sufficient to equip a person here and there for the work of evangelism. Much good evangelistic work does not result in church growth because the church itself is not equipped to assimilate the new people who are won to Christ. That is why I intentionally entitled this presentation, "Equipping the *Local Church* for Evangelism." What I am going to say from here on, then, I am saying to groups of Christians who constitute local churches, and to individuals only to the extent that they are expected to make their contribution to the activities of the group as a whole.

There are many traditional approaches to equipping a local church for evangelism which seem to be somewhat inadequate to me. I will list a few that will sound familiar to many church members:

1. Hire a preacher who knows how to lead people to Christ. After all, the preacher has been to seminary and they teach people how to be soul-winners there. If our pastor is an evangelist, we're equipped.
2. Hold a revival once or twice a year. It may cost some extra money, but if we get a good speaker and some good music we can pack our evangelism into a week or two. If people want to be saved they can come out to our revival services.
3. Elect an evangelism committee. If we can get five or six people to serve on a committee, they can concentrate on reaching out and bringing new people in.
4. Buy into a good evangelistic program. Many experts, both in our denomination and in parachurch agencies, have developed successful ways of sharing Christ with others. If our church gets a program like that and implements it, we will be adequately equipped to evangelize.
5. Join with other churches for a citywide crusade. If we pool our resources we can invite a big-name evangelist to come to town. It will draw a good bit of media exposure, Jesus Christ will become the topic of conversation, and the unchurched will be evangelized.

There is nothing intrinsically wrong with any of the traditional methods I have mentioned. In fact they are all good things to do. But collective Christian wisdom as well as actual field research have shown that no one of those approaches has been able to sustain vigorous and continuous evangelism. How, then, should a local church be equipped for evangelism?

Although the church growth is complex, I believe that the major key to equipping is *allowing the body of Christ to function as it was originally designed by God and explained in the Bible.* I have emphasized this because I believe it is the most important single sentence in this whole presentation.

I am using the term "body of Christ," of course, as the Bible uses it—meaning the church (see Ephesians 1:22, 23). For the purposes of evangelism the principal structural manifestation of the body of Christ is the local church. What, then, is God's design for the functioning of the body of Christ or the local church?

The body of Christ is an organism with Christ as the head and every member functioning with one or more spiritual gifts.

The key to equipping the church, then, lies in the area of spiritual gifts. If spiritual gifts are operating as they should, the body will be equipped for evangelism. We must be clear, however, as to what a spiritual gift is: A spiritual gift is a special attribute given by the Holy Spirit to every member of the body of Christ, according to God's grace, for use within the context of the body. Notice by that definition that every member of the body of Christ—including you yourself—has one or more spiritual gifts.

Knowing this is a tremendous help. It allows you, better than anything else, to understand what God's will is for your life (see Romans 12:1-6). It helps all the members of your church to know and appreciate where each of you fits best into the total picture of your church life and activities. It allows the nominating committee to place church members according to their divine giftedness rather than simply on the basis of their availability. It helps the body of Christ to become mature and to grow (see Ephesians 4:13, 16).

## *MORE ABOUT SPIRITUAL GIFTS*

It has been mentioned that spiritual gifts are given "according to God's grace." In fact the biblical word most used for spiritual gifts is *"charisma,"* which has as its root "charis," meaning "grace." In 1 Corinthians 12:11 and 12:18 we are told that the gifts are placed in the body as God sees fit. No one can order his own gift or gifts, nor can anyone work for a gift and receive it. God alone decides what gifts you have or do not have.

Scholars will differ as to how many spiritual gifts should be included in the list. Three chapters in the Bible contain the most distinctive lists of gifts: Romans 12, 1 Corinthians 12, and Ephesians 4. Most agree that a composite of these three lists yields twenty spiritual gifts: prophecy, service, teaching, exhortation, giving, leadership, mercy, wisdom, knowledge, faith, healing, miracles, discerning of spirits, tongues, interpretation of tongues, apostle, helps, administration, evangelist, and pastor. Mention is made elsewhere in the New Testament of five more, which brings the total so far to twenty-five: celibacy, voluntary poverty, martyrdom, hospitality, and missionary. Then the question arises: Are there gifts in the church being used today that are not mentioned specifically in the Bible? Some would say no. My opinion, and that of many others, is that there are. Some of the most commonly mentioned are music, preaching, writing, and craftsmanship. I personally do not include those in my list, but I do feel that two others should be included: intercession and exorcism. Adding these two to the twenty-five in the Bible brings my list up to twenty-seven. I have no quarrel with others who have lists of nineteen or twenty or twenty-five or thirty, or what have you, but I have settled on twenty-seven.

Another difference of opinion is whether all the gifts are in use today. Some feel strongly that certain "sign gifts" were valid only for the apostolic age, and that since then they are not in use. Some feel that they are all in use. My observation is that God honors both positions, and that he will bless you if you determine to discover, develop, and use the spiritual gifts that you feel are available to you and yours. While we need to listen to and try to understand each other's opinions, arguing, bitterness, and church splits over this issue are obviously not the fruit of the Spirit but the works of the flesh.

Not only is it important to know what the spiritual gifts are, it is equally important to know what they are not. Let me mention four key areas of potential confusion:

1. Do not confuse spiritual gifts with *natural talents.*
   Natural talents are God-given abilities that are distributed

to human beings in general. Spiritual gifts are given only to members of the body of Christ. Sometimes God will see fit to take a person's natural talent and supernaturally transform it into a spiritual gift. Sometimes a person's spiritual gifts will have no evident relationship to their natural talents. But spiritual gifts are given specifically for the ministry of the body, not for human activities in general.

2. Do not confuse spiritual gifts with the *fruit of the Spirit*. The fruit of the Spirit are listed in Galatians 5:22, 23. Love is the chief fruit of the Spirit. In 1 Corinthians 13, the Apostle Paul explains the relationship between the two. The Corinthians had all the spiritual gifts, but they were worthless. Why? Because they did not have love, the fruit of the Spirit. The fruit of the Spirit is the indispensable foundation upon which all the gifts of the Spirit must be exercised.

3. Do not confuse spiritual gifts with *Christian roles*. Many of the gifts in the list above describe qualities that should characterize every Christian. For example, all Christians must have faith, not just a few. I label that ordinary kind of faith as our Christian role. But it is qualitatively different from the special gift of faith that is given to only a few members of the body selected by God. The same applies to the gift of giving. All Christians are expected to give at least 10 percent of their income to God. We all have the role of tithing. But a few are given a very special gift of giving far above what the average Christian is expected to give.

4. Do not confuse spiritual gifts with *counterfeit gifts*. It is a sad but true fact of life that the devil can and does counterfeit spiritual gifts, but it should keep us on our toes. Those with the gift of discernment of spirits have a God-given ability to know the difference.

## *DISCOVERING YOUR SPIRITUAL GIFT*

In light of what has been said, it is clear that one of the most important spiritual exercises for any church member is to discover, develop, and use his spiritual gifts. This is the true starting point for equipping a local church for evangelism. How, then, does one discover spiritual gifts?

Before I list the five steps, it is necessary to realize that a person needs to be emotionally mature to come to realistic terms with gift discovery. In our society, emotional maturity usually arrives between eighteen and twenty-five years of age, although earlier for some and later for others. New Christians who are already emotionally mature should discover their gifts in a period of between four and twelve months after their conversion and incorporation into the body of Christ.

There is considerable agreement among scholars in the field that the following five steps will be extremely helpful in gift discovery. While this specific outline is mine, the ideas in it are commonplace:

1. *Explore the possibilities.* Accumulate as much knowledge as you can concerning the options. Study these options, compare them with your knowledge of the Scriptures, and then decide on your own definitions. The more you know about the gifts, the easier it will be for you to recognize yours.
2. *Experiment with as many as you can.* As you experiment with gifts, pray that God will help you discover not only the gifts you have but also the gifts you do not have. For many people, discovering a gift they do not have is a great source of relief from unnecessary guilt feelings, and a reasonable explanation of why they have tried hard to do some kind of Christian ministry with an obvious lack of success.
3. *Examine your feelings.* God, I believe, matches our gifts to our personalities and our temperaments in such a way that if you have a certain spiritual gift you will enjoy using it. Conversely, if you dislike doing a certain job in the church (after conscientiously experimenting with it) it may be a sign you do not have the gift.
4. *Evaluate your effectiveness.* If God has given you a certain spiritual gift, it will "work," so to speak. You will be successful in using it (other things being equal) because the Holy Spirit is working supernaturally through you to accomplish God's purpose.

5. *Expect confirmation from the body.* The body of Christ, like the human body, is a unit. The parts work in conjunction with each other. If you have a bona fide spiritual gift, other members of your church will affirm one way or another that you have the gift.

## SUGGESTIONS AND RESOURCES

The awareness of the need for spiritual gift discovery has been increasing rapidly over the past ten years in our churches. Hundreds of churches have now been renewed through awakening to spiritual gifts, and many of them have experienced vigorous growth as a result. From such churches, several specific recommendations have emerged to help others enter into the same exciting experience.

1. *Inform, motivate, and encourage the congregation.* This can be done, for example, by a series of sermons, and the pastor can mention spiritual gifts from the pulpit regularly. Many have found that spiritual gifts provide a stimulating subject for adult Sunday school classes or weeknight and home Bible study groups. For these I recommend three texts: the Bible, my book entitled *Your Spiritual Gifts Can Help Your Church Grow* (Regal Books), and the *Spiritual Gifts Bible Study* workbook available from the Charles E. Fuller Institute (P.O. Box 989, Pasadena, CA 91102). Churchwide reading programs can also help. In my book I list the ten books on spiritual gifts I consider at the top of the line. Films and other resources are also available.

2. *Hold a spiritual gifts workshop.* For this you will need quality materials. A growing number of denominations are designing materials for their constituency. In order to help meet the increasing demand, I myself have helped develop the well-known Spiritual Gifts Workshop produced by Charles E. Fuller Institute. It contains the *Bible Study Guide* mentioned above, a participant's manual for a six-hour gifts discovery workshop, including a Modified Houts Questionnaire of 125 self-examining questions for each participant. The leader's guide has all

those materials with instructions as to their use, plus two cassette tapes of my complete lecture on the subject, and a Mobilization Workbook to help the pastor match gifts to church jobs.

The leader of the workshop can be the pastor, a staff member, a lay leader with the gift of teaching, or an outside specialist. Hundreds of churches have used the discovery workshop to great profit.

3. *Build spiritual gifts into your regular program.* As the weeks and months go by, more and more churches are gearing their programs toward spiritual gifts. One church in the Detroit area, St. Paul Lutheran Church of Trenton, Michigan, has a staff member with the title "Minister of Spiritual Gifts." A church in western Pennsylvania, Grace United Methodist of Franklin, holds spiritual gifts discovery workshops three times a year on a regular basis. Each of these churches is sustaining a growth rate of over 300 percent per decade.

4. *Diagnose the health of your local body of Christ.* Some churches have tried spiritual gifts discovery and found that their evangelistic program did not thereby become more effective. Discovering spiritual gifts is not a panacea for all church problems. Church growth is always complex. Part of equipping the local church for effective evangelism is making sure that the church is healthy in all ways. In order to evaluate this you should know the vital signs of a healthy church (see my book, *Your Church Can Grow*, Regal Books) and you should be able to identify the major growth-inhibiting diseases (see my book, *Your Church Can Be Healthy*, Abingdon). A very popular do-it-yourself resource, called the Diagnostic Clinic, is available from the Fuller Institute. This can be used profitably by professional church leadership for making sure that obstacles to growth are removed and that opportunities for growth are appropriated.

5. *Establish a regular, structured witnessing program.* Evangelism takes doing. Part of equipping the local church is providing a program that will make evangelism intentional and constant. Many denominational supply houses have such programs. Also parachurch

organizations such as Evangelism Explosion (Fort Lauderdale, Florida) or Campus Crusade for Christ (San Bernardino, California) have excellent programs that can furnish channels for ministry to those who have the gift of evangelism and to others as well. My suggestion is that all church members, old and new, prayerfully go through a program which trains them to share their faith with others. Through it those with the gift of evangelism will discover their gift, and those with simply the role of witness will be better witnesses for Christ for the rest of their lives.

## USING SPIRITUAL GIFTS FOR EVANGELISM

The most important person for equipping the local church is the pastor. This may be less than true in some very small churches, but in most medium and large churches it is a recognized fact. My advice to lay people who get excited about spiritual gifts is to pray that your pastor will share the excitement. If he or she does not, it is usually not productive to attempt an end run around the pastor to make changes in church life.

While the whole body must be equipped for evangelism, the gift of being an evangelist is the primary gift for the task. My studies have shown that in most congregations somewhere between 5 and 10 percent of the active members will have the gift of an evangelist. They need to discover their gift, be recognized by the other church members, and be given full opportunity to use their gift to win people to Christ. At the same time, all Christians have the role of witness and should be sharing their faith with others as the opportunity arises. But the 90 percent who do not have the gift of evangelism have other important gifts they need to be using. If they do not, the new converts will not be assimilated into the body, the evangelistic effort will be curtailed, and the church will not grow.

Equipping the local church for effective evangelism is not easy. It requires motivation, dedication, and just plain hard work. But the rewards are abundant. If the angels in heaven rejoice when one soul comes to repentance, how much more should we also rejoice when our efforts open the way for the Lord to "add daily to the church such as are being saved."

Peter Wagner is one of the most outstanding teachers of evangelism in America today. Professor of Church Growth at Fuller Theological Seminary, he has served on the Lausanne Committee for International Evangelization, has written a host of books, produced several movies, and was a missionary for fifteen years in Bolivia. Here is a man who knows his subject, and who informs us on how to organize a sound parish program of evangelism— how to equip people to be effective evangelizers within their own parish community.

Dr. C. Peter Wagner, Professor of Church Growth, Fuller Theological Seminary, 135 N. Oakland Ave., Pasadena, CA 91101.

# BILLY GRAHAM SCHOOLS OF EVANGELISM
## MINNEAPOLIS, MINNESOTA
## THE REV. JOHN DILLON, DIRECTOR
## EVANGELISM TRAINING FOR PASTORS

CHAPTER

37

WE are all aware of the great Billy Graham Crusades held around the nation, and the millions of people who have attended them. But few people, especially pastors, are aware of the Billy Graham Schools of Evangelism that are held at the same time and in the same place the crusades are held.

They began as the special project of one Presbyterian layman from California. While attending a Graham Crusade for the first time, Mr. Lowell Berry suggested that such successful evangelization should be shared with local pastors. He asked himself, as he sat in the stands at the stadium, "Why can't my pastor preach like that?" "Why don't we reach out to the unchurched?" "Why can't we have special materials to use in reaching the inactives?" Realizing that evangelism was a specialized ministry, and that the Billy Graham Team is certainly the best in the field (and being himself a most successful businessman) he thought that such methods and skills needed to be taught and shared.

Mr. Berry approached the Billy Graham Team and suggested

that they conduct a school for pastors at each of their crusades. Starting at the bottom, he made his suggestion. "That's a good idea," was the reply; but no action took place. He began to attend other crusades and at each one he would make the same suggestion, this time to a higher ranked member of the team—until one day he was standing before Billy Graham himself.

"Dr. Graham," Mr. Berry said, "why don't you teach pastors your evangelism skills? Why not have a school of evangelism for pastors everywhere you have a crusade?"

Billy said, "Lowell, that's a great idea, but it would cost a lot of money which we don't have."

Mr. Berry quickly replied, "But I have a lot of money," and the Schools of Evangelism were begun with the outstanding financial backing of this dedicated Presbyterian layman.

The first one was held in Kansas City, and the turnout of one thousand pastors brought Lowell Berry's dream to fruition. The schools begin on Monday afternoon and continue until Friday noon. They are intensive training programs using the very best instructors from all over the world. The finest in the field conduct lectures and workshops that equip pastors with the latest evangelization skills to be found anywhere. There is an interdenominational cooperation that would amaze you. In the introductory remarks made by the schools' dean, Dr. Kenneth Chafin, he told the assembled ministers and priests, "Don't tell your neighbor what denomination you belong to—keep them guessing." And guess you would have to do. At one recent school over ninety-two denominations were represented. At the average school you'll find Roman Catholic priests, Salvation Army Officers, Serbian Orthodox, Southern Baptists, Presbyterians, Methodists—the list goes on and on.

One pastor said, "Just being together for this week is an education in itself." The schools are directed by the Rev. John Dillon, who has his office at the Billy Graham National Headquarters in Minneapolis, Minnesota. Pastors are asked to register as soon as possible, and generally there are three such schools conducted in a year. Since that first School of Evangelism held in Kansas City in 1967, there have been forty-nine schools held with over 47,275 pastors having attended.

Lowell Berry died a few years ago, but before he did, he

established the Lowell Berry Foundation to insure that his great idea would continue. Through his generosity, scholarships are offered to pastors that provide for books, transportation, and housing during the school. Realizing how important it was for the pastor's wife also to attend, Lowell made arrangements for pastors to bring along their wives to these schools, and special programs are presented to them while their pastor husbands attend specialized seminars. Not all the costs are paid for by the foundation, but the foundation does make possible the opportunity for all pastors to be able to attend.

Now what exactly is a Billy Graham School of Evangelism? Director John W. Dillon states it to be an event which is designed to focus your attention on the dynamic of the gospel. The emphasis is threefold: church growth, evangelism, and personal renewal. It is a supplement to seminary studies designed to inspire pastors, ministerial students, and key lay leaders to a greater emphasis on evangelistic activity, together with tested methods for local church outreach.

The general objectives of the school are fourfold: (1) to demonstrate both in prepared lectures and crusade meetings the inherent power of the gospel message in such a way that the student will be able to impart this message to others; (2) to present evangelism in such a way that the student will be able to develop lay evangelism in the local church; (3) to provide a biblically centered theological basis for evangelism; (4) to present the why and how of evangelism so clearly that there will be a new commitment to its message and effectiveness.

The schools will provide the pastor student with several days of intellectually and spiritually exciting moments. It will be a time to make new friends, to find out what is working for others, to discuss with one's peers the programs you are using, and to find out what they are doing that works.

The dean for the schools, Dr. Kenneth Chafin, is also pastor of one of the nation's finest churches, located in Houston, Texas. He pastors the 7,000-member South Main Street Baptist Church and was formerly his denomination's professor of evangelization. Dr. Chafin says of the schools, "Every pastor I know would like to be more effective in leadership but feels he needs some assistance. He would like to have help with his own life; to better understand the world in which he lives and its needs; to develop skills in communication and leadership; and to find within himself a new sense of mission.

"This School of Evangelism is an honest effort to meet these needs. The faculty has great variety, insight, and commitment to Christ and his work."

The principal objective is to equip pastors and pastoral staff for the work of evangelization. Specifically, this means both the spiritual and physical preparations necessary to do evangelism, as well as the appropriate discipling of those who place their faith in Christ.

## THE DAILY PROGRAM

The day is divided into three parts. The morning is spent from 8:00 A.M. until lunchtime in the main hall where lectures are given by outstanding persons in the field of evangelism. It is a "back to back" preaching/lecture program interspersed with a time of worship, a few moments of song, and always a guest from the music staff of the Billy Graham Association. Men such as Dr. D. James Kennedy, Dr. George Hunter, Dr. Charles Allen, Dr. Robert Schuller, Dr. Charles Swindoll, and many more will give a presentation.

The afternoon is divided into optional seminars so that the student is able to select two each day. There are over twenty to pick from and cover fields of communications, media, preaching, how to reach ethnics, unchurched, and inactives. No seminary could possibly offer the quality, the experience, and the courses that are provided at these seminars. The top men in the field are selected to lead these.

The evening is spent at the crusade. Dr. Chafin says, "Evangelism is better caught than taught," and attending the crusades provides a firsthand experience of hearing a master evangelist such as Dr. Billy Graham preaching, and then watching the people around you responding to his message, his reasoning, his call for response. It is an amazing experience to see hundreds, sometimes thousands of men, women, and children respond to his call. It removes the cynical judgments of the sceptics who claim it is all emotional, and proves through experience the real power of the gospel message.

## BOOKS AND EVANGELISM MATERIALS

Throughout the school, the students will have the opportunity to review some of the finest evangelism materials ever produced. Films, booklets, textbooks are displayed, and special discounts are offered to the students. In addition, usually two books are handed out free of charge each day. The student goes home, not only with information from lectures and seminars, but with a bag full of the finest printed materials available.

At the end of each day, the students are required to complete a worksheet on special topics in the field covered that day. They are asked to comment on the Billy Graham sermons during the crusades, and to outline for themselves his method of presenting the gospel and his final request for a response to the message. This process helps the student to organize his own approach to lead to effective evangelistic outreach.

The day usually ends with groups of pastors coming together in the hotel that has been selected for their housing, and as you pass through the lobby or the coffee shop you see these groups talking over their own programs, asking one another how it is in their church, and oftentimes, praying together. If nothing else happened at the school, this time of fellowship and professional sharing would make the time well spent.

## MUCH MORE THAN INFORMATION

One of the amazing things that happens at every School of Evangelism is the great number of pastors who come away with a totally new outlook upon their life as a minister or priest. It would be impossible to number them, but at every school, you can see pastors responding to Billy Graham's call to "give your life to Jesus." These pastors are meeting Jesus Christ in a real way for the very first time in their lives. One pastor who had such a "conversion experience" said, "I knew the twenty-third Psalm but I didn't know the Shepherd. This experience brought me not only to *knowing* the Lord, but to the Lord himself."

Almost every pastor who attends leaves with a new commitment—a new outlook on his ministry. Dr. Kenneth Chafin likes to say, "Wouldn't you just love to be in their church the Sunday they get back home?"

# SUBJECTS PRESENTED

At a recent school, the following lectures were offered:

1. Evangelism Today—Dr. Oswald Hoffman
2. The Anatomy of Leadership—Dr. Kenneth Chafin
3. Burned Out, Burned Up—Mrs. Millie Dienert
4. Building an Evangelistic Church—Dr. Mervin Thompson
5. Starting a Branch Church—Dr. Robert Ricker
6. Is My Neighbor Really Lost?—Dr. Charles Swindoll
7. If I Could Preach a Thousand Sermons—
   Dr. Charles Allen
8. The Inner City Needs the Gospel—
   Dr. C. Philip Hinerman
9. Communicating with Secular People—
   Dr. George Hunter, III
10. Equipping the Laity—Dr. D. James Kennedy
11. Challenge for Special Ministry—
    Mrs. Joni Eareckson Tada
12. A Lay Witness—Mr. Charlie Branagh

If these twelve outstanding lecturers were not enough, the afternoon seminars offered were as follows:

1. Reaching Young People through Your Church—Dr. Jay Kesler
2. Principles of Successful Evangelism—Dr. Sterling Huston
3. Ministry as a Basis for Evangelism—Dr. Kenneth Chafin
4. Evangelizing with Film and Media—Mr. Larry Backlund
5. Ministry to Singles and Formerly Married—
   Dr. Mervin Thompson
6. Getting Our Act Together—Mrs. Millie Dienert
7. Reaching Young Adults—Dr. Milton Cunningham
8. How to Give an Invitation—Dr. Ralph Bell
9. The Ordinary Doing the Unlikely—Dr. Charles Swindoll
10. Evangelism in Everything—Dr. Robert Ricker
11. Preparation for Preaching—Dr. Charles Allen
12. A Discipling Tool—Dr. Tom Phillips
13. Writing—A Wider Ministry—Dr. Roger Palms
14. Mobilizing the Congregation for Continuous Outreach—
    Dr. Norman Pell

15. Witness of Christian Arts—Mrs. Jeanette Clift George
16. Communicating for Secular People—
    Dr. George Hunter, III
17. Methods for Equipping the Laity—Dr. D. James Kennedy
18. Media Relations and Evangelism—Mr. Ted Dienert
19. Follow Up Seminars—Dr. Tom Phillips
20. The Role of Music in Evangelism—Mr. Thomas Bledsoe
21. On Finding God in the City—Dr. C. Philip Hinerman

Reading through that impressive list, and realizing all this takes place within one week's time, you can appreciate what a great opportunity any pastor has. Without question, the Billy Graham Schools of Evangelism provide the pastor of today with the latest materials, the best proven methods, the finest people involved in evangelism, and the most opportune time to see those methods in action at the crusades. Little wonder that almost 50,000 pastors have attended these week-long schools, and one can only imagine what these 50,000 pastors have done with their newly found "tools" within their own communities and churches.

## THE BILLY GRAHAM STAFF

We have all witnessed the crusades on television and have enjoyed the artistry of the Billy Graham musicians. Throughout the week of studies, the lectures are interspersed with presentations from the Billy Graham staff. Dr. Graham himself comes and speaks with the students. George Beverly Shea comes and sings. Tedd Smith and Bill Fasig play the organ and piano and Cliff Barrows leads in the daily singing of hymns. Other artists appear, and the time flies by so quickly. The morning worship time is especially prepared for pastors and is a time for renewal and spiritual development so often overlooked in a busy pastor's life.

## THE FINAL MOMENT OF COMMITMENT

With the experience of over fifteen years, the dean knows that the final moment of the school is the most important. It is a moment for commitment—for rededication—a very special time for a pastor. The week gone, the work done, the school gathers for those last moments together. The spiritual impact of that moment is truly awesome! Tears fill the eyes of most, as they pray for the Holy Spirit to make them true evangelists for Jesus Christ—that their ministry will bear new fruit in reaching the unchurched, the inactives, the alienated, and the lost for Jesus Christ. It's an experience every pastor should have. The dream of one man, Lowell Berry, has come to pass. There exists a place that every minister of the gospel can now learn "How to be an evangelist!"

## HOW TO APPLY FOR A SCHOLARSHIP

Remember that this is a school for all who name themselves Christian, regardless of what denominational affiliation they belong to. Catholics and Protestants alike are invited and attend. To receive information and dates about the next School of Evangelism along with an application for a scholarship and a list of subjects to be offered, write to:

Rev. W. Dillon, Director
Schools of Evangelism
The Billy Graham Evangelistic Association
P.O. Box 9313
Minneapolis, MN 55440

## WHY SHOULD YOU ATTEND THE SCHOOL OF EVANGELISM?

First of all, *it will be a great blessing to you.* In the past, many ministers and priests, after attending the school, have written to tell how helpful it was, how much they learned, how significant it was in their spiritual renewal and growth.

Second, *you will benefit professionally.* Some of the most dynamic and effective people in the church come to the school to share information, insights, strategies, concerns, and guidance. Your ministry cannot help but be strengthened.

Last, but not least, *you will really enjoy this time with fellow ministers and members of the Billy Graham Team,* sharing concerns and experiences. It will all take place in a beautiful setting—a quality hotel in a fascinating city—which will make your stay even more memorable. Each night during the school everyone will be the special guest of the Billy Graham Evangelistic Association and will attend crusade meetings, sitting in special reserved seats.

Remember, the B.G.E.A. has available scholarships for ministers who request assistance that will provide: (1) lodging—for the clergyman and his spouse in a quality hotel for four nights, absolutely free; and (2) travel assistance—at ten cents a mile up to 1,500 miles.